Omniocracy

A Government that Represents All Living Beings

CHARLOTTE LAWS

For information about this title or to order other books and/or electronic media, contact the publisher or author.

Stroud House Publishing
Offices in NY and CA

Charlotte Laws, Ph.D.
CharlotteLaws.com
OfficeofCharlotteLaws@yahoo.com

ISBNs:
(Print) 978-1-7333410-1-1
(eBooks) 978-1-7333410-2-8

Printed in the United States of America

"If you like books that are extremely thought-provoking, highly controversial and make you question everything you thought you knew, then this book is for you."

Jane Velez-Mitchell, journalist / author

"A life-changing scholarly book and much needed in a world that is dominated by and for the human. As the author convincingly states: Nonhuman animals will remain in chains until they are recognized within the political system."

Gene Bauer, president of Farm Sanctuary

"From an emotionally-charged Introduction to an argument-based twelve chapters, Charlotte Laws succeeds in outlining a new philosophy for the animal movement and a revolutionary political structure that values all living beings. Omniocracy is a provocative and scholarly work of art."

Dr. Bruce Goldberg, bestselling author

"Omniocracy is compelling, courageous, original, and well-written. It will be seen as one of the most important animal rights books in history. You will never view society, life, or politics in the same way again."

Sue Jones, investigative reporter

"A challenge to the greatest inequity of all: human supremacy over non-humans. Charlotte Laws confronts us with the question: Do we believe in equality, or just the appearance of it? What are the merits of a political system that leaves the majority

of beings without representation or consideration? Omniocracy is the blueprint for a truly just world."

PETER YOUNG, AUTHOR / ANIMAL ACTIVIST

"[Charlotte Laws's] goal is not simply more humane policies but political inclusion; [she is] trying to expand the prevailing conception of the political community."

KIMBERLY K. SMITH, PROFESSOR / AUTHOR

"Laws states her case that both animal and earth advocates must encourage political leaders to widen their lens by embracing nonhumans as constituents."

ALL CREATURES MAGAZINE

"Charlotte Laws has written another winner! She leans on science, philosophy, and common sense to convince the reader that a government that represents all living beings is the only way forward. Eloquently written and sure to be a classic!"

PAMELYN FERDIN, ACTRESS / ANIMAL ACTIVIST

"Anyone interested in policy, political science, philosophy, animal liberation, or environmentalism must read this comprehensive and vitally important book! Lucid, compelling, and insightful."

RICHARD RIIS, AUTHOR

To the nonhuman victims of prejudice. You are truly the oppressed, the voiceless, and the forgotten. It is my hope that this book will educate Homo sapiens about your plight. You are forever in my heart.

To animal liberationists throughout the world. Keep up the good work.

To my vegan granddaughters, Atlas Jade and Blake Capri, who are destined to lead compassionate lives. I love you.

Contents

Introduction

Discard your trendy moral coat; this is a rebel in a binder.

Coats are bulky and restrict movement. Traditional (objective or absolute) morality is problematic in a similar way. It is arbitrary, not supported by science, and harmful to the planet. It leads to hatred, divisiveness, and an unhealthy chasm between species—an argument that will be detailed later. This book, *Omniocracy,* begins by deconstructing the hodgepodge of philosophical ideas that dominate Western society. Later, it constructs (or, in some cases, reconstructs) pieces—while leaning on scientific evidence and reason—to reach a structure of what I believe would allow for a better society.

You might call this project utopian. Even if I were to buy into this notion, things that seem utopian at one time may be commonplace at a later date. Commercial air travel and indoor plumbing would have been dismissed as unrealistic in the seventeenth century. In addition, a theory or societal framework with a few utopian features may include other elements that are immediately handy. The lofty or visionary aspects can motivate scientists, engineers, politicians, policymakers, and the like; these people can sink time and energy into making them a reality.

I have criticized traditional (objective or absolute) morality as a destructive fiction in general terms, but this book is primarily about the animal rights (AR) movement's philosophy and how its arguments could be adjusted to better align with science. AR activists tend to rely upon objective morality and a metaphysic of free will, which coincide with the perspective of mainstream society. The positive side of promoting this misinformation is that it might be easier to sway the masses who already believe in such myths. For example, many children believe in Santa Claus. If you want to convince a child to eat her vegetables, it might be more expedient to tell her that Santa will bring her lots of presents if she eats her greens. You might encounter greater resistance—or blank stares—if you were to explain how vegetables promote good health, lowering blood pressure and cancer risk and reducing the chance of heart disease and stroke. You would encounter even more blank stares if you were to detail the benefits of antioxidants, dietary fiber, phytoestrogens, and anti-inflammatory agents.

People can be astute, especially with specializations or subjects they deem practical or a clear boon to their lives. For example, some individuals are brilliant in computer science, others with oil painting, and still others with brain surgery. Some are adroit at fixing broken radios or with do-it-yourself projects. But most people could be likened to children when it comes to subjects that they believe to be less pragmatic, such as metaphysics and epistemology. They lack interest in what they think are futile or dead subjects. In addition to philosophy, Latin might fall into this category despite the fact that this language aids with vocabulary. Many English words are derived from classical and medieval Latin.

The risk in perpetuating misinformation as an AR activist is that some non-AR folks may realize—if only on a subconscious level—that these ethical and metaphysical pillars are at variance with the movement's conclusions. This awareness could derail the ultimate mission: to be persuasive and confident about one's position and protect nonhuman lives. Plus, inconsistency could be personally distressing to the activist herself. She may want to feel steady and true in her heart and mind. The metaphysical and political advice advanced in this text may help her feel more self-assured and consistent; it could aid her in endorsing a non-speciesist world in which nonhuman animals are treated as valuable and as ends in themselves.

This book admittedly offers a new and radical path for the AR movement. It does not rely on magic beans, invisible gods, or new age gurus. It is radical because it deviates sharply from what most people want to believe and are comfortable with believing. It is radical because it renounces the fundamental preachings of established political leaders, religious figures, corporate CEOs, and other power brokers who serve up ideological hallucinogens to the public, in part because they think it will help them maintain control and facilitate mass obedience. It is radical because it diverges from the teachings of most traditional Western philosophers—a necessary move for the AR activist because these theories tend to be speciesist.

Speciesism is a belief in human superiority, which is then used to justify exploiting and killing nonhuman animals. There are countless examples of speciesist philosophies. For example, Kantian moral principles and the Rawlsian veil of ignorance apply only to humans. Many celebrated utilitarian philosophers of the past, such as John Stuart Mill and R. M. Hare, limit consequentialist calculations to *Homo sapiens* while ignoring the needs of other living beings. (A non-moral and more inclusive utilitarian system will be explored later.)

Although I am critical of the AR movement's reliance upon traditional morality and free will, AR ideology is accurate in one important respect: its conclusion. Nonhumans have interests and needs; they are of equal value to humans and worthy of equal consideration. I will provide arguments in this book as to why this conclusion holds—a conclusion based on consistency, reason, and available scientific evidence.

Omniocracy is a government with representation for all living beings. Unlike democracy, it is inclusive. It does not ignore the needs of those without power—nonhuman animals. I define democracy as a totalitarian regime in which the powerful (people) use, abuse, manipulate, and murder the powerless (nonhumans) for the former's own perceived gain. Democracy provides representation for only the elite, also known as humans. Even the most down-and-out person has legal rights and societal protections. Democracy is of, by, and for one species: *Homo sapiens*. It is baffling as to why so many people trumpet democracy, especially those who are AR activists and deep ecologists because it is a system built on prejudice—more specifically, on speciesism.

Although humans are animals and no more important than any other species, this book occasionally uses the term "animals" to describe nonhumans. This is for one reason only: ease of writing. It should be noted, however, that philosopher Jacques Derrida is correct. He says that when you categorize nonhuman animals as "animals," you've already "started to enclose the animal into a cage . . . . [It is a] very violent gesture . . . . It partakes of the very real violence that humans exercise towards animals, that leads to slaughterhouses, their industrial treatment, their consumption . . . . There are very few . . . philosophers who don't give into this prejudice against animals."[1]

Speaking of language, I have recently relabeled the term used to describe prejudice against other living beings. I often call it "racism"—instead of "speciesism"—because the phrase "human race" is bantered about so frequently. If humans are a race (as some people apparently like to think), then I figure I can tag the arrogant bias against nonhuman animals as "racism."

Words are powerful and perception is (or often becomes) reality. The word *speciesism* is confusing to the masses; they tend to be unclear of the definition. *Racism*, however, is a trigger. It is viewed as unacceptable, even heinous, in today's society and equated with other politically incorrect "isms," such as sexism and anti-Semitism.

As David Ernst writes, "The power to shut others up by merely insinuating that they are a bigot is subtle, but its potency is difficult to overstate."[2] When discussing "isms," the word *Hitler* is often introduced into the conversation because Nazis are viewed as the Mount Everest of vileness. Most people do not want to think of themselves as racists or Nazis, thus might be willing to discontinue their use and abuse of nonhumans in order to avoid the odious label.

The Emotional Toll

Before delving into my proposed changes for both the AR movement and, by extension, society at large, I would like to focus on the emotional toll experienced by many dedicated animal advocates. Later, I will propose a theory and direction for society that I hope will alleviate much of the anxiety, rage, despair, and turmoil the AR activist may feel.

Warning: Those who believe humans to be superior to other life forms will undoubtedly take offense at the passages below, just as Nazis would have been offended by Germans who defended Jews. "How dare you equate them with us!" is a comment I have heard more than once while advocating for nonhumans.

People tend to demonize animals and glorify humans; thus, they often become indignant, even outraged, when the plight of the former is compared with the plight of the latter. But it is important that the feelings and experiences of the average

AR activist be communicated: animal rights texts tend to avoid this sensitive topic for fear of alienating those who endorse the supremacy of *Homo sapiens*.

Issac Bashevis Singer was a Jewish-American novelist and the recipient of the 1978 Nobel Prize for Literature. His words, which touch on the Nazi discussion above, are particularly relevant:

What do they know—all these scholars, all these philosophers, all the leaders of the world . . . . They have convinced themselves that man, the worst transgressor of all the species, is the crown of creation. All other creatures were created merely to provide him with food, pelts, to be tormented, exterminated. In relation to them, all people are Nazis; for the animals it is an eternal Treblinka.[3]

I would like to expand on this. True, the world is a hell-hole, slaughterhouse, and never-ending Auschwitz from the perspective of nonhumans. But this is *also* the perspective of many (if not most) dedicated animal activists, whether they publicly admit it or not. In their minds, the planet suffers from Nazi occupation. It is crawling with millions of little Hitlers, wantonly splattering blood, asserting unfettered dominance, desperately clinging to the theory that "might makes right," and deluding themselves into believing humans are the anointed ones. There is no escape from the pain because Nazi, Germany, is everywhere; it is an anthropocentric world of abusers who do not care about the helpless creatures they crush, oppress, mutilate, and exterminate. The activist is expected to defer to, even salute, the Führer. For her, Earth is a "heil human" planet.

The AR activist knows it is impossible to eliminate the wall-to-wall human arrogance, the rampant complacency, and the racist hatred for anything not human. The problem is just too widespread. She feels helpless, distraught, and often angry. It is an emotional nightmare. Is she an alien? She often feels like she comes from a different planet and has been dropped into a place she cannot understand. She is constantly shaking her head in disbelief. How can so many people not care while claiming to be moral? Do they not see their hypocrisy? How can they not recognize what they do to innocent nonhumans while condemning Bin Laden, Jeffrey Dahmer, and others who kill their own precious species?

She quickly realizes that most people do not want to open their eyes. They have no interest in giving up their luxuries: their dead animal food, their fur coats, their zoo exhibits, their animal circus acts, their bullfighting and backyard cockfighting, their inhumane horse races (over 900 thoroughbreds died in 2022 alone[4]), and their fancy cosmetics, which are often tested by mutilating rabbits, guinea pigs, and other victims in labs. They prefer to ignore the fact that millions of male baby chicks are thrown alive into electric grinding machines because the factory farm system has no use for them. Or, as an alternative, they are dumped into huge plastic bags and piled up like trash, one live chick on top of another until they all suffocate. Most people wish to ignore the fact that a hen lives her entire life in darkness, on a painful wire surface, crammed into a seven-by-nine-inch area while feces falls onto her head. After a hellish, short life, she is murdered—many years before a natural death.

Offensive images and racist language slam into the AR activist every day. It is like being sandwiched between two Mack trucks. It is inescapable. The brutal images and words are depicted on billboards and in TV commercials (even those pitching non-animal products such as insurance and vacation packages). They are prevalent in movies and newspaper articles, on plates in restaurants, in grocery stores, in social media posts, and in conversations at the park. Every group imaginable—Democrats, Republicans, capitalists, socialists, and even most environmental groups—seems to be complicit.

Dead animal meals are often served at environmental fundraisers despite the fact that meat is a major cause of climate change.[5] Vice President Al Gore conveniently omitted the discussion of food from his environmental book *An Inconvenient Truth*. Meat is a taboo subject; it is considered too controversial to be mentioned. Asking members of environmental organizations to eliminate it from their diets or eat less of it might lead to a loss of donations. Meat is a symbol of power and masculinity. It is "extremely hard to ask people to change their habits."[6]

A few years ago, I offered to give a speech about veganism to Extinction Rebellion activists but was met with a firm no; it was not part of their message.[7] I was informed that many members of the group eat meat.

Society expects the AR activist to keep a stiff upper lip. She is supposed to suffer in silence. She is expected to tolerate images of corpses and verbal grenades—despite the fact that it seems like every other "offended group" is catered to in today's woke society. Special groups get "safe zones." Statues are removed. The names of schools are changed. Some of Dr. Seuss's books have been discontinued due to problematic content.[8] The list goes on. But the AR activist enjoys no such consideration. She is implicitly told, "Those groups matter, but you and the nonhuman victims can go to hell."

For those of you who cannot relate to my Nazi analogy, I will provide another example. Let us assume you are trapped on an island with thousands of adults and children. There are fruits, vegetables, and grains to eat, but the brown-haired people (Brunts) believe the redheaded people (Reds) are inferior beings. The Brunts behead the Reds, cut off their limbs, and fry or bake the parts for consumption. The Reds are used in painful lab testing and dissected in middle school science classes. The Brunts make fashionable polka-dot purses out of the freckled skin of Reds and show them off to their peers. There are images of dead Reds (or their body parts) everywhere: on television, in newspapers, and on billboards. The billboards depict so-called yummy images of Red ribs, fried Red legs, and Red Velvet Cake (a delicacy made from the livers, intestines, and tongues of redheads). The place is abuzz with racist talk and well-stocked with subtle messaging that seek to confirm the inferiority of Reds.

Although you are a privileged Brunt (with flowing brunette hair), you empathize with the Reds and want to protect them. You hate the prejudice, arrogance, and suffering, but you are outnumbered. Brunts have all the power. When you speak out, you are marginalized. You are called a kook, a radical, or mentally ill. You become a victim of "cancel culture," losing your job. If you try to rescue a Red, you will be jailed and possibly tagged as a terrorist. There is no "right to rescue." If you try to videotape a Red in distress in the "agriculture area" or the "vivisection zone," you are punished. The torture and annihilation of redheads is legal, and it is designed to occur in secrecy. Videotaping is prohibited. You feel helpless and defeated. You feel like an alien and an outcast.

The government on this island is a Brunt-ocracy. It is of, by, and for the Brunts. Laws, culture, and the political system exist to benefit Brunts. The Reds have no standing in court. Brunts have dominion. Reds are perceived as mere objects, put on the island for the benefit of the Brunts. After all, the sacred doctrine says so. It is argued, "The Supreme Being agrees."

Brunette mommies and daddies teach their brunette children about the intelligence and goodness of Brunts. Reds are either disparaged or omitted from the conversation. Instructors teach the Brunt children, both implicitly and explicitly, that Reds are lesser and lack free will. They say, "Reds operate due to instinct. They are subordinate." Reds are raised to be meat, lab victims, articles of clothing, dissection tools, or entertainment for Brunts. They are no more valuable than a lamp or sofa. Apart from their usefulness to Brunts, they are as worthless as trash.

What would it be like to be trapped on this island without the possibility of escape? And without an ability to change the entrenched system? Would you feel rage and sorrow? Would you feel paralyzed and powerless? If so, you can identify with the AR activist's heart.

Going forward, this book focuses on philosophy and science—rather than on the emotional—in order to pave the way toward an omniocratic society in which all members—human and nonhuman—are valued. I hope that my theory and suggestions will alleviate some of the pain that the dedicated AR activist feels in society today.

Chapter One

THE PHILOSOPHY OF TODAY'S ANIMAL RIGHTS MOVEMENT

Animal rights advocates criticize the anthropocentric outlook that posits human beings as the final end of God's creation and as inherently superior to all Others, and they ask that society shed the antiquated and catastrophic notion that nonhuman animals are tools to be manipulated or murdered for a human end. The biocentrism they promote affirms equal value and equal consideration for all sentient life forms. It typically stems from either a deontological argument (i.e., per philosopher Tom Regan) or a utilitarian one (i.e., per philosopher Peter Singer). Regan appeals to animal *rights,* and Singer suggests a moral imperative for animal *liberation.* (Keep in mind, I am generally using the terms "animal rights" and "animal liberation" interchangeably in this book for ease of writing.)

To fully comprehend the animal rights ethic, one might want to embark upon a discussion of "essentialism." In other words, one might want to evaluate whether there is a particular attribute, such as the size of a brain, which "morally" differentiates humans from their nonhuman brothers and sisters. Charles Darwin—who once said that "animals whom we have made our slaves, we do not like to consider our equal"[9]—uprooted the traditional theologies and philosophies of his time with the theory of natural selection. This theory discounts the significance of the human brain by suggesting it is "no different from the hawk's keen eyes, the gazelle's swiftness, or the chameleon's camouflage."[10]

AR thinkers know that by displacing essentialist criteria and demonstrating that intelligence, communication skills, consensual ability, and moral agency are inconsequential when making evaluations about the inherent value of a being, they can give their cause force. Any onlooker who cannot be convinced, who ignores the durability and power of these arguments, is hopelessly condemned to speciesist quarters.

A speciesist is, according to AR activists, a bigot, giving refuge to a deplorable "ism" no less severe than anti-Semitism, sexism, or racism. Believing humans to be superior to nonhumans is, in their view, morally equivalent to assuming that Whites are superior to Blacks, men are superior to women, or Christians are superior to Jews. From an AR perspective, speciesism places nonhumans in concentration camps and gases them to death.

Intelligence

Throughout history, intelligence has been touted as the best way to "prove" the superiority of certain peoples, races, and sexes, and it has been used to sanction the abuse of those deemed less intellectually endowed. This was the belief in Nazi Europe when the Germans tampered with Jews, Gypsies, and other non-Aryans in numerous research studies. Due to his fascination for twins, dwarfs, and "abnormal humans," Josef Mengele gathered up prisoners at Auschwitz, especially children, weighing them, measuring them, and dissecting them. Nyziszli, a prisoner pathologist, said in a 1945 deposition that Mengele once "shot two boys in the neck and that while they were still warm, began to examine them: lungs first, and then each organ,"[11] and on another occasion, Mengele is said to have "brought in two heads . . . wrapped in newspaper . . . children's heads . . . smelling of phenol."[12] One concentration camp survivor reported seeing his high school gymnasium teacher stuffed (mummified) on Block 10.[13] Nazis tinkered with humans in a range of research projects, from sterilization and castration experiments to typhus contagion testing and artificial insemination procedures.

The assumption that superior intelligence entitles one to violate the bodies and minds of those considered "lesser" has not been limited to Eastern Europe. American Blacks suffered at the whim of racist scientists in the Tuskegee, Alabama, study of 1932, a forty-year longitudinal survey that victimized poor Black males by observing the course of untreated syphilis without offering these men treatment or even bothering to inform them that they had the affliction.[14]

Some believe that the U.S. government injected the Black men with the disease because it seems inconceivable that such a large pool of syphilis-inflicted research subjects could have been located in such a limited geographical area and within such a brief period. Aside from Tuskegee, dozens of other experiments have been documented using Blacks, the mentally incapacitated, the aged, and other so-called inferior beings.[15]

Intelligence is difficult to define. Is it manifested via the ability to solve advanced calculus or to successfully conduct brain surgery? Is it demonstrated through street smarts or manipulation of the sociopolitical system? Instead, does it involve having the ability to do the waggle dance, a skill far too complex for any human to replicate, by which bees measure angular distances and exchange detailed information?[16] Perhaps intelligence is best exemplified as a sixth sense, such as when an animal recognizes the onset of an earthquake or other natural disaster.[17]

Nonhumans possess abilities that humans lack, and some of those abilities could arguably qualify as "intelligence." An article in *Discover* magazine lists five of these special nonhuman abilities: echolocation, electroreception, infrared vision, magnetoreception, and polarized light vision.[18] But there are more specific examples. Butterflies have the equivalent of a GPS in their antennae,[19] and some chimpanzees have surpassed humans on the cognitive task of taking a brief glance (faster than a human can blink) at a series of numbers and then tapping them in the right order.[20] Wild orangutans know how to find and use medicinal plants to treat their wounds. They do it with intention. Researchers recently observed a Sumatran orangutan "treating an open facial wound with sap and chewed leaves from a plant known to have anti-inflammatory and pain-relieving properties . . . . Five days later, the facial wound was closed, while within a few weeks it had healed, leaving only a small scar."[21] Most people would have no clue how to locate and apply shrubbery to mend a skin laceration.

According to the *New York Times,* dogs can detect cancer in humans by merely taking a whiff of a human breath sample.[22] They can also detect cancerous growth in members of their own species.[23]

Some animals seem to be able to detect earthquakes a day or more before the event because of what scientists guess may be an ability to hear higher frequencies or zero in on the existence of electromagnetic changes.[24] There are eyewitness accounts of animal movement prior to a disaster; one article states that "elephants ran for higher ground, flamingos abandoned low-lying nesting areas . . . and cows, goats, cats, and birds deliberately mov[ed] inland."[25]

Perhaps intelligence is best characterized by wisely withdrawing during a fight rather than feuding until death, a pacifist tactic notoriously attributed to animals rather than humans. Perhaps reckless stupidity is best exemplified by those who build nuclear weaponry and trash the environment. Or better yet, perhaps the only intellectually inferior beings are those who believe nonhumans are of lesser value than humans. In other words, it is a matter of definition.

As has been the case historically with human oppressors and their subjugated victims, biases favor the definers rather than the definees. People establish the criteria for judging intelligence; thus, they emphasize their own strengths rather than those attributed to other species.

At the time of the syphilis testing, Whites invented intelligence tests that Blacks reportedly failed. The non-passing scores reflected the subjective nature of measuring intelligence and how the creators of the questionnaire unconsciously (or perhaps consciously) designed and administered a test that their own race would pass and outsiders would fail. Amazingly enough, the intellectual leaders of society had full confidence in the viability of the tests, and therefore, "did not doubt the racial ranking with Indians below Whites, and Blacks below everybody else."[26]

Another inherent difficulty with intelligence centers around its immeasurability and fluctuations. Not only is it impossible to quantify, but the amount of intelligence in a being must necessarily change from moment to moment as he or she gains new insights from the environment or experiences mental deterioration due to internal and/or external stimuli. Scientists note that true measurement of anything is impossible because even the act of measuring alters the results.

Let us suppose that one is unconvinced by the above arguments and still wishes to bank on an "essentialist" distinction between clever humans and less intelligent nonhumans. Does this provide a basis for eliminating the latter from moral concern? Animal rights proponents say no, for if one claims that only the rational have innate value, one must concede that newborn infants and "marginal" humans, such as the severely mentally incapacitated, also lack intrinsic worth. If it is acceptable to vivisect or consume dogs, pigs, or cows, by analogy, it must be acceptable to experiment on or eat some severely "handicapped" humans. There are canines, swine, and bovines with markedly higher levels of intelligence and reasoning ability than certain humans.

If one maintains that babies or mentally incapacitated humans are more important because there are loved ones who care about their welfare, what happens to the "unwanted" humans, such as homeless alcoholics who lack family and friends? Can they be disposed of like nonhumans?

Some may try to escape from this difficulty by appealing to the "general tendency of the species." They might argue that *most* humans are intelligent and *most* animals are not; therefore, the former should be protected whereas the latter should be available for use and exploitation. However, a flaw in this reasoning surfaces when one embarks upon a hypothetical case in which 51 percent of the human population contracts a harrowing disease that transforms them into mental vegetables, unable to reason, unable to think with the level of clarity found in a dog, pig, or cow. Would this make it acceptable to kill, vivisect, or devour all humans, including those with "normal" mental capacity?

The person relying upon the "general tendency of the species" is, of course, unlikely to allow for the ingestion or dissection of his entire, now (predominantly) mentally "inferior" species and would probably even object to the murder and/or torture of the defective 51 percent, many of whom may be his friends and relatives. Thus, this person would be exposed for what AR activists initially assumed him to be: a speciesist.

Moral Agency

Philosopher Richard A. Watson deploys a different tactic against standard animal rights philosophy. He asserts that nonhumans are unworthy of moral consideration because they are not moral agents. Watson says there must be a reciprocal moral relationship for there to be duties and obligations. He suggests that a being must possess the necessary qualities of self-consciousness, free will, the capacity to understand moral principles, the Kantian ability to act for the sake of duty, and the physical capacity (or what he calls "potentiality") to act.

Watson's position is again one of essentialism, and his use of the word "potentiality" would arouse suspicion in most AR activists. It gives the impression that this was a last-minute thought serving only one purpose: that of including the entirety of the species *Homo sapiens*—including the previously discussed infants and mentally impaired humans. Watson confesses uncertainty as to which animals are self-conscious, if any, but then guesses that perhaps "some chimpanzees, gorillas, dolphins, elephants, whales, dogs, pigs, and maybe cats are moral agents."[27] He bases his findings on subjective, personal experiences of watching the behavior of nonhumans—not very convincing on scientific grounds.

Author and philosopher Steven Sapontzis rejects the essentialist position hinging on moral agency but believes that animals may be moral agents anyway. He focuses on the altruistic behavior of a "mother bird that feigns a broken wing and risks her life to distract a fox from her nest . . . [and then discusses] loyal dogs, courageous lions, responsible wolves, and industrious beavers."[28] Some researchers maintain that even rats are altruistic and have metacognition.[29]

But it is unclear why moral agency or lack of moral agency would matter, as morality dictates how an agent should behave regardless of the moral or immoral behavior of the "other." A newborn baby that stabs her mother with a knife is not suddenly judged unworthy of moral consideration. The mother is not granted the moral or legal right to stab the baby back. So why should it be different with nonhumans?

To take another example, let us assume a woman gets robbed. She is now the victim of theft, but she is not suddenly morally entitled to steal. The Golden Rule does not say "Do unto others as you would have them do unto you *unless*, of course, they do something bad to you first."

Immanuel Kant's categorical imperative dictates a universal maxim that must be followed, yet the failure of others to comply in no way diminishes a moral agent's obligation. Utilitarianism is no different: One "right" action is calculated for every situation, and it is not contingent upon whether others treat you properly or whether they have the ability to choose. Thus, it is a weak argument to hinge moral consideration and intrinsic value on the capacity for moral agency.

Philosopher Paul Taylor believes that only humans can be moral agents but argues that this "essentialist distinction" does not damage AR arguments. He asserts that it is a logical flaw to assume that humans are morally superior due to their ability to be moral agents because only beings who "have the capacities of a moral agent can properly be judged to be either moral or immoral. Moral standards are simply not applicable to beings that lack such capacities."[30] Taylor reasons that animals and plants cannot, therefore, be said to be morally inferior in merit to humans.

Communication

Some people argue that communicative ability is the factor that should determine who is worthy of moral concern. They state that animals cannot communicate in the sophisticated way that humans can. Therefore, they should not be entitled to moral consideration.

I will set aside the fact that humans are not privy to the full communicative capabilities of other species. I will simply explain how drawing the line at communication is another problematic "essentialist" distinction. It can be condemned per the arguments about incapacitated humans in the "intelligence" section. An impaired human may have less ability to communicate than a pig, horse, or cow.

Furthermore, there is evidence that some animals have penetrated the human–nonhuman communication/intelligence barrier, such as a pygmy chimp named Kanzi, who has demonstrated not only aptitude but also communicative skills.

UCLA psychology professor Patricia Marks says his abilities "compare favorably with those of a two-year-old child. Kanzi's syntax skills imply that a potential for primitive language is not unique to humans but existed in our apelike ancestors."[31] By 1991, Kanzi had proved his understanding of 650 sentences, quite remarkable considering the tight controls used during the testing procedures, which convinced even skeptics of his extraordinary ability. Kanzi broke a "two-decade deadlock during which language experimentation with animals was paralyzed by concerns that the animals were responding to cues from their trainers rather than demonstrating true abstract abilities."[32] Today, Kanzi knows more than 3,000 spoken words[33] and can light fires and cook.[34]

Kanzi is not alone. There are numerous examples of communicative prowess (and intelligence) in nonhumans.

Expressing oneself is often a prerequisite for proving aptitude. Rhesus monkeys display a talent for ordering numerals at a research lab at the University of Georgia,[35] and pigs are smarter than three-year-old children.[36] Octopuses can process, store, and apply data; they stand out with respect to "discriminative learning . . . and can retain this information for several months."[37] They can also navigate simple mazes and unscrew jars[38] and are "very skilled at communicating with humans."[39]

At the University of Arizona, an African gray parrot named Alex could communicate his feelings and had learned more than 71 labels denoting objects, actions, colors, shapes, and materials. He died in 2007, but at the time, he had the intelligence of a five-year-old child.[40]

Dolphins can understand simple language and communicate with people. Researchers at the Kewalo Basin Marine Mammal Laboratory have learned that "dolphins can understand not only a complex vocabulary but also syntax, or word order—a basic rule of sentence formation that constitutes language as humans define the term."[41]

Sea lions also have a "grasp of human communication skills,"[42] and studies done on East African Vervet monkeys indicate similarities between animal calls and human language.[43] Some green-backed herons actually fish with bait, which "suggests that they are indeed thinking about what they are doing."[44]

A 2017 segment on *BBC Earth* focuses on a dog who understands 1,022 words and can figure out the names of new objects via a process of elimination.[45] I could go on with examples, but suffice it to say, there are numerous others. A *Huffington Post* piece lists several "Animal Einsteins" and adept communicators; the article admits that science has "put a dent in human uniqueness claims."[46]

Would Watson, who determines the moral agency of animals

by watching their behavior, revise his list of those deserving of consideration in light of this evidence? What would a policy look like that includes herons, octopi, butterflies, and parrots? And if they can be included, it is reasonable to assume that many—if not all—nonhumans have such capacities, regardless of whether humans can tap into them.

Despite the evidence, some claim that "all animal cognition is unconscious . . . and . . . [even if animals do have conscious mental experiences] they are hopelessly inaccessible to scientific analysis . . . . [Thus,] hypotheses about them cannot be objectively tested."[47] Yet, it is a fallacy to deny animals moral consideration based on this theory because even hypotheses about the consciousness of other humans cannot be proved. How do we know about another person's mental state? We have no access to their inner thoughts or experiences. Professor John A. Fisher says there is "no way to formulate the other minds problem so that it applies to animals but not to fellow humans."[48] There is always a logical gap between behavior and mental state.

Additionally, relying upon behavior and verbal evidence from humans is problematic in that people sometimes pretend to have mental states that they do not indeed have. For example, an individual may feign pain when none exists. She may lie, be under a psychological delusion, or be playing a practical joke. As Fisher states, "Skeptics about animals do not suppose that they are capable of this sort of deception,"[49] and if one attributes this type of deception to them, it arguably makes them as intelligent and as conscious as humans are said to be.

Can Animals Consent?

Another question revolves around whether a nonhuman can consent to assume the role of research subject, zoo prisoner, factory farm egg producer, or steak house entrée. An AR activist might assert that an animal cannot autonomously agree to any of the above. Because it would be appropriate to use, abuse, or kill only those who can consent (if appropriate at all), it must be concluded that nonhumans should not be the subject of enslavement or slaughter.

Surprisingly, the aforementioned Sapontzis believes that animals can consent, and relates a story about monkeys raised in a research facility who are permitted to wander in and out of the compound each day in search of food and entertainment. Because they always return, Sapontzis interprets this as voluntary and consensual. He contrasts this with another case in which cats involved in a sleep deprivation test repeatedly try to escape the painful procedures and thus cannot be said to give permission.

Sapontzis says that in order for animals to give informed consent, they must be sane and capable of understanding "how the experiments will likely affect (their) interests."[50] Although animals cannot sign a release form, he thinks they can make behavioristic, consensual decisions in much the same way as Socrates believes that people consent to a social contract when they live in a free society.

John Stuart Mill argues that one cannot consent to be a slave, and even if Sapontzis's monkeys are repeatedly given opportunities to resign from the project, they could be psychological slaves. Perhaps they have been raised in captivity and are frightened by the prospect of fending for themselves on a full-time basis, unaware of wild monkey protocol. Perhaps they have been, in a sense, brainwashed and are oblivious to the option of fleeing from the research facility. They may fear the consequences of deserting the scientists or simply love a certain kind of edible that cannot be found in the woods. Additionally, how do we evaluate whether the monkeys are sane?

Psychological motivation can be complicated. Numerous wives go to the supermarket, dry cleaners, and department store, yet return home each night to be beaten by their husbands. Do these women consent to abuse? Have they given permission like Sapontzis's monkeys? Some say the women should be independent enough to flee, whereas others call them "victims" and insist that they have no control over their impulse to return. Are the monkeys similarly victims? It could be argued that some animals are more dependent by nature, as in the case of dogs who are known to return for further maltreatment. It is logical that Sapontzis's cats would try to escape because felines are notably self-reliant creatures.

Although it can be difficult to determine whether a person is sane and able to rationally agree to be a research subject, it is easier to ascertain human autonomy due to ease of communication and the mounds of psychological data relating to the behavior and motivation of *Homo sapiens,* which can assist in the process of judging true consent. Thus, an animal advocate who attributes equal value to animals would elect consenting and financially compensated humans as research subjects in lieu of nonhumans—the latter being incapable of making easily identifiable and binding decisions. It would be illogical and speciesist to do otherwise.

The Speciesism Defense

Before discussing how most animal activists consider "sentience" to be the pivotal factor for determining innate value and moral consideration, I will examine what it means to rely upon speciesism as a philosophical defense. Philosophers J.A. Gray, Mary Midgley, Robert Nozick, and R.G. Frey maintain that speciesism is a wholly defensible position. J.A. Gray argues that a mother has a special duty to a child for biological reasons in that natural selection forces her "to maximize survival of the genes (she) carries." He adds that as humans, we have special duties toward the members of our own species and that "much of the concern for the welfare of people unrelated to ourselves is very likely the extension of the genetically-based concerns we feel for kin."[51]

There are convincing objections to this line of reasoning. First, some people feel more connected to nonhumans than humans; thus, it seems incorrect to insist that a biological factor predisposes one to prefer members of one's own species. Secondly, the love a mother has for her child is in no way lessened when the child is adopted; therefore, the assumption that her feelings stem from biology seems wholly inaccurate. Thirdly, Gray's argument could lead to serious consequences in that a White person could argue that she has greater affinity for another White, and thus no moral concern for or obligation toward Blacks; after all, the White could argue that she remains genetically closer to those of her own race. It could lead to other biases, such as in the case of men who mount this argument in favor of hiring only males in the workplace. Fourthly, "is" does not translate to "ought," and "natural" is not necessarily the preferential state of affairs. Even if evolutionary factors contribute to the perpetuation of a species and any partialities thereof, this does not indicate that a moral theory should be based upon these factors. To take an example, so-called progress—which could be touted as a "natural" and inevitable occurrence in history, much like Gray's "natural" feelings for kin—has arguably led to the deterioration of the environment and emphasis on monetary gain, but this in no way indicates that an ethic should be based upon ravaging nature and making money.

Mary Midgley likewise distinguishes herself as a speciesist but attempts to dispel the racist repercussions of the theory by suggesting that "race" in humans is not a significant grouping because one does not need to know the race to which a person belongs to know how to treat her. She argues that this is not the case with animals because "species" is a significant grouping: one must know from which species an animal comes to know how to behave toward the animal. But do not most animals, including humans, require the same basics: food, water, shelter, and warmth of some sort? And is Midgley correct in assuming that the nature of *Homo sapiens* requires a particular type of treatment? I say no, for treatment would differ vastly for a headhunter, an Aborigine, an American Indian, a White Wall Street stockbroker, an Amish farmer, a Black female, a Hindu, and a Jain monk. Treatment may have little to do with race, but it has much to do with culture in addition to the individual's beliefs, personality, and desires.

Midgley says that nonhumans "have entirely different needs about temperature and water-supply, bedding, exercise-space, solitude, company and many other things. Their vision and experience of the world must therefore be profoundly different [from those of humans]."[52] Her focus on "species" as the demarcating factor would be quickly countered by the animal activist who might point out major differences between people. A person plagued with agoraphobia has requirements unlike a person suffering from claustrophobia. The recluse who prefers staying alone in a six-thousand-square-foot mansion in the Hamptons differs greatly from the person who enjoys living with three others in a one-room flat, and the individual who needs the 102-degree heat of Phoenix to combat acute arthritis has contrary needs from the person who favors the bitter chill of Minnesota. There are food allergies, psychological and physical demands, and other personal considerations. Thus, each human, like each animal, has unique requirements that largely dictate her needs, and these needs may diverge—sometimes substantially—from others in her species.

Midgley then follows Gray's line of thought (which, of course, can be similarly criticized). She insists that "the natural preference for one's own species does exist. It is not, like race-prejudice, a product of culture. It is found in all human cultures, and in cases of real competition it tends to operate very strongly . . . . Our nature dictates where the border of morality shall fall, and aligns itself with it once and for all with the species-barrier."[53] However, interestingly enough, Midgley seems to refute her theory later in her essay when she cites examples of wolf-children who care more about wolves than humans, a duck who is reared by chickens and thus prefers chickens to other ducks, and a chimp who has a greater affinity for baboons than those of his own species. Apart from Midgley's article, other sources discuss how animals can leap over the species barrier. Reuters singles out a tortoise and baby hippo who are inseparable,[54] and the *Daily Mail* reports a farm dog who is raising a tiny pot-bellied pig as her child.[55]

Midgley also discusses how some tribes fail to view human outsiders as "persons." She adds that "there are some people who actually prefer [horses] to humans [although she says] this attitude is generally frowned upon . . ."[56] These exceptions seem to lead Midgley into a zone of doubt at the end of her essay and support the conclusion that Midgley's theory is severely flawed.

Robert Nozick, a speciesist, argues that "any species may legitimately give their fellows more weight than they give members of other species. Lions, too, if they were moral agents, could not be criticized for putting the interests of other lions first."[57] Yet the animal activist might ask why this argument does not likewise hold for race, class, gender, and sexual orientation. And if it does hold, why do we criticize Nazis for putting the interests of other Aryans first or slaveholders for putting the interests of masters above those of slaves?

Perhaps the movie *Planet of the Apes* best illustrates how people would react to Nozick's speculation about lions having power. In the film, when apes refuse to give moral and legal consideration to another species—namely, the humans they hold as slaves—the movie's protagonists are morally outraged, and the audience is compelled to feel the same way. It isn't until one human, Charlton Heston, proves he can speak English (the same language as the apes) that he is finally considered somewhat of an "equal." However, he is still slated to be vivisected by the scientific community. He is rescued by two radical ape activists who would no doubt be declared terrorists today under the repressive laws that target the AR movement, such as the Animal Enterprise Terrorism Act.

In the movie, the ape activists ignore the laws of their land and risk their freedom to save Heston's life. Of course, the nonspeaking humans remain inferior and enslaved. One suspects that if lions were to dominate humans and if they could vivisect, eat, maim, and murder people at will, people would violently object to speciesism. Because lions cannot currently abuse and dispose of the human population, Nozick may not be able to fathom his true reaction.

R.G. Frey is also a self-proclaimed speciesist, yet he does not try to uphold the view that all humans are equal. He believes the life of a mentally disabled person is of less value than that of a "normal" human, for "life is a function of its quality, its quality a function of its richness, and its richness a function of the scope or potential for enrichment."[58] The error with this argument is that it could be used to condone the murder of a child with Down Syndrome (a so-called defective human) in order to save the life of Hitler (a supposedly normal person). It might even allow for experimentation on the mentally inferior and other similarly objectionable acts.

Feminist Deborah Slicer does not call herself a speciesist but follows an argument that, in the end, promotes prejudice and gives preferential treatment to humans. She argues against grounding an ethic in "reason." Instead, she suggests that we base our moral actions on the special ties we feel for others. She seeks to promote the significance of "familial relationships or friendships" and thinks a rational grounding "strips an individual of his or her specific history, identity, and affective-emotional constitution."[59] She hopes to replace this rational grounding with "respect, gratitude, compassion, fellow or sisterly feeling, and wonder."[60] Slicer does not seem to consider two points. First, the strength of "reason" is that it is not inherently biased. It does not eliminate some from moral concern based on personal preference or feelings of kinship. Reason—in conjunction with morality—tells us that we are not justified in throwing the one Jew out of the lifeboat because we feel kinship with the Christians on board.

Secondly, acting in a particular way in a stressful situation can differ from how one *ought* to act in the situation. Let us assume a homeowner adheres to an ethic of nonviolence (ahimsa), and a felon breaks into her house with a gun, aiming to murder her sister. The homeowner has the opportunity to shoot the felon first and does so. Although the killing could be legally justified due to the situation, the woman could still maintain that her murderous action was immoral. It is in no way inconsistent to say that it is always wrong to take another life intentionally and to simultaneously admit that one might act immorally when under tremendous stress. Although it may be reasonable to act upon emotional feelings when a criminal bursts into one's home, it is arguably unnecessary and dangerous to build an ethic on this basis.

Sentience

Now that intelligence, moral agency, communicative ability, autonomous consent, and speciesism have failed to prove viable measures for distinguishing who is worthy of moral concern, upon what criterion do animal activists rely? The AR movement almost unanimously rallies around "sentience," as championed within the basic theories of Peter Singer and Tom Regan. I emphasize their "basic theories" because there are specific, dubious statements that Singer and Regan make with which an activist might disagree. Most activists do not scrutinize these questionable statements. Instead, they adopt the general or overall philosophies of Singer and Regan.

According to animal rights philosophy, sentience is neither dubious nor discriminatory if one is seeking an impartial gauge to determine the inclusion or exclusion of *sentient* beings within the arena of moral consideration. This is because it is the lowest common denominator for all sentients.

The desire to avoid physical pain is a recognized goal of all sentient beings; thus, it harbors no bias in connection with elite abilities and talents, genetic composition, cultural complexity, species membership, or other erroneous factors. Although only sentients are shielded under AR's moral umbrella, the animal advocate might argue that insentients are not necessarily excluded from moral concern. Insentients are simply outside the parameters of the movement's particular focus. Therefore, nothing needs to be said about them.[61]

An AR activist might compare this with a feminist organization that strives to free Afghan women from sexism. The lowest common denominator for the victims is that they live in

Afghanistan, are female, and are oppressed; the activist might argue that this focus in no way suggests that the feminists favor the subjugation of women in other countries, nor does it sanction the subjugation of men in Afghanistan or abroad.[62]

Jeremy Bentham, perhaps the first philosopher to argue that the utilitarian calculation should not be confined to humans but instead extended to all sentient living things, says, "The interests of every being affected by an action are to be taken into account and given the same weight as the like interests of any other being."[63] In his famous quote, he asks, "The question is not, Can they [animals] reason? nor Can they talk? but, Can they suffer?"[64]

Like Bentham, Peter Singer—often revered as the founder of the animal liberation movement[65]—is a utilitarian who concludes that sentient creatures are of equal value to humans and worthy of equal consideration. However, this does not necessarily translate into equal treatment. Because of differing interests or abilities, treatment may vary. For example, a bird need not be given the legal right to vote or the freedom to worship, just as a human need not be given the right to flap her wings and fly.

The theory of deontologist Tom Regan parallels that of Singer in many relevant ways; Regan asserts that animals are not our resources "to be eaten, surgically manipulated, or exploited for sport or money"[66] and calls for the complete replacement of animal models in science and a total dissolution of animal agriculture.

George P. Cave, the president of the animal liberation organization Trans-Species Unlimited, agrees with the general theories of Singer and Regan. He says, "We must always choose to avoid the greater pain. This applies no less to ethical conflicts between a human being and a nonhuman being than to those between two or more nonhuman animals. Yet where the pain suffered is determinable as equal, the conflict cannot be resolved by utilitarianism . . . . . . [and when we embark upon] a qualitative standard of good and evil we are in danger of speciesism."[67] Cave asserts that "equal pain" warrants an impartial tossing of a coin.

Is pain truly equal for nonhumans and humans alike? Of course, the pain threshold necessarily varies from one individual to another regardless of species. Still, some contend that nonhumans encounter less pain overall as a result of what they call their "limited mental capacity," in much the same way as they assume brain-damaged people suffer less. Perhaps the nonhumans and the "incapacitated" humans do not experience the anticipatory dread that "normal" humans would.

On the other hand, some argue the pain of nonhumans is greater because of their inability to comprehend the situation. Philosopher Baruch Spinoza reasons that "understanding the cause of a sensation diminishes its severity,"[68] and common sense supports this argument, such as when a suspected heart attack turns out to be heartburn. Steven Sapontzis concurs: "The distress and frustration experienced by a human prisoner of war can be alleviated by recollections of past freedom and hope for future release, while a dog trapped in a laboratory cage (supposedly) has no such recollection or hope to ease its distress and frustration."[69] Because arguments on both sides of this issue are convincing and because the extent of individual pain remains scientifically indeterminable, it must be assumed to be equal between sentient living beings.

Subject of a Life and Quality of Life

Although Peter Singer and Tom Regan brilliantly advance the general notion of equal value and equal consideration for all sentient creatures, they sabotage their models with internal inconsistencies regarding "quality of life" claims. For example, Singer states that a human generally has more interests than an animal and is, therefore, capable of a fuller life. So, when a conflict arises between a human and a nonhuman, one should save the one with the fuller life, usually the human.

To Singer's credit, he acknowledges that a dog should, in many cases, be saved over an incapacitated human because the dog has a fuller life. Yet, to Singer's discredit, he seems oblivious to the fact that he has shifted his focus from the lowest common denominator of sentience to "having a fuller life," an essentialist claim with repercussions as problematic as those associated with intelligence, communicative abilities, and moral agency. He has secretly moved the goal post or, more precisely, switched the measuring stick.

Philosopher James Rachels faces the same criticism as Singer. Although he does not appeal to sentience, he builds his argument on a Singer-like criterion: by giving moral consideration only to beings who are "subjects of a life." He says that "when there is reason to choose between the death of a human and the death of a dog, there is reason to choose in favor of the human . . . because when a mentally complex thing dies, much more can be said about why its death was a bad thing."[70]

In *The Case for Animal Rights,* Tom Regan errs in much the same way as Singer and Rachels when he discusses a lifeboat situation with five on board: four humans and one dog. The situation demands that one be thrown overboard, otherwise all will die. Regan concedes that the dog should be sacrificed because "death for the dog, in short, though a harm, is not comparable to the harm that death would be for any of the humans."[71] In fact, Regan goes on to say that it would be better to save one human rather than a million dogs and adds that the reason for this is not speciesist but simply based on assessing the losses each individual faces and measuring these losses equitably.

First, how do Singer, Rachels, and Regan know that a human has a fuller life than a dog? Science certainly lacks the capacity to assess this immeasurable quality. In addition, there are countless examples of mentally alert jet-setters who complain of a "lack" in their lives and even sometimes resort to suicide, whereas there are mentally impaired individuals who gleefully report that they have very full and happy lives.

Secondly, surely the million dogs (in Regan's example) have a fuller life combined than one human. Although Regan is not a utilitarian and is therefore disinclined to evaluate the total sum of pain and suffering, it seems that ignoring this fact could potentially lead to the annihilation of every nonhuman in the world in favor of one human life, thus defeating his entire AR theory. Thirdly, if one million nonhumans, with their less full lives, can be killed in favor of saving one human being, why does Regan claim to be opposed to vivisection and other animal use? It would seem that he does not support animal rights at all.

Lastly, Regan's and Singer's (and Rachels's) "quality of life" concerns could take us down a slippery slope toward racism and other objectionable "isms," toward the moral imperative to preserve human life with a higher perceived "quality" (i.e., the jet-setters) over those of ordinary or "substandard" humans. The "quality of life" distinction could require choosing the life of a rich, smart world traveler over that of a depressed and financially impoverished couch potato, just as it could mandate the rescuing of Hitler from Regan's infamous lifeboat while tossing a child with Down Syndrome over the side. Of course, it goes without saying that (per Regan's theory) one would be ethically required to rescue Hitler in lieu of Regan's beloved dog, the latter whom we could suppose, for argument's sake, has recently saved Regan's little girl from drowning.

Many critics have blasted both Singer and Regan for these inconsistencies. However, animal activists, in general, if they notice these problems, remain focused on "sentience" and the overall theories of these well-respected philosophers—theories that promote equal value and equal consideration for all sentient beings.

Going forward, I set aside the traditional animal rights arguments—in effect, wiping the theoretical slate clean—and address what I believe is a better way to construct AR philosophy and establish a non-speciesist society. Later in the book, I will focus on politics and the need for an omniocracy.

Let us begin with everybody's favorite subject: metaphysics.

Chapter Two

FREE WILL: AN INVISIBLE MONSTER

The average AR activist in Western society subscribes to the metaphysic of free will despite the fact that this view is misguided. Scientific evidence supports a (hard) determined universe, meaning humans and nonhumans act, react, and move like marbles in a vast pinball machine or billiard balls on a universe-sized pool table. People are not mini-gods with the ability to rise above the rest of creation. They are metaphysically determined. They are equal to all creatures in this way.

A determined universe is one without accidents, random acts, irregularity, contingency, or freedom of the will. Every event, result, effect, desire, feeling, thought, choice, and action is caused. Although humans cannot comprehend the myriad triggers that produce a given effect, this in no way suggests these triggers do not exist. Within this theory, all inanimate objects and living things, including people, are governed solely by cause and effect.

Both internal factors, such as one's constitution and heredity, and external influences, such as societal mores and laws, create silent and invisible imprints that arguably dupe a person into believing she has free will. If it were possible to comprehensively explore the biological and environmental stimuli that have impinged upon a particular individual throughout her life, one could accurately predict her future behavior.

Determinism should not be confused with fatalism, which holds that an outcome is predestined. The characters in the movie *Final Destination* were hunted down by Death when it was their time to die, just as Oedipus was doomed to marry his mother in the end. No matter what path the Greek king took, he was sure to find himself in the same dreadful predicament.

Fatalism assumes that high-level motives emanate from a creator or designer of the universe; every person has a detailed and inescapable life plan. Determinism is much simpler; it does not attribute actions to a God or wise architect. It merely describes how the whirling, swirling universe impacts one thing, which in turn impacts another, and so forth. It outlines a domino effect.

If freedom of the will existed, it would allow humans to make unhampered choices and act on these choices without influence from causal forces. It would transform people into virtually omnipotent deities with the magical skill of detethering themselves from their genes, their upbringing, and their circumstances. It would catapult humans to the pinnacle of the great chain of being, second only to a maker, first mover, or God. It would reinforce the notion that humans are superior to other living beings.

You can think of the determined universe like a soccer match; the players engage in a game of cause and effect. There is a constant reaction to the forces. A ball bounces up and down, ricochets, hits a head, and spins through the air. The players run here and there, push, tumble, leap, have multiple thoughts, claw each other, and drive for the goal. It happens in a flash; there are millions of tiny actions that even the most advanced computer cannot compute. The players are the ball; the ball is the player. None have choices. All react.

"Free" Deception

The oafish character Castle in the novel *Walden Two* says: "A simple personal experience makes [determinism] untenable . . . . [I rely upon] the experience of freedom. I know that I am free."[72] But is Castle right? The perceived inner struggle that one may experience between so-called options, whether to smoke a cigar or refrain, go the theater or stay home, indulge in a chocolate eclair or diet, all add to the presumption that one could do otherwise. Since science maintains that every event is caused, is this sense of grappling with options merely an illusion? Is this internal tug-of-war nothing more than a verbalization or clarification of some of the causes bearing upon a person, some of which might be viewed as duties and others of which might be described as pleasures?[73]

The only so-called evidence for the existence of free will revolves around what Castle mentions—a supposed *feeling* that some people claim to have, a subjective notion that they are somehow free.[74] But a mere feeling is not science. It is not a repeatable experiment. It is not logic or reason-based. It is not evidence of anything. As philosopher Baruch Spinoza says, those "who believe that they . . . do anything from free mental decision are dreaming with their eyes open."[75]

Perceptions are fallible, as evidenced by a mirage in the desert, a straight but crooked-looking stick in a pond, computer images of virtual reality, motion picture special effects, the impression of a flat earth, and a portrait with eyes that mysteriously seem to follow wherever one moves. All can induce perceptual errors when one is not privy to the latest scientific findings. Any experience of free will is arguably a similar consequence of error, faulty judgment, confusion, or inadequate knowledge about causality.

Many explanations exist for why humans may deem themselves free: from a subconscious, Nietzschean desire for power and control to being duped by that which is nothing other than a by-product of consciousness. I call the latter the "body protection theory." This theory asserts that consciousness is required in order to differentiate oneself from the rest of the world. On a subatomic level, the quarks flow to and fro, deleting the divide between objects and merging them into one. But on a grander scale, there is a practical need to distinguish one's body from that of another. Without this ability, a living being might not survive. If she could not make a distinction between her arm and a fire, she could burn. If she could not perceive a difference between herself and a pond, she could drown. She arguably needs to be conscious to protect her body. It is possible that a by-product of this consciousness may be a feeling of freedom, the illusion that one has the unhampered ability to direct one's actions.

There is direct scientific evidence that free will is a parlor trick, and people are mesmerized by its spell. Experiments dating back to the 1970s have shown that individuals are fooled about the ownership of their actions. They react or take responsibility for decisions *prior* to receiving the necessary stimuli to their brains. Some studies have shown that there is a full 11-second discrepancy.[76] In other words, people make decisions *before* thinking about the issue at hand. Reactions are simply from the body.[77] Research has found that "a participant's brain activity [can] predict their eventual choices before the individual [is] even asked to make a choice."[78]

Philip Merkle, a psychiatrist at the University of Waterloo, Ontario, maintains that the "unconscious circuits of the brain are processing sensory information"[79] of which the conscious "you" is unaware but which could account for that which we describe as intuitive feelings. In effect, our brain may "know" things to which "we" have no access and thereby make "moral" decisions without "our" permission.

Soft Determinism

In addition to (hard) determinism and free will, there is a third theory called soft determinism or compatibilism. It is nonsensical. Soft determinists (a.k.a. compatibilists) are arguably more concerned with coming up with the *right* conclusion than following logic. They say that everything is determined, yet they also hold that human freedom exists in a limited sense. Despite this controversial statement, they do not locate the mechanism that allows for this partial freedom. Descartes (although a free-willer) is an exception. He claimed the pineal gland was the mechanism or handle that controls freedom and the soul.[80] (The pineal gland is adjacent to the thalamus in the brain, and it functions to release melatonin.) Descartes was criticized for this baseless claim. He could have just as easily proclaimed that freedom comes from the right pinky finger or the left ear.

Some compatibilists argue that certain people have a greater degree of free will than others.[81] Who these people are and how they obtain these extra "freedom bonus points" is never explored. Do the rich have greater free will than the poor? Do Harvard alums have more than community college graduates? Do churchgoers have more than atheists?

In addition, soft determinists may argue that some choices are free and others are not but fail to explain this fanciful claim. According to the book *Ethical Theory and Practice*, compatibilists subscribe to the notion that " . . .to some extent [perhaps even] (varying considerably from person to person) and over a considerable span of time, we are free to desire or not to desire, to choose or not to choose, and to act or not to act."[82] Are choices "free" on Friday but "determined" on Monday? Perhaps they are 20 percent "free" on Tuesday and 40 percent "free" on Wednesday. Some compatibilists claim that freedom exists within a person's character, but this is a flawed argument because character is the result of nature and nurture, of genetics and environment. If one traces causes back far enough, they are found to be outside of human control—a point that compatibilists have difficulty countering since they do not dispute universal causation.

A foremost concern of soft determinists and free-willers seems to involve retaining autonomy and moral responsibility, praise and blame, and rewards and punishment. They may worry that a society without these would be chaotic. They may fear that public acceptance of a determined world would lead to a collapse in society—an outcome that is unlikely based on evidence from Eastern cultures where determinism is generally accepted as fact. The compatibilist acknowledges that the scientific evidence for determinism is compelling and that the notion of an undetermined world is absurd yet desperately wants to retain human freedom. Therefore, she tries to reconcile the two. But free will and determinism are like barbed wire and sand: they do not coalesce. Embracing both leads to a contradiction.

In addition to the fear of increased crime and anarchy, compatibilists and free-willers may not want to believe that humans are powerless when it comes to their destiny, and by extension, no different from the rest of creation. As the book *Free Will* states, soft determinists (like the free-willers) are often "struck . . . by the disquieting thought that free will is an illusion [and that we are] . . . puppets or machines . . . [or are like] the falling rain."[83] Do compatibilists and free-willers latch on to their illogical theories so as to relieve themselves from these troublesome thoughts?

Author Eric Hoffer confirms that this may indeed be true: "You dehumanize a man as much by returning him to nature—by making him one with the rocks, vegetation, and animals—as by turning him into a machine."[84] But philosophy is supposed to be about seeking truth, not avoiding an uncomfortable situation. Otherwise, one becomes no different from the fraudulent researcher who fudges an experiment to achieve a particular result. Soft determinists and free-willers arguably want to keep humans at the crown of creation, pretending they have the power to make unhampered choices. Humans have viewed themselves as mini-gods for centuries. Soft determinists and free-willers seem reluctant to dismantle that myth.

In the *New York Times* piece "Humans Are Animals. Let's Get Over It," professor Crispin Sartwell makes a convincing argument in line with Hamlet's famous quote "The lady doth protest too much." He says people have throughout history repeated—again and again—in philosophy books and other Western texts that humans are free, moral, rational, and conscious while claiming—over and over—that nonhuman animals are the reverse. He sarcastically says, "We can congratulate ourselves on the threat averted . . . . [And then he asks] If we truly believed we were so much better than [nonhuman animals], why have we spent thousands of years driving home the point? It's almost as though the existence of animals, and their various similarities to humans, constituted insults."[85]

I recently listened to a podcast in which the host and guest struggled with how to support the theory of free will. There was a desperation in their voices, an urgency to figure out how freedom could exist, to brainstorm as if their lives depended on it, and to pinpoint a mechanism that might allow for the possibility. They never came up with a solution. Their bias was obvious to me, although clearly not to them. Why were they fixated on this subject? After all, they were not fiercely searching for ways to prove that green tigers float through the air or probing how grass might be red. They had chosen free will for a reason: they had a personal stake in the outcome. Free will stems from the Abrahamic religions but could be described as a religion unto itself. It leans on hope and belief, not evidence and science. It is centered around labeling *Homo sapiens* as sacred and powerful, as worthy of special reverence, and as unique creatures who possess a supernatural ability.

Determinism need not be scary or destructive of society—a topic I will explore in depth later. It is, to my mind, beautiful and comforting. It is the dancing, frolicking, swirling universe at play without burdens, without judgment, without hatred. There is equality, balance, acceptance, and connectedness to all living beings. Causality is impartial; the blind and deaf forces do not care about the human ego, excessive pride, or pettiness. Determinism embraces oneness and whimsy, love and humor, science and art. A lovely passage in professor John D. Caputo's book *Against Ethics* describes the profound elegance and symmetry of a determined universe.[86] It can be soothing to be part of a whole and equal with all aspects of nature.

Superficial Freedom

Superficial freedom explains the surface or veneer of a situation. It does not address the underlying deterministic factors at play. When you choose an orange instead of an apple, your thoughts and actions are determined by biology and the environment, but picking one fruit over the other amounts to what I call "superficial freedom." Your mind is likely weighing the pros and cons during the decision-making process: The orange has more liquid, and I am thirsty due to the hot weather; I had an apple for breakfast, so I don't really want another one now; I need to save the only apple for my sister, or she will be angry, and so on. Some of these calculations may be fleeting or subconscious. These thoughts are causes (along with others) that lead to the ultimate decision: favoring the orange. If someone ties you up, preventing you from having that orange, you lack the superficial freedom to accomplish your culinary goal.

Superficial freedom is more like choosing or selecting, similar to what an oak tree does when a branch grows outward and similar to what a cockroach does when he decides to scurry across a kitchen floor instead of remaining in the pantry. If no one chops off the branch or impedes the oak in a restrictive way, the tree can be said to have superficial freedom. It is growing in accordance with its essence. If nothing obstructs the cockroach from the kitchen, he uses his superficial freedom to move in that direction. He is operating in accordance with what he wants to do.

I call this type of freedom superficial because it is surface level. Deep down, behavior and thoughts are wholly caused. But the "superficial" is still important. Being able to select the apple or orange is an action revered by the chooser. Moving across the kitchen is valuable to the cockroach, and arguably, spreading branches is desired by the oak tree.

There are two categories related to superficial freedom: *mental* and *physical*. The former leads to an expansion of cognitive possibilities and thus tends to be appealing. Having multiple choices generally makes it easier for the human or nonhuman to follow her essence, inner voice, desires, or needs. (One could argue, of course, that too many choices could stifle action, but this would be rare.) Having several potential avenues or paths tends to feel freeing; living beings do not typically want to be in a limiting circumstance. Options allow for possibilities and opportunities. "Possibilities" and "opportunities" should not be interpreted as having the ability to pursue A or B or C in an unhampered, libertarian, or compatibilist sense but instead, as being presented with three avenues and having a heightened (but, of course, still determined) chance to pursue the one that will most benefit the self—the one that will most conform to "essence." I will present examples of different scenarios.

Let us assume that a person has a dog she thinks might enjoy playing in the lake behind her house because she has learned that this breed loves water. She introduces the dog to the lake, hoping that swimming will enhance his life. Lo and behold, he loves the experience and paddles around in the lake, thereafter on a daily basis. The dog need not be credited with free will when he "decides" to swim every day. The introduction of water merely brings new information to his attention. It is the cause that thrusts him in a better direction (toward fulfilling his desires or essence). He uses his superficial freedom to choose to swim in the lake.

Let us assume that ants are invading our home, so we take measures to redirect their route to some distant garbage cans. Additionally, we think their lives will be improved by the abundant leftovers located there. Thus, we lead the ants to the cans with a trail of bread crumbs and, lo and behold, they crawl around in the trash day after day. The ants need not be credited with free will when they "decide" to no longer invade the home and instead "decide" to stay with the garbage. The new information has heightened their superficial freedom and enhanced their lives.

Let us look at another case. A person only knows about alternatives A and B, although C would be a better option for her, leading to greater self-preservation or self-realization. Because she has no knowledge of C, she is determined to pursue A. On the other hand, if she has knowledge of A, B, and

C, she will be predisposed to "choose" C, the better alternative for her. Perhaps Susan is this person, and she has a brain disease but is unaware that surgery is an option. She will perish without an operation, a state contrary to her best interest. If she gains knowledge about her malady, she will have the freedom or opportunity to seek treatment from a doctor and the freedom or opportunity to get well. The possibility for improving her situation is increased simply due to previously inaccessible information to which she now has access.

One might argue that although Susan gains information about her affliction, this in no way assures that she will be compelled to do that which is in her actual best interest. If she, for example, still decides to forgo treatment for her brain disease—and chooses instead to pray to a statue in her garden—how has she bettered her predicament? The answer is that she gained valuable information when C (the surgery option) was introduced. Her choices expanded. She had a heightened chance of following the path that would benefit her most.

As will be discussed later, all living beings necessarily operate from the doctrine of psychological hedonism, whereby they are designed to strive toward maximizing their own expected utility. They pursue that which they regard or estimate to be in their own best interest. This mental and physical compulsion toward the greatest expected utility (for themselves) means that they are necessarily striving to realize their essence (as they see fit). Perhaps Susan does not "choose" surgery because she thinks praying comports better with her essence. That is her choice. That is what she wants to do with her superficial freedom and life. Perhaps she is the kind of person who does not want to endure a serious medical procedure.

I want to briefly insert the topic of "altruism" into the discussion, even though it will be examined later. A person who appears to be altruistic is operating from the view that helping others is likely to bring (to herself) the most personal happiness or fulfillment, even when it puts her physical body in harm's way. The mother who gives up her life for her child is, on some level, calculating that she could not live with herself if she were to let her offspring die. The psychological drive to assist others must necessarily comport with psychological hedonism even when it seems, appearance-wise, to be against the interest of the doer or actor. It is part of her essence.

Now let's turn to the physical aspect of superficial freedom. This pertains to whether a body is confined. Examples of restriction are as follows: a lion in a cage, a fish in a tank, a dog tied by a rope, or a human child locked in a closet. All of these beings lack freedom of the will, but they also lack superficial freedom. They are slaves to others. They cannot get past the iron bars, the glass enclosure, the thick cord, or the locked door. Physical restriction hinders one from activity and, in most cases, from fulfilling one's essence or existence. When a being is released from bondage, her possibilities or opportunities are usually increased, and so is her "freedom."

For a final example of physical restraint, let us assume the existence of a lever that is determined by electricity and other causal forces to move backward and forward at a 90-degree angle. This mechanical device would have the potential to open to a 180-degree angle if it were not for a metal bar that prohibits its full movement. On one particular day, the scenario changes. Another causal force removes the restrictive bar, thus allowing the lever to be free in a superficial sense. The lever can realize its full potential by moving the width of the 180-degree angle. The situation would, naturally, be the same if the lever had been programmed to remove the metal bar itself at some point without the aid of an outside force. A human or other living being can be likened to the lever in that she is compelled by forces to shift one way or another. An increase in understanding, knowledge, introspection, or self-reflection (the mental) and in movement (the physical) can drastically alter a situation, elevating superficial freedom and moving a being closer to realizing her essence.

Is superficial freedom truly relevant in a determined world? Although meaning or purpose has no significance to the swirling and disinterested universe, it has great significance to individuals within that whole—humans and nonhumans. If the aforementioned lever were a living being rather than an inanimate object—a being with a stake in the outcome of going 180 degrees rather than 90 degrees—then its newly acquired freedom might be quite important from its subjective perspective. It could derive a feeling of happiness from this freedom, or a flourishing or a fulfillment of some need or desire.

Humans, nonhuman animals, and arguably all living things can be said to have interests, needs, or a stake in a particular state of affairs. It is important to consider the subjective interests of all, as best as possible, if one wants to create what I call a "definitionally good" (DG) society. This topic will be explored later.

Earlier, I touched on John Caputo's book *Against Ethics*. My favorite section includes a parable that focuses on determinism and (absolute) "morality." The passage celebrates the amoral swirling of cause and effect and depicts Being as a great cosmic game corrupted by humans with their perverted invention of moral truth. The story begins, "The forces vied with each other . . . (and) there was no meanness in Being, no ill will, no will at all, and hence no guilt . . . (for) there is nothing unjust in the little victories that the forces win, nothing unfair in their harshness with one another, nothing cruel in their little contests. Being itself is not cruel or benevolent; It is without good will or bad; It is without any will at all . . ."[87]

Then the story introduces the sick forces, man and woman,

who complain that "the Game is Evil . . . . War is a cruel father . . . . More and less, stronger and weaker are unfair. Becoming is unjust. Life itself . . . is unjust. Movement is wicked and causes pain," and then these "large, black, bloated [human] words crawl into the throats of the healthy forces and choke them, suffocating them, making them ill."[88] Humans had found a way to lame the healthy forces, a "way to cope with the Great Game, but it was a base and mean way, which cursed the game."[89]

This book, *Omniocracy,* reinforces the message about the frolicking, free-flowing forces and the debilitating effects of (absolute) morality. Some may think there is a contradiction here . . . in that, those who read this book cannot freely choose to adopt or reject these espoused theories. This is indeed true. The forces of nature and nurture may persuade or discourage; they may transform readers into sympathizers or dissenters. Some might say this negates the purpose of these ideas, so why propose them if they cannot be freely accepted?

First, just as one may be *determined* to read a book, one can likewise be *determined* to write it. And secondly, this book could be option C for a person who previously believed there were only alternatives A and B. Ideas influence and expand horizons. They can be the cause that brings about an effect, a positive effect that may better lives and, in turn, establish a happier society.

Chapter Three

DETERMINISM AND SCIENCE

Science reinforces philosophical determinism. As mentioned previously, scientists have learned that they can predict the behavior of research subjects up to 11 seconds before the subjects actually grapple with or think about an issue.[90] In other words, it seems that the "unconscious person" makes decisions before the "conscious person" is aware—thus defeating the notion that "free will" is behind human decision making.[91] But this is only a sliver of the evidence that supports determinism; the theory is buttressed from all corners of the scientific world—including quantum physics.

In this chapter, I provide a rapid-fire list of scientific investigations and research results (with corresponding citations) that damage—often fatally—the argument in favor of the existence of "free will." Each piece of evidence chips away at the notion that human beliefs, values, and actions are self-directed. The underlying causes might point to biology, the environment, or both. Regardless, the data hurts the claim that human decisions are—or can be—self-directed in an uncaused way. If you are already convinced that humans and other living beings are determined, this chapter may be superfluous.

Let us begin.

Some studies link genetics with various qualities, attitudes, or tendencies, such as happiness,[92] an outgoing personality,[93] sexual orientation,[94] a propensity for crime and violence,[95] particular moral beliefs,[96] an embrace of certain political candidates,[97] coffee consumption,[98] and even a fear of certain foods.[99] In other words, biology does not merely impact eye color, height, and hair texture, it can influence beliefs, likes, dislikes, and values. Author and cognitive scientist Steven Pinker argues that 70 percent of personality stems from genetics, whereas 30 percent originates from the environment. Others place even greater emphasis on hereditary factors. Psychologist Eric Turkheimer makes the sensationalistic comment, "The nature-nurture debate is over . . . . All human behavioral traits are heritable."[100]

In 1998, a group of scientists uncovered evidence that shoplifting—traditionally assumed to be a moral malady—stems from a brain defect, thus is curable with Prozac and other antidepressants,[101] and many alcoholics and heroin addicts have an "unusually long version of a gene on chromosome 11—the same gene that is common in risk takers."[102] Attention deficit hyperactivity disorder, which can lead to unruly or destructive behavior, was once thought to be largely, if not solely, correlated to social factors, but a Stanford research study has found that the genetic disorder can be cleverly detected with a magnetic resonance imaging test, which measures the amount of blood flow to a hyperactive child's brain.[103] Even babies—once assumed to be blank slates—have been found to have their own value systems.[104]

Scientists from MIT, Harvard University, and Beth Israel Deaconess Medical Center have discovered that powerful magnets applied above the right ear in a location called the temporo-parietal junction can alter people's "moral" beliefs—in effect, scrambling their sense of right or wrong.[105] During the study, scientists related a story about potential danger to a loved one while applying the magnetic field. This caused the research subjects to have trouble differentiating between pure intentions and harmful consequences. Liane Young (a scientist on the project) says, "It's one thing to 'know' that we'll find morality in the brain. It's another to 'knock out' that brain area and change people's moral judgments."[106] How can values and beliefs stem from free will when they can be so easily maneuvered by a magnet?

Twin Studies and Adoption Studies

Twin studies and adoption research bolster the argument that values and beliefs—as well as likes, dislikes, and interests—are related to genetics. In 1999, *60 Minutes* aired a segment about Jeff Landrigan, a young man who was adopted at birth by a law-abiding family but who was found guilty of murder and executed by the state of Arizona in 2010. Landrigan's adoptive sister speculated that her brother had bad genes, adding, "I personally think that the day my brother was born, his fate was probably sealed."[107] While on death row, Landrigan found out that his birth father was imprisoned on death row in another state, and his family tree was peppered with felons. He told *60 Minutes* that he believed crime was passed down in his family "like cancer or heart disease."

A number of adoption studies point to a link between genetics and crime. Dr. Sarnoff A. Mednick's study of 1,500 adopted children reveals how a propensity to chronic criminal behavior may be passed through the genes.[108] He found that "sons whose fathers had a prison record were almost six times as likely to have a prison record themselves."[109] Researcher R.J. Herrnstein agrees with this finding and states, "In adoption data, blood relatives act criminally in similar ways even though they have not shared a family environment."[110]

British and Australian research conducted on 4,635 pairs of twins determined that subjects who were reared apart thought similarly on subjects ranging from religion, sex, politics, divorce, and apartheid to crime and punishment, and tough-mindedness,[111] and later at the University of Minnesota, "twin research" amassed similar data. The head of the department reported that "genes may indirectly affect attitudes by introducing a perceptual bias, making an individual more interested in certain aspects of his or her environment."[112]

A Few Points about Determinism and Crime

In the appendix, I discuss research that links genetics with crime for those of you who seek additional references on this topic. In a nutshell, studies show that by investigating the brain, one can predict whether the very young—sometimes even babies—are likely to grow up to be "deviants" or criminals. Irregularities with the frontal lobes, atypical brain wave patterns, and metabolic abnormalities are, for example, considered very telling with respect to a child's future.

Other factors increase the chance of a person becoming what could be described as violent, aberrant, erratic, immoral, or antisocial—or falling into a life of crime. Some of these indicators are the XYY chromosome, MAO-A, a hyperactive cingulate gyrus, and low levels of chemical serotonin in the brain. Interestingly, the National Institute of Health conducted a study on the serotonin levels of prison inmates and was able to predict with 84 percent accuracy who would return to crime upon release.

Some researchers say that tampering with the brain could someday be seen as the remedy for "deviant" or illegal conduct, and "someday" may be sooner than we think. James McClellan of the University of Pittsburgh says that scientists may eventually be able to medically or surgically alter people in such a way as to eliminate racism and other stereotypes. Neuroplasticity could lead to transforming the brain, not only to maximize intelligence or reduce depression but also to modify "moral" behavior. A reconfiguring of the electrical impulses that correlate to the cluster of neurons associated with fear or hatred could, in effect, "train the brain to have a different reaction."[113]

The compelling scientific data presented in this section and in the appendix explains how deterministic predispositions affect personal values and/or "moral" behavior in the areas of shoplifting, political affiliation, incitement of violence, use of illegal drugs, murder of one's neighbor, sexual orientation, and culinary preferences, to name a few. If beliefs and behavior are nothing more than the consequence of nature (biology) and nurture (both inside and outside of the womb) at play, then a human crutch called freedom of the will cannot exist. However, if you are still not wholly convinced, perhaps you will keep reading about how the social sciences and the field of quantum physics also lend weight to deterministic theory.

Determinism, Society, and Conformity

People have a genetic predisposition toward particular beliefs and behavior, but they are also impacted by environmental factors. Countless studies have demonstrated that individuals are inclined toward conformity and ethnocentrism because these traits aid in survival. We cannot live without the assistance of others, and societal cooperation requires some adherence to established rules.

Cultural group selection is essential in the same way that natural selection is. Numerous experiments have found that a person's behavior is often drastically altered by those around her and her overall circumstances. Below, I continue with an inventory of data that supports the notion that values and actions are not the product of free will; however, this time, the data is linked more closely with "the environment" as opposed to genetics.

At the Princeton Theological Seminary, two psychologists conducted a study in which seminary students were asked to relate the parable of the Good Samaritan into a tape recorder at a nearby building.[114] A "victim" (an actor) feigning physical distress and asking for help was positioned en route. The instructor warned half the students that they were late to make the recording and should hurry to the proper location, while telling the other half that there was no need to rush but they might as well head over to the building early. Of those in a hurry, 90 percent walked around the injured "victim" or stepped over him to reach the destination. Of those with time to spare, 63 percent assisted the man in need. The context of the situation proved essential: the desire to obey orders and conform to the perceived time limitation played a significant role in whether the seminarians were predisposed to become a Good Samaritan.

Social psychologist Solomon Asch conducted experiments in 1951.[115] He wanted to see whether an ordinary person would conform to a group decision when it was clear that this decision was erroneous.

An unsuspecting subject was placed in a classroom with seven actors (pretending to be students) who agreed, one after the other, that two lines were equal in length when there was, in fact, a huge discrepancy: One line was short, and the other was long. Then the subject was asked for his opinion. After running the test with a large number of research subjects, only 29 percent of those questioned deviated from the majority, thus establishing the power of conformity. Those who answered correctly reported feeling uncomfortable when doing so. If the decision making had been related to ethics or aesthetics rather than the empirically verifiable length of two lines, experts agree that compliance with the group decision would have been higher.

Asch's work was inspired by Stanley Milgram, a Yale University psychologist who wondered whether people would execute strangers if they were told to do so. Milgram was fascinated with the Nuremberg trials and wondered if Adolf Eichmann, a high-ranking official of the Nazi Party, was inherently evil or had just followed orders in such a way as any person would. Milgram invited ordinary Americans, whom he labeled "teachers," to give electric shocks to a stranger he called the "learner" when the latter could not provide the correct response in a memory test.[116]

There were no real shocks, and memory was not being tested, but each teacher was unaware of this. The learner (an actor) screamed with pain and continually begged the teacher to release him from his straps. The testing device was labeled from level 0 to 450. Level 100 to 150 supposedly delivered mild shock, whereas higher levels were labeled "very strong," "extreme severity," "danger, severe shock," and finally "XXX" (or fatal). Milgram had asked accredited colleagues in advance to guess what they thought the outcome would be; they hypothesized that no one would go above 150 volts, except for the rare sadist who would push the lethal 450 lever.

The actual results were quite different: 66 percent of the teachers "executed" the victim merely because they were told to do so by the authoritative figure, the psychologist. Of those who refused to go to 450, no one stopped before reaching 300 volts; nobody helped the victim, thus proving to Milgram that part of the human condition is blind obedience. Milgram's experiment has been replicated by numerous researchers in the United States, Australia, South Africa, and several European countries with similar results. In a German study, more than 85 percent of the subjects administered a "lethal electric shock" to the learner.

Philip Zimbardo conducted a study at Stanford University in 1971 by creating a mock prison and drafting university students to be prisoners and guards.[117] The participants passed mental and physical exams, and coins were tossed to see who would assume which role. The authoritative impact of the guard uniform with the accompanying nightstick and mirrored sunglasses converted previously docile students into violent enforcers. The inferior status of the convicts—reinforced by their low-ranking garb, prison numbers (rather than names), and confinement to tiny cells—transformed them into victims. Formerly active prisoners became passive; healthy ones became sick.

Both sets of students said they lost their identities and forgot they were part of an experiment. The illusion became a reality. The two-week study was called off after only six days because the treatment of the prisoners became brutal and humiliating. The 2004 photos revealing the abuse at the Abu Ghraib prison in Iraq are astoundingly similar to the video footage of the Zimbardo experiment.[118]

Scientific Indeterminism versus Philosophical Indeterminism

Physicist Stephen Hawking agrees with most scientists that free will is an illusion. In his book *The Grand Design,* he states, "Though we feel we can choose what we do, our understanding of the molecular basis of biology shows that biological processes are governed by the laws of physics and chemistry and they are as determined as the orbits of the planets."[119] Despite this, there are those in the field of science who embrace what they call "indeterminism," thus giving the false impression that they are referring to the existence of free will. The confusion lies in the definition of "indeterminism" within science versus the definition within philosophy. The term means something quite different in each of these disciplines.

Indeterminism within science means that *humans cannot predict accurate results from the limited information available*. In other words, Newtonian deterministic laws of motion are inaccessible when investigated on a quantum level. This differs from the previous belief that man could eventually understand everything. The "modern" assumption (of the past) was that nature could be "brought under control by means of the systematic development of scientific knowledge through observation, experiment, and rational thought."[120]

Indeterminism within philosophy has an altogether different meaning. It conveys the idea that *cause and effect do not operate in the universe, period*. Philosophy endeavors to know the truth. It is relatively *unconcerned with whether those truths butt up against the limitations of man*.

All fields of science above the quantum level—biology, genetics, chemistry, botany, zoology, sociology, anthropology, psychology, geology, meteorology, astronomy, and so on—conform nicely with philosophical and scientific determinism. In addition, Einstein's theory of relativity poses no threat to deterministic models because it "requires strict continuity, strict determinism, and strict locality." [121]

The problem comes with the study of quantum mechanics, where all is not knowable by man and only loose predictions can be made. This is when some individuals seem to confuse scientific indeterminism with philosophical indeterminism.

Quantum Fraud or Quantum Friend?

The discovery of quantum mechanics occurred in conjunction with a disillusionment of science and a rejection of its fundamental tenet: causality. After World War I, the Germans held science and its causal principles responsible for precipitating the war, for providing tools of destruction, and for begetting mass death and destruction. Amidst this despair, a reaction against the scientific and the determined quickly unfolded, followed by an embrace of the mysterious and indeterminate. Thus, the quantum world was born.

In the dictionary, *indeterminism* implies that some events are without a cause; however, as stated above, quantum scientists redefine this concept to mean "that which dodges human detection." They say that if one cannot measure something, it is meaningless to talk about it. Philosophers disagree. They will talk about anything regardless of whether it can be measured, and they look to create theories based on logic and the best available data. They may argue that causality is the foundation for all events—physical and mental—despite what may appear, at first glance, to be bizarre findings in the quantum world.

Sir Isaac Newton—a physicist, mathematician, and astronomer—did not assume it was meaningless to talk about a theoretic possibility. He stated that humans will never be able to understand all causes within the universe and thereby derive all effects; he instead allowed for contingency. He was in agreement with Pierre La Place, a nineteenth-century mathematician who communicated the idea that "if a person of great intelligence knew the exact configuration of atoms at any specific time, as well as the laws that govern the movement of matter, that person could predict every future state of the universe with absolute certainty."[122]

"If" speaks to a form of conditionality and contingency that could perhaps be accessible to no one other than an omniscient, Godlike being. It is true that much of Newton's theory has been overturned by the exploration of the subatomic world—such as the fact that atoms have now been broken down into smaller units, namely, into six types of quarks, and the lowest common denominator is currently viewed as a wave-particle function rather than as a strict particle—but this in no way means that his reliance upon philosophical determinism falters.

The Copenhagen School versus the Hidden-Variable Theory

There are two schools of thought in quantum physics: the hidden-variable theory and the Copenhagen theory. Quantum physicists from the Copenhagen school—such as Werner Heisenberg, Max Born, and Paul Dirac—focus on the nonlocal and scientifically indeterministic nature of the subatomic world and thus may erroneously communicate the idea that free will exists. However, it is interesting to note that they rely on a number of causal factors within their quantum research, and they use (philosophically) deterministic language to describe quantum processes. They may insinuate that quantum physics hurts the case for philosophical determinism, but they make it clear that they are talking about only that which escapes human detection. In other words, they are not speaking about whether the world is determined; they are merely saying that humans do not have the ability to locate or measure causal factors. They are explicitly referring to science's definition of "determinism"—not philosophy's definition.

Boston University theorist Abner Shimony subscribes to the Copenhagen school. He says, "[Quantum mechanics] is spooky in the sense that causation is a more subtle relation than we had ever realized,"[123] implying that *there are "determined" hidden variables to which humans are simply not privy.* Max Born proposes a probability wave interpretation of Schrodinger's wave function, yet *probability presumes a deterministic relationship*. The result will be within a particular range rather than completely erratic. If there is a statistical range within which one can repeatedly and accurately find a photon or electron—as is the case in the quantum world—then it seems likely that determined factors are behind this element of predictability. This is clear in Thomas Young's famous two-slit experiment and Heisenberg's uncertainty principle. In the former, a particular range can be established for where a photon will appear; in the latter, one can determine a range for the velocity and a range for the position of an electron in motion because both cannot be measured simultaneously with high precision.

When humans observe the overall result in the two-slit experiment, light behaves like a wave interference pattern. Yet, when humans tamper with the experiment and try to extract specific information, light appears to be a particle. This is indeed the case every time this research is repeated, bringing one to the conclusion that *consistency of this sort indicates the presence of deterministic forces*, secretly hidden, perhaps laughing at human limitation. Author Lewis Schipper agrees. He analyzes whether philosophical determinism is in any way jeopardized by quantum theory and concludes that it is not because "perfect randomness contains in itself a lawfulness. Such randomness gives rise to stable probability distributions."[124]

Statistics, *probability*, and *chance* are terms frequently employed by quantum physicists. These words imply that only surface data is accessible, whereas something deeper is out of reach. *Webster's Dictionary* says probability is that which is "supported by evidence strong enough to establish presumption . . .," and chance is defined as "of dice, . . . something that befalls the result of unknown or unconsidered forces." Neither definition precludes the possibility of veiled but determined forces at work.

For example, when one rolls dice in a game of backgammon, one may say that obtaining double sixes is a matter of chance, probability, or statistics. Yet, one does not discount the underlying determinism that prompts the numbers to appear. One does not presume the dice escape causal forces: the configuration of the table, the force of the roll, momentum, and gravity. Even though a backgammon player cannot devise a method for assuring double sixes and even though she is incapable of predicting the outcome of a roll, this is not to say the dice have free will.

Hidden-variable scientists insist that any illusion of randomness within quantum physics merely indicates the limitations of the human mind. They assert that humans cannot know the causes; however, these causes clearly exist. For example, in *Does God Play Dice?*, Ian Stewart discusses chaos, a "lawless behavior governed entirely by [the] law [of determinism, in which] not all [deterministic] predictions lead to repeatable experiments."[125] He superimposes chaos theory over the quantum world and attempts to discredit any suggestion of acausality, such as with Schrodinger's Cat paradox, by arguing that " . . .while the statistics of radioactive decay, say, follow definite laws, nobody can predict when a given atom will take it into its head to decay . . . [and this may be because] each radioactive atom is obeying some kind of internal dynamic, culminating in a decay to a non-radioactive state."[126]

Stewart concludes his book solidly in the determinist camp by asserting, "All is predetermined; but we're too stupid to see the pattern . . . . An infinitely intelligent being with perfect senses—God, Vast Intelligence, or Deep Thought—might actually be able to predict exactly when a given atom of radium will decay, a given electron shift in its orbit. But, with our limited intellects and imperfect senses, we may never be able to find the trick."[127]

Phillip Frank likewise notes that determinism is behind the quantum world's seemingly haphazard behavior: "The [subatomic] function that determines the distribution or probability . . . obeys a causal law."[128] This view coincides with that of David Bohm,[129] Louis De Broglie, and Albert Einstein, all of whom rely upon the assumption of hidden variables. Einstein avidly supported subatomic determinism until his death in 1955, insisting that God does not play dice.[130]

Indeterminism: Could It Really Help Free Will Anyway?

Even if quantum physicists could prove the presence of (philosophically) indeterminable gaps in subatomic physics, this would not assist the free will cause unless one could uncover a mechanism—or handle—for these unexplained irregularities. In other words, there would need to be a way to link humans with an ability to independently control their actions. Scientists do not speculate that there is any such connecting force or mechanism and, in fact, tend to describe these quantum gaps as erratic, random, bizarre, and uncontrollable, with "electrons jump[ing] from one locale to another without passing in between."[131]

In layperson lingo, free will would have to come from someplace within our anatomy: the kneecap, the pineal gland, the left ventricle of the heart, the right eyeball, and so on. It cannot appear out of thin air and then mysteriously disappear. It cannot be magic. Scientific testing would then need to confirm that a particular section of the anatomy is indeed the "freedom center." Without this scientific confirmation, any talk of free will is nonsensical.

Pure Chance and an Evil Deceiver

What would it mean if pure chance were behind events in the quantum world? How would this affect the notion of free will? When I say "pure chance," I do not mean to imply that underlying, determined forces are at work as they were in the earlier backgammon example but that there is complete randomness, senselessness, and uncontrollability from the macro-level all the way down to the micro-level.[132]

This would mean a backgammon player could toss the dice and the dice could disappear into the void and then reappear in another country or another century. Any semblance of regularity, such as with the gravitational pull of Earth, would have to be attributed to a force such as Rene Descartes's evil deceiver,[133] who tricks us into thinking there is order to our world. This could, of course, account for the semblance of order and pattern found in quantum experiments. Yet, this would not give humans access to free will, because the evil deceiver would be in control. He would be the cause of all effects.

There is another problem. Humans—whether controlled by the evil deceiver or composed of haywire quarks—could not be held morally responsible for factors over which they have no control. Immanuel Kant recognized the absurdity inherent in morally condemning "oneself or anyone else for a quality that is not within the control of the will [because] condemnation implies that you should not be like that . . .,"[134] whereas luck, fate, and chance suggest that you have no choice in the matter.

God Manipulating Quarks?

Let us turn from the evil deceiver to God, as 81 percent of Americans believe in his existence.[135] Although Einstein says it is absurd to think that a deity could tamper in the events of his creation, this could theoretically account for the perceived haphazardness of photon and electron activity in the quantum world. God could be meddling; he could be manipulating the particles and waves like puppets. However, this explanation does not help the free-willer's cause; the world would still be outside human control. God would be the cause, just as the evil deceiver was the cause in the earlier example. The absence of harmony on the quantum level would be an illusion, and freedom of the will would still be a myth.

Quarks with Free Will?

A third possibility could be that electrons and photons have free will and *choose* which path to take in a subatomic experiment. They *decide* whether to exist, whether to be here or there. However, if this were true, the present concept of free will would become worthless because a person, tree, and rock could all be said to possess the same type of free choice due to their "free" subatomic composition. Freedom would lose all value as a precursor for moral responsibility. Rocks and trees would have to be held as morally accountable as we hold ourselves.

Evidence Supports Determinism Beyond a Reasonable Doubt

In conclusion, the whole of science, including quantum physics, currently supports the presence of (philosophical) determinism. Free will cannot be taken seriously as it is merely a *subjective feeling* by some people who *believe* they have choices.

Going forward in this book, I will explain why (absolute) "morality" is also fiction; it is free will's partner in crime. It is destructive to individuals and society at large. A determined and amoral world promotes less hatred against the self and others. It provides harmony and unity between all living beings—a stated goal of the animal rights movement.

Chapter Four

MORALITY: A PARTNER IN CRIME

Morality is sabotaged by a determined universe. In a totally caused world, there can be no right or wrong, no praise or blame. Free will cannot survive when every act, every thought, and every belief, human or otherwise, is an unquestioned product of cause and effect.[136] If a deed, whether it be to steal a loaf of bread or murder another human, is the result of neurons in the brain, hereditary predispositions, genes, estrogen, progesterone, or other such bodily mechanisms, solely or in combination with environmental triggers (e.g., being abused as a child or being prodded by gang members to commit a crime), how can this "natural" act be "evil" and how can the perpetrator of this deed be blamed for that which eludes her control? Can an utterly helpless individual—a pawn, if you will—be expected to comply with "moral" truths and should she be morally castigated for noncompliance?

John Hospers notes, "The more thoroughly and in detail we

know the causal factors leading a person to behave as he does, the more we tend to exempt him from responsibility."[137] Stuart Hampshire says, "When the behavior now causally explained [in terms of physical causes] is what was formerly regarded morally wicked, we come to regard it as a symptom of a disease, curable, if at all by the removal of its cause; expressions of moral disapproval come to seem useless and irrelevant."[138] If humans have no control over their genetic makeup and environment, holding them morally responsible for their character, thoughts, choices, or behavior seems absurd. Almost all philosophers agree that "a necessary condition for holding an agent responsible for an act is believing that agent could have refrained from performing that act."[139]

After all, a tree would not be condemned for fatally wounding a passerby who tripped over its root, nor would a baby be criticized for stabbing her mother. Humans and nonhumans who ostensibly lack the ability to do otherwise are rarely held responsible for acts considered "immoral." If reason and science demonstrate that adult humans lack authority over their actions, they should also be exempt from moral blame.

This is not to say they should be exempt from legal responsibility and spared from legal consequences. As the philosopher Baruch Spinoza writes, "The judge who condemns a man not through hatred or anger [stemming from the popular morality of blame and praise] but solely through love of public welfare [such as through compliance with the law] is guided only by reason."[140] The law calmly and methodically informs a guilty person that she must pay a fine, go to jail, or surrender to some other form of punishment, such as community service, whereas morality shouts.

Wrongdoing is that which is forbidden by law. Illegal acts can be punishable because just as a criminal is the product of cause and effect, so too is the judge or prosecutor who condemns this person to jail. Determinism explains behavior on both sides of the law. Criminals are no less dangerous when they act on the basis of causality than if they had been able to operate via free will.

Webster's Dictionary seems to separate moral responsibility from legal responsibility. It offers that within the area of ethics, responsibility means "having the character of a free moral agent,"[141] yet it does not mention "freedom" in association with legal responsibility, financial responsibility, or other forms of obligation. Instead, it speaks in relatively vague terms about being answerable or reliable.

Outside of the moral sphere, "responsibility" seems to revolve around an agreement or a contract, as in "I will be responsible for taking the children to school," or around a command or mandate, as in "You are responsible for not carrying a concealed weapon," or "You are responsible for paying damages stemming from your children's irresponsible actions." One can have a mutual understanding about a certain behavior, or one can be compelled by an authority to act in some way, but neither of these requires free will.

It could be argued that legal responsibility is primarily, if not completely, a practical designation invented to assist with organization, orderliness, and peace. One is expected to know the laws and abide by them; if one does not, and thereafter gets caught, one must suffer the consequences. Typically, one is held legally responsible even if one is ignorant of the law or determined (by nature and nurture) to do otherwise. Of course, one could say that responsibility harbors moral overtones, but the law seems to mean something altogether different than ethics when this word is used.

"Responsibility" is perhaps an improper term for describing that which the law asks. *Mission* or *job* might be more accurate. According to the criminal justice system, a citizen is given a mission—to comply with the legal rules of her community or face the consequences. The criminal justice system does not want her to think about whether to fulfill her mission, grapple with the choices, or use her "free will" to ignore its directives. It simply wants obedience. It provides the data to be inputted (in the form of laws) and expects the correct output (in the form of behavior), making little to no allowance for malfunctions. If the output is unacceptable, she will be punished in the hope that these penalties will sway her and others in the future.

To better clarify this, one could assume that a business owner tells an employee, "You have a responsibility to make sure all of the boxes are moved to the back of the store." This "responsibility" has been forced upon the worker, just as the law thrusts rules upon the citizenry. The boss does not mean to suggest that the worker must worry over what to do or use his supposed "free will" to properly carry out the act. As in the case of the law, the employer has made the worker's mission clear and assumes the boxes will be moved. If they are not (as with the law), the employee may face sanctions, such as losing his job.

There are countless examples of how legal responsibility is more like a task or an assignment rather than a decision-making process and how the government expects citizens to blindly adhere to the rules set forth rather than use any "free will" they may have to do otherwise. If a person receives a speeding ticket and contends in court that she did not see the sign or that she did not realize she was speeding, the judge will likely pronounce her guilty nonetheless. If she asserts that she freely decided to disobey the sign because the speed limit should have been higher, she will gain no sympathy. Her lack of knowledge about the law, her inability to abide by the law (e.g., because of biological composition or environmental factors), or her rebellious resolution to amend the law is not an acceptable excuse.

If a court tells a man that he has a legal responsibility to catch up on back alimony payments, his access to or lack of access to "free will" is not brought into the proceedings. A murderer may testify that he was drunk or compelled by bad genes to commit a crime, and although he could potentially get a lighter sentence, the jury is still likely to penalize him. Of course, the law makes special provisions for those who qualify as legally insane, and it designates that manslaughter is a lesser offense than first-degree or second-degree murder, but it typically punishes or restrains, in some fashion, even those who rely upon these sorts of defenses. Studies reveal that jurors sometimes dole out a less severe sentence when they realize the perpetrator lacks control over her actions. However, judges tend not to be influenced; they rule instead on the basis of precedent and deterrence.[142]

Unlike legal obligation, moral responsibility implies that there is ultimately a free decision to be made by an autonomous agent. This process has a creative aspect, a perceived or real tussling with options that legal responsibility does not so obviously seem to require. Moral responsibility is a decidedly more onerous enterprise. It squarely depends upon free will.

You may have noticed that the (absolute or popular) "moral" is often embraced by quotation marks in this book, as is the term "free will." This is because they are fictions or what the modern world might call misinformation. Man's freedom is "a fabricated freedom, and he pays a price for it [and] he must at all times defend the utter fragility of his delicately constituted fiction, deny its artificiality."[143]

Moral absolutes are illusions and human inventions, whether they stem from religion, the categorical imperative, utilitarianism, natural rights, intuition, natural law, or some other means.

An apt parallel can be found in Peter Berger's book *A Sacred Canopy*, in which the author lays a foundation for postmodern thought with his assertion that humans are creators of values and society. He claims that people forget they are the architects of their beliefs due to the process of "externalization, objectivation, and internalization."[144] By virtue of this Bergerian formula, human inventions are falsely disguised as absolutes.

Morality and Religion

Traditional Satanism is an interesting religion in that it is readily definable by its moral position, flaunting it front and center, conspicuous, screaming out, "I am evil. I am bad. And I like being this way." The Satan-related "moral" is not hazy or ill-defined and does not hide in the black pot in the corner but does a striptease for all to see. Few people nod or smile when face-to-face with the Satanist because they are too busy judging, hating, and running. Yet the Satanist may not be "immoral" by society's standards or worship the Bible's devil. She may embrace her religion to be eccentric and rebel against her parents, or she may like dressing up in a pointy hat, painting her fingernails black, reciting Latin phrases, and pretending they are spells. Maybe she has reinterpreted the religion into a personal spirituality that bears no resemblance to what the masses think it is. Perhaps the Satanist is a fraud: she may give money to impoverished children, adopt stray dogs, and volunteer at a convalescent home.

Some may contend that there is nothing inherently fear-evoking or hatred-arousing with regard to incantations and black robes. Still, these same people may rebuke Satanism because of its commingling with the (im)moral. Moral labels and imagery hold great sway; thus, the Satanist likely finds herself on the receiving end of stares, whispers, and stabbing words. It is not only her religion that is loathed but also her perceived lack of morals. She is seen as the ultimate deviant and the enemy of common values.

Western religions rely heavily on "morality." It is immersed within their precepts and community. However, unlike Satanism, believers think they occupy the right side of the ethical divide. They are often taught—subtly or otherwise—to harbor a "good versus evil" and an "us versus them" mentality. This can lead to punishing outsiders in astonishingly brutal ways. Historically speaking, the howls of agony have echoed through scores of sacred halls. For example, Christian leaders branded thousands of people heretics and executed them during the Crusades and Spanish Inquisition. Until the 1700s, torture was an ordinary investigative procedure for the Catholic Church. Priests were trained at seminaries on how to inflict the greatest pain upon their victims.

A mass revolt in Germany, commencing in the 1520s between the nobility and peasants—which led to the death of thousands—was condoned by the Protestant leader Martin Luther. He wrote a pamphlet telling the lords to stab the rebels "like mad dogs" because Jesus never spoke against the sword. Jesus specifically said, "He that hath no sword, let him sell his garment and buy one,"[145] and Anabaptist Jan Matthys said, "The righteous must take up the sword and actively prepare the way for Christ by cleansing the earth of the ungodly."[146]

Religions have been—and still are, in many cases—on the intolerant end of the moral spectrum. Women and the LGBTQ+ community are denied equal rights in many instances, and animals are typically viewed as property. Most religious leaders of the past defended slavery. Although cannibalism is taboo throughout most of the world and only still practiced in parts of New Guinea and on some isolated islands in the Pacific Ocean, at one time it was "almost universal, and in most cases, it was connected with religion."[147]

There have been numerous bloody battles over faith. Buddhists and Hindus have killed each other in Ceylon; Hindus and Sikhs have killed each other in India; Christians and Muslims have killed each other in Armenia; Muslims and Jews have killed each other in the Middle East; Sunnites and Shiites have killed each other in the Persian Gulf; and Protestants and Catholics have killed each other in Ireland.

A number of thinkers—from Bertrand Russell to Christopher Hitchens—have chastised religion for the atrocities perpetrated in its name. Friedrich Nietzsche declared himself the anti-Christ while warning of the stifling and calamitous nature of Christianity. On the stifling side, he writes, " . . .The Christian faith is a sacrifice . . . of all freedom, all pride, all self-confidence of the spirit [and] at the same time [is] enslavement and self-mockery, self-mutilation."[148] On the calamitous side, he says, "There is a great ladder of religious cruelty, with many rungs . . . . . . [such as] the sacrifice of the first-born . . ."[149]

Sigmund Freud describes religion as an "appeasing . . . lullaby . . .,"[150] a neurosis, a poison that can intimidate, make threats, and be dangerous to the self.[151] The early Karl Marx witnesses it as a placating illusion utilized to manipulate and exploit the proletariat. Marx writes, "Religion is the sigh of the oppressed creature, the sentiment of a heartless world, and the soul of a soulless condition. It is the opium of the people."[152] Although Nietzsche, Freud, Marx, and Hitchens, as well as others, have denounced the sacred, most philosophers reinforce the importance of the "moral." John Stuart Mill, for example, says that religion is inutile, but " . . .the power of . . . praise and blame . . . of favor and disfavor . . . is a source of strength."[153]

This text argues that Mill is wrong. "Morality" is a dangerous illusion, and it matters not whether it is nestled within religious precepts or stands proudly on its own—a topic that will be examined in a later chapter. The dual dimensions of the moral—the maso-moral (masochism) and the sado-moral (sadism)—are detrimental to the individual and society at large. The maso-moral leads to internal dissonance and repression of one's true self. The sado-moral begets hatred, hierarchy, disconnectedness, and a chasm between humans and other living beings.

What Is "Morality" and the "Definitional Good"?

Apples and oranges are fruit. If these two very different foods could be described only as "fruit," discussions about them would be limited and ultimately absurd. Rather than state, "Let's eat apples and not eat oranges," one would be required to say, "Let's eat fruit and not eat fruit," a nonsensical and contradictory statement.

Although countless philosophers use the term "morality" interchangeably to describe that which is objective, impersonal, and absolute as well as that which is subjective, personal, and relative, this results in confusion. A belief that is nothing more than a matter of opinion differs greatly from one that is said to be a truth of the universe.

Within ordinary language, there is no delineation between a moral state presented as objective truth and one based on opinion. This book argues that there is a need for the term "morality"—which relies upon absolutes and firm "oughts"—to be separate from what I call "lessalities" and "leastalities" (terms that are discussed later in this chapter). Lessalities and leastalities rely upon subjectivism or emotivism. They reflect mere sentiment or opinion. With the suggested language adjustment, a person can logically say, "Abortion is not immoral (in other words, not in conflict with right or wrong according to the universe), but my leastality (personal belief system) disallows abortion." Without a terminological distinction, the sentence would be nonsensical; it would state that "Abortion is not immoral, but abortion is immoral."

The statement "I personally find your behavior wrong" differs from "Your behavior is wrong." The former implies a possibly flawed, subjective opinion, whereas the latter states a fact, an absolute truth stemming from an authoritative source, such as an omniscient being or a perfect principle. A subjective statement is soft, less judgmental, less confrontational, and only a mere mortal's opinion, whereas the latter is tough, brutal, and highly judgmental and dares not be refuted because it stems from a reliable and masterly source. The subjective opens the door to discussion and friendly debate, whereas the objective silences the "other," openly offends her, and does not furnish her with an opportunity to defend herself.

Subjective and objective statements differ in content and practical consequences when they venture out of the "moral" realm. Let's assume an individual is sprawled out on the highway changing a tire while another person watches for oncoming traffic. There is an important contrast between the *fact* "There is no car coming" and a potentially faulty assertion or *opinion*, "There is no car coming." If the first statement is known to be true, irrespective of the human communicator of these words—perhaps imparted by an omniscient being—then the tire changer need not worry about being injured or killed by a motorist.

The second statement does not provide such certainty. The person on the pavement changing the tire may consider many factors. Is this person telling the truth? Is she a good friend who can be trusted or does she have malevolent intentions? Is she wearing her glasses, and does she have enough light to see a car without headlights? Fact or flawed perceptions? It could mean the difference between life and death.

The factual statement "There are pink and purple elephants

floating around the room" creates different assumptions, beliefs, and ultimately a different reality than the phrase "I personally believe I see pink and purple elephants floating around the room." The first sentence is known to be true. But in the latter case, one could assume that the observer is in error, that she is insane or hallucinating, that she is not truthful, or that she is the instigator of a practical joke.

Everyday reality need not be altered to understand the second subjective statement. Whereas it would be necessary to overhaul one's conception of the universe in order to accept the first, objective one. The practical implications are, of course, obvious. Should we dodge these elephants or feed them? Should we place our hallucinatory friend in a mental institution?

An absolute morality expresses certainty akin to the statements "There is no car coming" and "There are pink and purple elephants floating around the room." Its directives regarding right and wrong conduct are not to be countered or challenged but accepted and followed. It expresses a certain type of reality: a moral reality, which is wholly different from one with an amoral fabric adorned with what I call lessalities and leastalities.

There is also a need for a nonmoral term that is descriptive rather than prescriptive. I call this the "definitional good," and it means exactly what it says: something is good by definition. Philosopher Ludwig Wittgenstein would welcome terminology of this sort because he likewise argues for two categories. He names the first "objective ethics" (which I call "morality") and the latter "trivial ethics" or "relative ethics" (which lines up with my definitional good). He goes on to explain that trivial or relative ethics does not really qualify as ethics at all[154] because it does not convey an "ought" but is used for the purpose of description (e.g., a good chair, a good piano player, a good tennis player, or a good runner).

Wittgenstein explains that it is not immoral or wrong to be a bad chair, a bad piano player, a bad tennis player, or a bad runner. These statements do not suggest a moral state but are "a mere description of . . . facts,"[155] often representing a usefulness, or lack thereof. William K. Frankena agrees these nonmoral judgments are "not the kinds of things that can be morally good or bad . . . . They are not a part of ethics or moral philosophy."[156]

As per my "definitional good" or Wittgenstein's "trivial ethics," a "good criminal" might describe someone adept at robbing banks. A "bad criminal" might refer to one who immediately gets caught by the police because he recklessly sets off an alarm in the midst of a burglary or shoots himself in the foot. The FBI created the nickname Fumbles to identify a "bad robber" whose bungled but amusing attempt to hold up a bank was captured on video. Fumbles dropped his gun when entering the bank, knocked his face mask off again and again during the holdup, repeatedly dropped the money he had stolen, kept bending to pick it up, and then left a trail of cash to the getaway car. He was thereafter captured.[157] Calling someone a good criminal or a bad criminal—as in the case of Fumbles—has nothing to do with the adherence to, or lack of, respect for "right" conduct; it merely points to commonly held notions about what being a criminal entail.

A woman could be described as a "bad nun" because she does not always abide by the rules of her convent. Perhaps she sneaks into the kitchen at night for a snack, wears her habit in a sloppy manner, belts out show tunes in her room, cannot sit still during prayers, or behaves in other ways contrary to what is expected of her. She need not be considered immoral because she is untidy, restless, or a crooner, yet she could still be described as not well suited for a nunnery. She could be characterized as a "bad nun."

In addition to allowing for the term "objective ethics" (which I call "morality"), Wittgenstein concurs with my thesis that moral absolutes do not exist. He says, "The absolute good . . . is a chimera [for] no state of affairs has, in itself, what I would like to call the coercive power of an absolute judge."[158]

More about Morality

As stated above, I define "morality" as objective. It is not subject to negotiation or modification, and it stems from God, reason, natural rights, intuition, utilitarianism, natural law, or another authoritative and unalterable source. Its survival is dependent upon the existence of freedom of the will. The "moral" implies a single ultimate standard and is never part of the postmodern, the relative, the subjective, the deconstructed, the determined, or the aesthetic, but instead stands strong and proud like a steel skyscraper.

That which falls under the hardy umbrella of the "moral" includes (a) God's commandments, such as "Thou shalt not kill" and "Honor thy mother and father," because, of course, the Creator is (according to Christians) never to be questioned or ignored; (b) philosopher Jeffrey Stout's (reliance upon an) "epistemic authority" called intuition, which he says enables individuals to differentiate between that which is right and that which is wrong, the latter including " . . .the injustice of whimsical eyeball-plucking . . . and the evil of slavery"[159] (in spite of the fact that Southern slave holders at the turn of the century failed to recognize the supposedly intuitive wickedness associated with holding slaves); (c) Immanuel Kant's categorical imperative, which states, "We have a perfect duty to not use ourselves or others merely as a means to the satisfaction of our inclinations"[160]; and (d) John Locke's absolutist premise, which reveals that "the state of nature has a law of nature to govern it, which obliges everyone . . . [not to] . . . harm another in his life, liberty, health, or possessions."[161]

The "murder of innocent humans" is an example of an act commonly considered an absolute evil. It is not perceived as morally acceptable on Monday and unacceptable on Tuesday, or permissible in Chicago and inappropriate in Houston, but describes that which people call a "universal wrong" regardless of culture or conditions—a fact evidenced by the success of the Nuremberg trials in which many ex-Nazis were prosecuted for failing to obey a "higher moral law" despite heeding the laws of their nation at the time.[162]

Even act and rule utilitarianism qualify for the "moral" distinction because they, too, are peremptory, normative theories. They provide concrete methods for establishing what behavior is forbidden, permissible, or obligatory. They demand obedience to their principle(s). Utilitarian John Stewart Mill argues that the general principle of happiness is "intuitively obligatory . . . . . . (and should be) recognized as the ethical standard,"[163] for " . . .actions are right in proportion as they tend to promote happiness, wrong as they tend to promote the reverse of happiness."[164]

Although act utilitarianism takes each unique circumstance into account, it provides one definitive and nonnegotiable answer to a moral dilemma in much the same way as deontological doctrine. After calculating the expected, actual, hedonistic, or eudemonistic utility for a particular situation or applying the utilitarian rule, one arrives at a fixed solution or an "ought." One does not end up with a tentative or experimental guideline or a mere reflection of personal taste. Utilitarianism reflects a duty or mandate that should be honored if one wishes to be virtuous or conform to ethical conduct. It claims authority in this way.

To recap: Absolute morality expresses certainty akin to

the statements "There is no car coming" and "There are pink and purple elephants floating around the room." Its directives regarding "right" and "wrong" conduct are not to be countered or challenged but accepted and followed. It expresses a certain type of reality: a "moral" reality, which is wholly different from one with an amoral fabric adorned with lessalities and leastalities.

What Are Lessalities and Leastalities?

Lessalities and leastalities fall on the subjective or emotive side of the divide. The term "lessality" describes a belief and/or set of values held by two or more persons, which is, in fact, *less* fixed, *less* inflexible, and *less* false than "morality" could ever hope to be. Lessalities are not frozen, stiff, crusty, unyielding, or anchored in restrictive, cement-like absolutes but instead point to the fact that humans themselves decide what qualifies as "right" or "wrong," establishing a societal conventionalism of sorts. This amounts to nothing more than a majority (or sometimes minority) opinion about values. Abortion, for example, would not be described as immoral but as distasteful or acceptable, depending upon the perspectives of those who interpret and judge the act at that time. It is much the same as saying, "Yuck, abortion" or "Yeah, abortion is okay."[165] Even the murder of babies cannot be described as "immoral" (with a lessality) but as unsavory or permissible depending upon the situation and perspectives of the deciders—their opinions being subject to constant revision since they are not tied to an inflexible absolute.

To illustrate a "lessality," one might look to a throng of activists who have petitioned the city to lower the freeway speed limit from 65 miles per hour to 55 mph. These activists are merely asserting their personal opinion that 65 mph is a dangerous or undesirable speed. They are not saying that the current limit of 65 mph is immoral or that those who do not comply with their request for change are evil. Instead, they hope their unified presence will be a cause that produces an effect, a positive change for society at large.

A group of animal activists or anti-abortionists could assert a lessality rather than a morality—although the latter is more common. A lessality would be expressed as a consensus among organization members; it would convey personal disapproval regarding the death of nonhumans or the unborn. On the other hand, if the activists espouse a morality, their protest would be based upon an authoritative source and likely be riddled with moral outrage and accusatory language. They might even decry the killers as evil and selfish with an immoral disrespect for life, a tactic that animal rights supporter Henry Spira calls unproductive because it needlessly "divide(s) the world into saints and sinners."[166]

Now, we turn to a "leastality," which conforms most closely to truth. Why? Because no two individuals have an identical value system or the same exact opinion about anything due to the fact that no two people are subject to the same biological and environmental conditions. A belief is more accurately expressed as unique to only one individual rather than jointly held with others.

A leastality is simply an individual value system or a personal belief. It is the *least* restrictive of all ethics-related foundations, the *least* false, and consists of opinions from the *least* number of people: only one. It is not rooted in the stodgy, totalizing metanarratives of morality or in the less-totalizing metanarratives of lessality but it is exceedingly postmodern in its embrace of the subjective, single perception and its focus on the self-defined essence. Leastality sees the self as the nucleus, a subjective source of wisdom, a playful inventor of nonabsolutes, and an insightful judge for a personal better or worse. Leastality-based values mean that the self is respected rather than masochistically denied. No outward (moral) source is praised and blindly obeyed.

Although the aforementioned animal activists, anti-abortionists, and speed limit activists come together to express a general consensus or lessality, this in no way means that they agree on all of the subtleties associated with animal rights, abortion, speed laws, or any other subject. One animal activist, for example, may think nonhumans should never be vivisection victims, while another may think it acceptable to experiment on a few cats when seeking a cure for a deadly and rampant cat disease. One speed limit protester may think that, in a perfect world, cars would be banned on a particular street, while another protestor may simply want the speed lowered. One anti-abortion activist may feel rape is an exception to the no-abortion rule, while another may contend there are no exceptions.

Even two members of an identical religion with the same alleged moral foundation will diverge on issues and the ethical nuances implicit within them. For example, any two Christians could be questioned about what they believe to be right or wrong and different opinions would inevitably emerge. Church congregants, activists, political party members, protestors, or nonprofit donors may appear to espouse a unified view around a chosen cause or mission, but they represent, in truth, a cluster of leastalities masquerading as a lessality. The lessality requires ignoring or hiding crucial elements of individual belief systems in order to merge into one voice and hopefully create a greater impact.

Psychological Hedonism/Egoism

In a metaphysically determined universe, it is important to understand the built-in mechanism that urges living beings to go in one direction rather than another. Conscious living things are equipped with an inborn trigger or a compulsory law. If motivations were haphazard, there would be no order to the universe. Predictions—such as what goes up must come down—would be impossible. Psychological hedonism, psychological egoism, or something akin to them provides the only realistic explanation. These are descriptive theories rather than normative or prescriptive ones. They outline how things *are* rather than how they *should be*. They are not affiliated with right and wrong.

Psychological hedonism and psychological egoism presuppose individuals automatically—and often unconsciously—act in their own perceived self-interest. In the case of the former, actions and desires "are determined by pleasures or displeasures, whether prospective, actual, or past."[167] In the case of the latter, there is an inescapable inner compulsion to satisfy self-interest.[168]

Because of this inborn mechanism, an abstention from the so-called moral vices of gambling, drinking alcohol, or engaging in adultery are perceived as producing greater happiness for the people who deprive themselves, thus they refrain from these temptations—whereas others do a different calculation and succumb.

To take another example, Mother Teresa spent her life attending to the sickly and destitute, but, according to psychological hedonism / egoism, she was in fact aiming to bring herself pleasure (in a broad sense). This was a benefit that could not have been attained in other ways (for her), such as by living a luxurious or glamorous life. Helping others made her feel good about herself; this was the true reason behind her actions. In this view, what we call "altruism" is either an illusion or a superficial label that describes behavior that only incidentally profits another. Any benefit to the other does not negate the fact that the primary purpose is to benefit the self. The same can be said of a soldier who gives up his own life to rescue a friend. The pain of letting his buddy die would be unbearable. In this circumstance, self-sacrifice is perceived as the best option.

Explaining the Definitional Good

The definitional good (DG) is a nonmoral measure that describes an optimal state of affairs. It provides a society-wide[169] basis for attaining "the good life." This guideline for happiness[170] exists on an ever-fluctuating scale; it is not fixed. It focuses on two truths: (a) subjective perspectives[171] are important, often meaningful, to the beings who harbor them, and (b) a compilation of these perspectives equals an objective reality. The DG is where the objective and subjective overlap. The accumulation of positive feelings, an abundance of fulfilled interests, or a realization of essences may not matter to the gyrating, disinterested universe, but it matters greatly to the individuals who comprise the whole. This is the basis for the definitional good. Of course, the definitional bad (DB) corresponds with a worse state of affairs.

All living beings, including those deemed insentient, are included in calculations of the definitional good. They are equally important to the faceless universe. To exclude them would be arbitrary, discriminatory, and illogical. As philosopher David Hume said in 1783, "The life of a man is of no greater importance to the universe than the life of an oyster."[172] Although many species cannot communicate sufficiently with humans, they have interests[173] in surviving, propagating, nourishing themselves et al. This can be reasonably surmised by their behavior.

To better understand the DG, one could draw on the Kantian dichotomy between noumena and phenomena. What I call "noumena" signifies that which relates to objectivity or a thing-in-itself.[174] "Phenomena" corresponds with experience or appearance; it is subjective and dependent upon the senses.[175] The swirling forces of the universe are present on the level of noumena. They are indifferent to the pleasure, pain, or desire of individuals. However, within phenomena exist individual living beings who operate in a determined manner, pursuing pleasure, satisfying desire, and / or avoiding pain. They possess an inherent mechanism by which they necessarily act in accordance with psychological hedonism / egoism and conform to a personal (nonmoral) utilitarian calculation of sorts.[176] They care what happens to them.

Let us take a simple example by assuming everything on the planet is inanimate except for eight rabbits. One can reasonably suppose that inanimate objects have no desires, needs, or interests. However, the rabbits can be presumed to perceive[177] a better or worse state of affairs according to their subjective experiences—a postulate corroborated by scientific research and other empirical data. If all eight rabbits are happy, free from pain, healthy, and propagating their species, this is definitionally a better state of affairs (for these particular rabbits) than it would be if they were being tortured and killed. This assumption can be empirically verified because rabbits consistently try to escape pain and death.

The rabbits' situation has nothing whatsoever to do with "morality," for the universe tosses and swirls in accordance with cause and effect, and the rabbits (like humans) are not privy to freedom of the will. Although it does not matter to the faceless universe (noumena) whether the rabbits suffer or thrive, it arguably matters very much to the rabbits themselves (phenomena). As a result, a happy or definitionally good world is one in which the rabbits satisfy their interests. With the DG, interests are maximized, and hedons are increased. Dolors or sadness is decreased.

To take another example, let us imagine an orchestral performance. The sounds that emanate from the stage could represent noumena. They may be considered melodious or discordant, depending upon the aesthetic preferences of an impartial observer. Apart from these sounds, there is another position to consider—that which we will call phenomena for the purpose of this example: the viewpoints of the musicians. Even if the "noumenal" impartial observer is deaf—like the swirling cosmos—the feelings, desires, and needs of the instrumentalists are "phenomenally" significant. Do they have an itch they cannot scratch? Are their shoes too tight? Are they starving or thirsty? Are they depressed? Did they have a fight with their spouse on the previous night? The definitional good cannot be satisfied without considering the subjective perspectives or interests of the musicians. Like the swirling universe, the deaf "impartial observer" may not care about the feelings, needs, wants, or desires of the musicians—or even recognize their existence—but the performers care deeply.

Interestingly, the realms of noumena and phenomena intersect. The subjective translates into an objective reality. Let me repeat this important concept: *a compilation of the subjective perspectives*[178] *of all living things on the planet results in a fact or objective truth.* Lots of happy living beings equals a definitionally better world. Lots of sad living beings results in a definitionally worse world. There is no other measure by which to calculate a good or bad world because inanimate things are believed to have no interests.

Earlier, we discussed the good criminal and the bad nun.

This is the same idea. The definition of a good world is one in which the living beings in that world are fulfilling their interests. A definitionally bad world is one in which living beings are not fulfilling their interests. This is not to say that one can ever achieve a definitionally perfect world because there will always be conflicts of interest between living beings. But one can attempt to strive toward the DG in the same way we currently endeavor toward a crime-free nation or a hunger-free world.

How does this relate to establishing policy? It is true that calculations related to the definitional good are fallible; they depend upon the judgments of impartial observers or decision-makers sequestered behind an invisible and non-anthropocentric veil of ignorance. If an omniscient entity (i.e., a Supreme Being) knew the subjective needs, desires, and feelings of all living things and could weigh everything with precision, she could theoretically formulate the definitionally best world possible. Even though mortals cannot accomplish this sort of perfection, it is rational to create policies and laws based on an honest attempt at taking all interests into consideration.

The DG is at the crux of developing a peaceful and happy sociopolitical system. At its foundation are manmade laws, which are malleable and more useful than a "morality." These laws can be adjusted regularly or at intervals because there is no uncompromising deity to praise or ossified principle to worship. The DG also corresponds nicely with the natural process of psychological hedonism / egoism—the innate predisposition or inclination of all living organisms. The implementation of this theory and its applicability to the animal rights movement will be examined later.

There may be an intuition that these recommendations will be hard to achieve. However, even in the world today, there are barriers to overcome and conflicts to resolve between disagreeing factions of the population. There will always be disputes over laws and policies and controversies over public and private issues. But this does not mean that the goals of harmony and bettering society should be abandoned. Improvements can always be made.

Chapter Five

POSTMODERNISM AND THE CREATIVE ESSENCE

According to a number of sociologists and philosophers, a postmodern cloud has descended on American communities,[179] fogging up the air, confusing us, tarnishing public confidence, and making it no longer clear whether we should trust societal institutions, the political establishment, science's monopoly of truth, traditional religion, modernity's moral universals, Hegelian-like world views, and other formerly relied-upon absolutes. At the crux of this climactic change is what I would call a liberating belief that individuals can establish personal value systems rather than mindlessly adhere to the so-called ideals of one's society, religion, family, or peers. Adherence to "moral truths" arguably guides one away from true freedom and happiness, toward hatred, subjugation, and oppression, taking the focus away from the abandoned, the heretical, the silenced, the forgotten, the irrational, the disenfranchised, the marginal, the powerless, and the different. "Moral truths" tend to be anthropocentric in Western society and harm the most neglected and persecuted group of all: nonhuman animals.

The postmodern movement, which emerged sometime in the mid-twentieth century as backlash to the certainty of modernism, is difficult to characterize, in part, because it refutes universal truth thus any concrete explanation about its nature would require a contradiction in terms. Despite the fact that it " . . .celebrates its own schizophrenia . . . [and] renounce[s] self-classification,"[180] it is possible to identify some of its central or most frequent themes. For example, it often revolves around distrust of totalizing metanarratives, suspicion for all systems, rejection of unifying discourses, scrutiny of power relations, and a dislike of consensus—with one possible exception: on some level, it presents itself as preferable to the options.

It has a reputation for pulling apart language, overturning it, dissecting it, and deconstructing it in order to expose a subtext(s) where secret messages or codes may be embedded. It acts as a "form of discourse analysis that reveals hidden discourses of power by which privileged groups (e.g., males, Europeans, [humans]) establish and maintain dominance over marginalized groups (e.g., females, Africans, [nonhumans]) . . . .."[181] Relativism, subjectivism, emotivism, perspectivalism, difference, fluidity, originality, skepticism, imagination, and personal truths are all familiar elements within postmodernity.[182]

There are numerous interpretations of and ideas about this elusive movement, as well as so-called experts on it. Philosopher Jean-Francois Lyotard believes that postmodernism has instigated a (positive) explosion of dissensus and, therefore, provides individuals with the opportunity to express themselves in a unique and singular way; he feels that the absolutes of Western tradition have bullied, terrorized, and silenced the masses for too long.

In a similar vein, Friedrich Nietzsche targets what I call "morality" (or what he describes as the slave or Christian morality), linking it with weakness and a stifling of creativity and labeling it a false doctrine, or malady, that imposes guilt and blame on those who are duped by its counterfeit nature.[183] Nietzsche criticizes the common tendency to become a carbon copy of others and blindly follow the herd;[184] he extols individualism and freethinking. He also favors an emphasis on good versus bad rather than right versus wrong, a distinction that is quite postmodern and that, of course, conforms to the view presented in this book.

As living examples on this subject, we can examine the behavior of Presidents Bill Clinton and Donald Trump, arguably the only contemporary, postmodern presidents. Neither have admitted to such an association because it would no doubt be politically unwise. Social psychologist and author Walter Truett Anderson says a person cannot be president and "be seen as too postmodern—(or) say in public that truth is socially constructed."[185]

The link between Clinton and postmodernism surfaced during the Monica Lewinsky scandal of 1998. First, the country learned that the president parses words, reinterprets meanings, redefines and deconstructs language. He attempted to dodge indictment and impeachment by reaffirming his untruths, mistruths, or half-truths, including that "is" can have multiple meanings, "oral sex" is not sex at all, and "not alone" can simply reflect that there are others in the same building, city, or world at large.

Secondly, Clinton's ability to compartmentalize his life beckons us to the cut-and-paste character of postmodernity with its dispersions, differences, dismantlement, distractions, and segregated parts. "Modernity," on the other hand, is imbued with cohesiveness within its Hegelian-like worldviews and grand narratives.

Thirdly, Clinton is a baby boomer. According to a 1993 study by Wade Clark Roof, "1960s children" tend to embrace moral values based on personal preferences, employing a decision-making process not so different from the purchase of an automobile, television, or stock.[186] This subjectivism is said to be, in part, a reaction to John F. Kennedy's assassination, Watergate, the Vietnam War, and other disenfranchising events.

Now, let us turn to Donald Trump. He is said to be "the perfect manifestation of postmodernism,"[187] despite his plea to return to a less complicated, modern era with his pitch to "Make America Great Again." Trump's populist and norm-breaking stance coincides with the postmodern impulse to topple the elite, deconstruct custom, throw grand narratives into disarray, flatten privileged institutions, and drain the swamp. His lack of predictability and his normlessness align nicely with the movement's goal to diverge, inspect, unravel, and critique. His unique mode of communication revolves around counter-attacking his rivals rather than playing into their hands with traditional, modern defenses. Policy advisor and speechwriter Peter Franklin says he "operates primarily within a postmodern mode of communication . . . . It is all just narrative, which may be taken seriously or unseriously as the mood takes you."[188]

Journalist Salena Zito argues that members of the press take Trump "literally, but not seriously," yet his followers take him "seriously, but not literally"[189]—an astute observation. While relentlessly targeting his opponents as frauds and hypocrites, Trump comes off as authentic to his supporters. According to writer David Ernst, Trump is an anti-hero—flawed but oddly genuine. Trump has "ingratiated himself with [his] audiences for [his] gritty realism and . . . candor . . . . In a postmodern world, there is no greater virtue than authenticity, and there is no greater vice than phoniness."[190] He is a former reality TV star who embraces the notion that perception is reality. What could be more postmodern than that?

The Creative Essence, Green Lighting, and Psychological Hedonism

The amoral universe and the lessalities and leastalities positioned within it are arguably quite postmodern, as is what I call the "creative essence" (CE). The CE involves self-exploration, self-discovery, inventiveness, envisioning a personal ideal, and then moving forward with a self-described label. Self-preservation and self-realization are crucial elements in the process. Of course, the CE is not really an active pursuit because nature and nurture are the underlying craftsmen. It would perhaps be more accurate to substitute the word *create*—which suggests that one has the power to freely bring something into existence[191]—with a word like *assign* or *proclaim*, that is, "I assign the following characteristics to myself . . . ," "I assign meaning to my existence in this way . . . ," or "I proclaim myself to be a person who . . . ."

The leastality is only a small part of the creative essence. A value system is only a morsel in the feast called being. There are political beliefs, aesthetic preferences, and a myriad of other factors that comprise an individual and define her role in the world. Tina, for example, might proclaim her creative essence in this way: She may decide that she is philanthropic and thrifty, enjoys dark chocolate and talk radio, and should remain celibate. This psychological self-evaluation is a postmodern enterprise that requires the designing or wearing of Nietzschean masks. It is subject to fluctuation because heredity and environment continually impact the self. The creative essence thrives on metamorphosis, interpretation, and continual reinterpretation. It is not a constant force but one that vacillates in symphony with perspectival shifts. Every individual has an ever-changing nature; constant revision of the creative essence is natural.

Let us assume Tina believes that "having short hair" is part of her creative essence; however, the notion that short hair makes her more attractive is a fallacy in that others have no opinion about the length of her locks. The feeling of prettiness and of having the (superficial) ability to define herself and direct her life toward short hair brings Tina happiness. Her essence includes short hair. There is a creative (although illusory) element to saying, "I am a person who (I believe) looks best with short hair." This idea that Tina has about herself is part of her creative essence, even though it does not correspond to truth as discerned by the universe or an impartial observer. It coincides only with personal truth.

Tina's view of herself as "one who looks best with short hair" could change tomorrow. She might revise her essence. She might say to herself, I have changed my mind. I now think I am a person who should have long hair. Regardless of the reality of the situation (i.e., the causal forces that prompt her to react in a particular way), this move is perceived as artistic. She is unaware of the determined forces of nature and nurture impinging upon her. She can derive happiness from this feeling of exploration, inward searching, and perspectival self-definition.

Let us assume that Tina has never tasted kale and thus has no opinion as to whether it fits with her essence. However, later she tries it and finds she likes the taste. Plus, she learns that it is healthy and is a top food in relation to the Aggregate Nutrition Density Index. Now she has data that can be included in her creative essence. Tina can say, "I am a person who likes kale. It fits with who I am."

In addition to refining or recalculating aspects of her creative essence, Tina has stumbled upon a form of "green lighting" (in this case, kale green lighting) or the opening up of possibilities to essence-build and hopefully lead a fuller life. She has learned that she wants to include this vegetable in her diet. Another example of green lighting would be attending college classes and attaining a degree in order to pave the way to increased skills and greater employment opportunities.

"Red lighting," on the other hand, means decreasing one's ability to realize essence. Taking heroin could serve as an example; it is an activity that might hinder function and brain activity. It could drain one's bank account and creative juices and hamper one's ability to pursue goals.

"Yellow lighting" is equivalent to riding on cruise control; it involves that which is routine, familiar, repetitive, dull, or unenlightening. It typically describes activities that keep a person going—financially, emotionally, and/or physically—but that would not be considered integral to life goals or happiness. Of course, in a postmodern world, deciding which activities fall into a particular category becomes a matter of perspective and personal definition.

Sustenance-related activities, or even full-fledged "red lights," could be viewed as "green lights" by some individuals in certain circumstances. For example, after acquiring five university degrees, my friend Ralph asked me, "When are you going to stop studying and start doing?" A bell went off in my head. I realized school had become a crutch. It was no longer a green light; it had become yellow. I revised my creative essence on the spot. I would no longer define myself as a student. I moved on to the next adventure.

Green lighting, yellow lighting, and red lighting take us back to the earlier discussion about superficial freedom. An individual can follow a green light or attain superficial freedom in two ways: mentally and physically. On the *mental* side, a woman named Cheryl knows she would be happier realizing her essence but repeatedly succumbs to the opinions and judgments of others, especially within the religion in which she was raised. She feels mentally manipulated—even brainwashed—by those around her and her childhood faith. Her life is in red light mode.

One day, her aunt advises her to be strong, leave her religion, and figure out who she is. These words become a trigger; they propel her to break free from this grip. Cheryl ceases to succumb to those adverse outside pressures and in so doing, opens up cognitive possibilities and opportunities. She redefines her creative essence and the leastality within. She is in green light mode. She views herself as a different person, a new and improved person, subjectively speaking.

Let us instead look at the *physical* embodiment of this idea by assuming the adherents of the religion have held Cheryl captive in a basement for months. One day, she escapes after a member of the congregation fails to secure the door. Cheryl runs from the property and goes to the police. She has used her superficial freedom and is in green light mode, bettering her situation and moving toward expected utility. Her creative essence no longer includes the label of "miserable kidnap victim." She now perceives herself as free to pursue a better life.

This idea need not be limited to individuals. It can be expanded into a useful tool for society. Polls frequently ask voters whether the country, state, or city is moving in the right or wrong direction. A respondent answers the question based on her subjective perspective at a particular moment in time. If the survey taker believes society is going in a desirable direction, it is green lighting. She holds that it is advancing in a positive way. If she instead perceives it as stagnant, it represents yellow light mode. If it is moving along an unfavorable path, it is red lighting. In an omniocracy, the community's decision-makers create laws and rules with an eye toward green lighting society toward the definitional good. They hope to improve the situation for all inhabitants, including the nonhuman ones.

The doctrine of psychological hedonism or psychological egoism has been touched on multiple times, but I want to reiterate how this important mechanism works. It should be noted that I am using these two terms interchangeably, although I realize the latter is technically broader in scope. They represent an inner drive by which all living beings operate. They illustrate how behavior works. All living beings are motivated to satisfy their interests, such as seeking pleasure and escaping pain. They naturally move toward what they deem will bring them the greatest *expected* utility. Various philosophers have spoken in favor of this principle, such as Epicurus, John Stuart Mill, and Jeremy Benthem. Psychological hedonism/egoism is an empirical theory; it is unrelated to values. It comports with scientific data and observation. It is consistent with a determined and amoral universe. There is no alternative theory that adequately describes actions and motivations.

It should be recognized that psychological hedonism/egoism does not claim that a living being will choose that which comports with *actual* utility. She could choose a poor alternative, empirically speaking. She is guided merely by that which she *regards*[192] to be in her best interest at that particular moment in time. Although a choice does not guarantee the best *actual* outcome (as only an omniscient being could weigh all consequences), the choice necessarily brings about the best *expected* scenario from that unique perspective.

As mentioned earlier, physical survival is not always deemed the best option; sometimes an individual feels that it is better to die for her convictions, such as the mother who gives up her life for her child. Altruism is merely an action based on an inner calculation that involves relinquishing self-benefit to help another because the decision-maker or actor believes it is better (via expected utility) to help the other rather than live with the pain of not assisting. In the end, even the altruistic act is benefitting the actor.

The creative essence is not uniquely human. All conscious beings perceive themselves in a particular way and endeavor to preserve and promote their essence via psychological hedonism/egoism. Just as with humans, the more information they gather about the world and their tendencies, the easier it usually becomes to attain their goals.

Can Animal Rights Philosophy Survive Within a Postmodern World?

As presented in this book, the postmodern is like a flame dancing above a mortar fire pit or steam wafting out of a cast iron pot of boiling water. In other words, it is ironically rooted in the modern because the amoral universe arises from the metaphysic of determinism and aligns with all branches of science. The subjective, relative, and unpredictable (to humans) emerges from a solid foundation. Philosopher Gary Steiner argues that any deviation from the modern will derail animal rights philosophy. He claims that one cannot support a pro-animal ethic, politic, or legal system with a subjective theory. I disagree.

In the book *Animals and the Limits of Postmodernism,* Steiner argues that postmodernism is a problem for any ethic or politic related to animals because it lacks concrete principles. He believes that "cosmic justice demands universal veganism . . . and postmodernists refuse to embrace anything like [this] . . . because of their epistemological and political opposition to principles."[193] Although "morality" is admittedly not possible within postmodern theory, lessalities and leastalities survive, and even flourish. The creative essence perseveres.

In addition, societal rules, laws, regulations, and the political system are not stifled or hampered. They need not be embedded in the moral. They need not be secured in concrete. They need not revolve around the wicked or pure, the monstrous or angelic. They can remain malleable and nonjudgmental. One can still have rules without a universal principle of right and wrong. To take the earlier example of the speed limit regulation, the law may set the speed at 55 mph, but it need not claim that 60 mph is evil. The same could go for any directive. Theft can be illegal yet not carry the stigma of being immoral. This could even be said of murder.

Despite the move in recent decades away from the "modern," I argue that America today is neither a land of postmodern mini-narratives nor a society of communitarian ideals. It is sandwiched between, wedged in the middle. Many individuals are in a quandary about the best route to take, unsure whether to look within or without for guidance. It is easy to retreat to the familiar, go back in time, and rekindle the universals as our moralistic forefathers did. But I maintain there is an advantage for both animal advocates and the rest of society to march forward and embrace a more postmodern approach.

Wokeism, Multiculturalism, and Tradition

"Wokeism" and multiculturalism—which are said to be contemporary offshoots of postmodernism—do not align with the protection of, or concern for, nonhumans. They support speciesism. They place culture above the lives of animals. They create exclusive clubs that celebrate a few select human groups while excoriating or ignoring outsiders. Postmodernism, on the other hand, is all-inclusive. It does not elevate a particular species, claim some groups are more important than others, or make a pitch for moral truth. It aims to deconstruct norms, many of which directly result in the torture, enslavement, mutilation, and death of nonhumans. It disassembles the toxic myths that place humans at the pinnacle of the great chain of being. It has no inherent bias in favor of one treasured principle. It is happy to bulldoze or pick apart anything that fails its authenticity test.

The term "woke" has existed in mainstream America since the 2010s, when it was defined as being attuned to racial injustice, sexism, and discrimination against the LGBTQ+ community. These are noble goals. However, wokeism goes further to place human culture above the lives of nonhumans. Advocates for a "woke" world may say, for example, that veganism is racist because it does not allow for ethnic meat-eating. Phrases like "white veganism" and "vegan privilege" are thrown about. Author and animal rights professor Gary Francione states that it is fairly common for "woke" academics and others to put cultural food traditions above the interests of nonhumans; he adds that "we should always reject the argument that tradition can justify a practice that harms others."[194]

Francione goes on to discuss how there is an assertion within the "woke world" that only certain people are allowed to speak about particular issues. He recounts the time two Black students condemned him for equating slavery with the treatment of nonhuman animals; they called it "appropriating slavery." Francione writes, "They explained that, because I was White, I had no business using a uniquely Black experience in my work. [Francione reasons that] their position, if accepted, would mean that only those who were members of a particular group could talk about an issue that affected that group . . . . Unfortunately, much 'woke' ideology is, far from being progressive or radical, nothing more than reactionary speciesist propaganda."[195]

Animal advocate and former political speechwriter Matthew Scully has candid advice for the "woke community." He writes, "The [animal] movement reflects a . . . spirit that might be exactly what is missing in our woke progressives, or that at least might help to shake them of their narcissism and self-pity . . . . Animals are without appeal against our every decree and whim . . . . We're all potential oppressors with 'privilege' to check [I advise you to do] . . . the work of studying animal cruelty—witness the things that some people and industries do to animals—and you'll think twice before ever again calling yourself a helpless victim."[196]

Since the early 2020s, the phrases "go woke or go broke" and the (Twitter) X hashtag "#wokeAF" have been routinely used by progressives to attack White privilege, promote gender fluidity, advertise the merits of identity politics, and elucidate structural racism. Part of the woke argument is that reason, science, and evidence are "white" and thus should be shelved in favor of "lived experience." In other words, wokeness is called upon, in part, to decimate "the modern."

Interestingly enough, there is an element of the creative essence within the call to define one's gender, and there is no shortage of "woke" options. Various websites and news articles articulate the dozens—and in some cases, hundreds—of choices. For example, Facebook allows fifty-eight gender options.[197] The Civil Service in the U.K. claims there are more than 100 gender identities and instructs employees to use the pronouns "zi" and "zir" when in doubt.[198] Some websites list upward of 250 different options.[199]

Not everyone agrees with the "woke" agenda. Many Americans, especially conservatives, view "wokeness" in a pejorative way due to how it has been applied. Although they may support the goal of abolishing discrimination, they argue that this particular movement is problematic in the following ways.

They say: It has been used to shut down free speech and create safe spaces for people who claim to be traumatized when faced with dissenting views; it has been used to impute guilt, "cancel" folks, and persecute ones opponents; it peddles the racist tenet that "all white people are automatically responsible for slavery, colonialism, and the slaughter of native peoples;"[200] it has been used to pressure politicians to defund the police and let criminals off the hook; it has a self-righteous, angry, and punitive tone; it has a myopic focus on racism and gender; it is the reason critical race theory has been inserted into the classroom and the reason minors are being hustled into getting puberty blockers and gender affirmation surgery; it comes off as an assault on feminism, requiring new terminology, such as "birthing people" while making it politically incorrect to define a woman. Finally, the opponents of the "woke" agenda oppose the directive to hire or advance people based on diversity, equity, and inclusion (DEI) rather than on equality, merit, and colorblindness.

The DEI framework and the "woke" movement, in general, are infused with moral tones, moral imagery, and moral outrage. They lean on calls for reparations and justice. This, of course, conflicts with the theory presented in this book.[201] Morality (implicit within the terms "reparations" and "justice") leads to hierarchy and a gaping chasm—which, as I will argue later, fatally wounds the assertion that nonhumans are of equal value to humans and worthy of equal consideration.

Like "wokeism," multiculturalism is a trend that, on the surface, appears to be dressed in postmodern clothes. But this is a mirage. In reality, it is nothing like postmodernism and harbors some of the "woke" movement's anthropocentric deficits. Specifically, multiculturalism backs the idea that identity and custom should take precedence over nonhuman lives. It is a crusade of the political left, a plea for cultural pluralism.

It demands minority cultures be recognized and their traditions be honored. It requests political neutrality for practices treasured by special groups (including practices that harm animals) and may even enjoin legal protections. It focuses on disenfranchised human groups: immigrants, the disabled, LGBTQ+, Indigenous peoples, cultural minorities, et al., while maintaining the speciesist view that nonhumans do not count.

Liberals and progressives often ignore the plight of animals and the pleas by AR advocates when multiculturalism is in the mix. They place culture on a pedestal. Customs are viewed as sacred, as divine stories that take precedence over the suffering of animals. To demonstrate this point, let us look back at the 2020 COVID-19 pandemic. The initial belief (prior to the lab leak theory) was that the virus sprang from wet markets in China. These markets were routinely in the news "complete with details of tortured wildlife and slaughtered dogs, [yet TV viewers] . . . heard rebukes from commentators on the left over the 'racism' and 'xenophobia' of those criticizing the markets . . . . In progressive circles, [people were] not allowed to talk [about how] the culinary habits tolerated in Asia are vicious and barbaric . . . [especially coming from] the shameful position of some white Westerner daring to judge another culture."[202]

The political right has a similar problem; it involves "tradition." Conservatives often emphasize their God-given right to hunt and fish, to eat meat, to wear animal skins, and to use the severed heads of wildlife to decorate their walls. They might call it "tradition" and tell a story about how their grandaddy shot deer, and then their daddy shot deer, and then they shot deer, and now they are teaching the skills to their sons. A hunter might be puffed up with pride about this ritual. It is sacred to him and he refuses to let anybody tamper with what he feels is his birthright—to do what he wants with "lesser creatures."

The desire to maintain tradition takes precedence over the pain, suffering, and lives of animals.

The political right's desire to respect "tradition" at almost all costs is no different from the political left's goal to respect "culture" again at almost all costs. These terms are basically interchangeable. Tradition is defined as the generational transfer of customs and beliefs. Culture is defined as the practices, communal convictions, and social institutions of a country or group of people. Tradition and culture allow treasured habits and dogma to be passed on to descendants. In effect, rituals, stories, and ideas become batons in a relay race.

Culture and tradition are subjective in that group members may highlight different aspects as integral or essential. For example, one American might assert that the culture or tradition of the country is baseball, hot dogs, apple pie, and church. Another person might disagree and say America is about ethnic diversity, reality television, and shopping. Someone else might claim it is about "innocent until proven guilty," free speech, and gas-guzzling cars.

The bottom line is that both conservatives and liberals tend to believe that practices from the past must be kept alive—often at the expense of other creatures. I contend that certain aspects of tradition and culture are best left behind, forever shed, and replaced with less harmful habits. An example of a problematic practice by the majority culture in the U.S. involves the eating of turkeys on Thanksgiving while ironically giving (or feigning to give) thanks to God. Approximately 46 million turkeys are killed each year for this single holiday.[203]

To cite another example, fireworks—a popular American tradition—terrifies animals; it causes many to die of fright. An article in *The Independent* is titled, "If You Go to Firework Displays, You Don't Love Animals." Sixty-two percent of dogs become distressed when hearing fireworks.[204] Horses, rabbits, and other animals may bolt into the street and get hit by cars, or they may get tangled in barbed wire, eventually perishing. Birds may fly into buildings. Pregnant animals may miscarry. Fish and sea animals can be killed by poisonous fireworks debris when it lands in the water. The list goes on. In addition, fireworks put toxins in the air. This damages air quality and can lead to serious health problems for people and animals.[205]

Outside of mainstream American culture and tradition, there are minority groups that cling to speciesist customs. These practices tend to be embraced by the defenders of multiculturalism. Examples can be found within the religions of Santeria, Voodoo, and "Hindu and the Goddess Kali." In these faiths, adherents partake in the ritual slaughter of animals. Hundreds, even thousands, of animals—including goats, dogs, sheep, chickens, and water buffalo—may be decapitated as part of a celebration. Then the bloody animal corpses may be strung up for the festival-goers to enjoy. Dead animals are viewed as a delightful treat in the cultural or traditional sense.

Centuries ago, the average person was unaware of animal rights arguments. Culture and tradition taught them to believe that other living beings were mere tools or objects to be used, abused, and killed for human gain. It is true that a majority of Americans embrace this mindset today; however, these same folks have likely been exposed to concerns about animal cruelty and calls for animal liberation. They have no doubt run into a vegan or AR advocate who has argued for the need to protect other species and terminate the deliberate pain and suffering that humans inflict upon other creatures. Activists have used their free speech to try to change culture and tradition, and most people have witnessed these arguments.

Although exposure to pro-animal views—and pleas to change culture and tradition—are more common today, the torture and killing of nonhumans has not diminished. It has skyrocketed. This is, in part, due to the explosive increase of humans on the planet and the advent of industries that can behead, dismember, and kill victims with speed and precision. Mechanization makes it easy to slaughter a huge number of animals within seconds. Approximately ten billion nonhumans are murdered on factory farms each year in America.[206]

There has been a rise in mega factory farms, and twice as many animals in the U.S. are butchered for food today (in the 2020s) as compared with the 1980s.[207] Journalist Marina Bolotnikova writes, "Thousands [of land animals are killed] in the time it takes to read this sentence . . . . [There is a] system of organized violence against our fellow creatures."[208] Author Ruth Harrison says, "If one person is unkind to an animal it is considered to be cruelty, but where a lot of people are unkind to animals, especially in the name of commerce, the cruelty is condoned and, once large sums of money are at stake, will be defended to the last by otherwise intelligent people."[209]

Polls routinely ask voters which topics they deem important, accompanied by a long list from which to choose. They do not mention animal issues in my seasoned experience. This bias has never been rectified despite the fact that people like me have been complaining to survey companies for decades. Concern for other creatures is seen as a niche issue that appeals only to crazies on the fringe. To most pollsters, animal issues are not worth the extra ink, the extra space on a form, or the extra computer memory. These questionnaires are molded by tradition and culture. The market researchers receive speciesist input from society and spit back speciesist results. They do not typically try to open minds or advance the conversation beyond human-centric concerns. They play into one big cultural loop. They contribute to the society-wide cycle of ignoring, rejecting, diminishing, marginalizing—even vilifying and despising—nonhumans and their human advocates.

"Morality" and "free will" are arguably the most revered, most destructive, and most entrenched components of culture in the U.S. They are traditions in and of themselves. They are particularly catastrophic because speciesism is embedded—secretly—within their hallowed walls. They are part of the fabric of society and marinated in what it means to be American. They are cooked into laws and political measures. They are woven into school lessons, and they bubble under the surface of dinnertime conversations across the country.

It is hard to remove stubborn stains. Thus, it will be challenging to pry the masses away from the "moral" and the "free," as well as the traditions and cultures that harm other living beings. But I submit it can happen, and it is best to begin the work now.

AR advocates can begin by inching their advocacy a little closer to the postmodern. A philosophy aligned with truth is stronger, more durable, and more convincing. It is a better foundation for a crusade. It is my hope that AR campaigners will wipe the philosophical slate clean by setting aside their own movement's traditions and take a hard look at the new paradigm advanced in this book—a paradigm that integrates the postmodern with the modern and advances an omniocratic vision.

Chapter Six

THE SADO-MORAL AND MASO-MORAL

The "moral," as defined in this text, is an absolutist intruder, asserting itself as the arbiter of truth, the judge of goodness and depravity. Jews, gypsies, drug addicts, tramps, the mentally ill, bohemians, atheists, hippies, geeks, feminists, socialists, adulterers, sluts, criminals, anarchists, Satanists, homosexuals, drunkards, environmentalists, communists, stutterers, the homeless, animal rights activists, and others have at some time been, or, in some cases still are, considered marginal members of society. These so-called deviants have been (or are) dismissed as morally inferior beings, either shunned for their oddities, quirks, eccentricity, indecency, or iconoclasm or pitied for their inherently "sinful" ways.

In pre-modern times, tribal cultures associated "evil" with the supernatural, other-worldly, and religious; this state emerged from a struggle between the benevolent and the Satanic forces of the universe in which the latter prevailed.

Because "evil" was attributed to an outside power, rather than to the perpetrators of questionable deeds, it was uncommon and illogical to blame or condemn those tainted by this force. This is called the classical model. Perpetrators were merely victims tempted beyond all willpower and in need of exorcism to restore them to their virtuous and natural state. Despite the lack of moral judgment against the pre-modern persons, the punishment for their immorality was quite severe and quite public. An open demonstration of reproof was necessary to reinforce social norms and strengthen the sacred order of the universe. Think Inquisition and the Salem Witch Trials.

When great thinkers decided that "the moral" needed to be supported by reason and science—rather than faith alone—"modern demonism" emerged, replacing the classical model. This modification was problematic because it placed moral culpability squarely on the individual rather than diverting it to a faceless entity. The determinism defense or claim that "the devil made me do it" could no longer be used, and this is still the case today in the Western world despite the fact that 58 percent of Americans believe in the existence of Satan;[210] it was 68 percent in 2001.[211]

With the classical model, there was only a bifurcated view of good and evil, but it is taken further with the modern version. There is a split of living, breathing individuals into two camps: those who are superior and those who are inferior, those who are fundamentally virtuous, and those who are fundamentally wicked. A 2021 Pew Research Center poll found that approximately half of Americans believe that things (and people) can be categorized as either good or evil, and those who self-identify as religious are more likely to express this point of view.[212]

The other half of respondents feel the issue is more complicated, the product of gray areas. According to one poll, when it comes to political identification, 21 percent of Democrats think Republicans are evil, and 23 percent of Republicans feel the same way about Democrats.[213] In another poll conducted around the same time, Democrats were found to be more likely than Republicans "to believe their opponents were 'evil' . . ." And they admitted to "occasionally thinking that we'd be better off as a country 'if large numbers of the opposing party . . . just died.'"[214] In short, both sides have a significant number of voters who view their political adversaries as immoral.

Modern demonic theory does not rely upon a supernatural conflict between the forces of good and evil like its classical counterpart. It involves an equally mysterious and illusory struggle: a war of the wills. It relies upon a battle of good will versus bad will. Free will is revered as the special vehicle by which one can overcome immoral tendencies and selfish interests in favor of moral and altruistic ones, and most laypeople in the U.S. "maintain a strong belief in free will."[215]

A person is expected to take full moral responsibility for a wrong decision. The outcome of this internal tug-of-war is not seen as significantly determined by genetics or environmental factors. The prevailing view is that it results from the unhampered decision of an autonomous individual. "Evil" is seen as intrinsic, residing in some people's (lack of) character. Think Adolf Hitler, Osama bin Laden, and Charles Manson. Most Americans would define these men as rotten to the core and incapable of rehabilitation. In other words, they are viewed as moral monsters, bad seeds, and beyond repair.

The word *evil* is a discussion-ender. It is a way to terminate a conversation. If one were to ask why the Holocaust occurred, the answer might be, "Because Hitler was evil." If one were to ask why 9-11 happened, the answer might be, "Because Bin Laden was an immoral extremist." If one were to ask why the Helter-Skelter crimes transpired, the answer might be, "Because Charles Manson was a psycho monster. End of story."

Laypeople often give these simple responses and expect them from the press and leaders of society. "Evil" is rarely, if ever, explored or defined. There is an assumption that everyone knows what the term means, and it is almost always applicable to how we treat other humans.[216] In other words, society almost never equates "evil" with the killing of nonhumans.

The field of mental health has arguably contributed to the perception that some individuals are irretrievably blemished. Terms such as "narcissist," "antisocial personality disorder," "mentally ill," "sociopath," and "psychopath" are seen as permanent moral failings. Today, almost everything that deviates from the so-called norm counts as mental illness—from a lack of enthusiasm for music[217] to garden-variety phobias, anxiety, and depression. Although studies reveal that 67 percent of those designated as mentally ill can recover,[218] there is a dominant societal view that mental ailments are virtue-related shortcomings. The mentally ill are generally perceived as irredeemable. Author Kristina Kopic says that people do not judge others for having a broken arm, but individuals are "very uncomfortable with the idea of mental illness and seem to believe that it is somehow a moral failing—a character flaw."[219]

To illustrate this further, one might look at how mentally ill criminals are portrayed on-screen. Examples are Norman Bates in *Psycho*, Hannibal Lecter in *The Silence of the Lambs*, Michael Myers in *Halloween*, and the butcherly threesome in *The Texas Chain Saw Massacre*. Although all are presented as mentally incompetent, audiences do not overlook their "sins" or exonerate them for their condition but instead tend to classify them as the most heinous and sinister villains of all time. Their lack of mental control seems to push them further into the pit of inferiority as contrasted with mentally stable but supposedly "immoral" characters such as Al Capone, the Godfather, Butch Cassidy and the Sundance Kid, and Bonnie and Clyde. Killers who (supposedly) have access to free will, moral agency, and mental competence are often cinematically glorified, whereas those who lack these qualities are scorned and feared. The mentally ill are never (or rarely) portrayed in a sympathetic way.

Charles Manson was diagnosed as an acute psychotic in 1974 but is nonetheless demonized (even in death) by a majority of Americans, as evidenced by an MSNBC documentary calling him "The Evil Madman."[220] Serial killer Edward Theodore Gein is another case in point. He was found innocent by reason of insanity and confined to a mental institution for the remainder of his life, where he died of natural causes in 1984.[221] The same can be said of Edmund Kemper III, who killed and sexually assaulted various females.[222]

Justice Somerville of Alabama once said, "The disease of insanity can so affect the power of the mind as to subvert the freedom of the will, and thereby destroy the power of the victim to choose between right and wrong, though he perceives it."[223] Despite Somerville's words, the criminally insane are not commonly held as "victims," but more typically find themselves the target of moral condemnation; they may be associated with grim animal stereotypes, such as mad dogs or crazed beasts. Being mentally ill—thus lacking access to the "moral" and the "free"—is in many ways seen as worse than being a typical deviant. It involves being tagged with eternal inferiority. It means being un-human, beast-like, ill-fated, chained, programmed, a puppet, trapped in an inferior state, like an animal.

Mental illness is routinely associated with those who deviate from the customs or values of society. Therefore, a slaughterhouse worker who murders thousands of animals each week is seen as psychologically normal. He may spend each day electrocuting terrified pigs, slitting the throats of chickens, or blasting bullets into the skulls of cows. A scientist who tortures dogs and rabbits in lab experiments is embraced as an upstanding member of the community. She may even be honored at a special ceremony and given a golden plaque. A hunter who bludgeons baby seals to death is perceived as someone who is simply doing a job. None of these murderers would be called "sociopaths," "psychopaths," or "mentally ill" because people (including those within the fields of psychology and sociology) generally only label individuals as "sick" or "evil" when they harm or commit crimes against other humans.

Animals tend to be off the radar; they fall outside of the anthropocentric bubble of protection. Their suffering and lives are invisible. Murdering nonhumans amounts to business as usual. As a BBC article states, "A rational human being shouldn't care too much about bugs' feelings"[224]—a statement that is not surprising since dominant groups have, throughout history, dismissed the feelings of outgroups, (i.e., Native Americans, enslaved African Americans, Jews, nonhuman animals). Humans have broadly adopted in-group favoritism and discrimination against outsiders. Although *rational* is a neutral word, it is often used to protect the controlling class and decimate the powerless. Thankfully, within an omniocracy, all living beings count—even the tiny ones.

Before moving on to the sado-moral and the maso-moral, I would like to briefly touch on one discipline that has a refreshingly un-antagonistic view toward the individual: astrology. Although it is characterized as pseudoscience or simply an amusing pastime, astrology is similar to the aforementioned classical model of demonism, which places moral failings outside of the individual. A person is born into a particular zodiac sign through no fault of her own. She may have certain behavioral tendencies, untoward thoughts, criminal outbursts, or unsavory character traits, but she is not deemed inherently evil. She is not to blame. The culprits are the stars, the moon, the cosmos, or the astrological chart itself. The malefactor is the venomous scorpion, the stubborn bull, or those troublemaking twins. Perhaps there is a rogue rising sign, or the sun is in a nefarious position. Whatever the case, blame and hatred are distanced from the individual. The person is not forever tainted, irreparable, inferior, or irredeemable.

Sado-Morality

The term "sado-moral" comes from the word *sadism,* which roughly means to derive satisfaction from causing others pain or to enjoy slinging blame and humiliation in their direction. Morality embodies this sadistic side. It is detrimental to human happiness and nonsensical within the deterministic universe in which we live, for it is not constructive or rational to blame someone for so-called misdeeds that elude the perpetrator's control.

To realize that a human act stems from an uncontrollable array of causal factors—some biological and others environmental—is to settle into an insightful and calming perception. It allows for a continually positive and supportive state of mind in which moral rebuke makes no sense, and it permits a person or the legal system to deal with a situation pragmatically rather than by ranting, raving, pointing fingers, and creating ill will and animosity. In an amoral and determined universe, feelings of wrath and hatred must at least partially subside. They are replaced by some sense of patience, tolerance, communication, cooperation, and compassion. Determinism acts as a mediating force, optimizing conflict resolution and thereby elevating the chance that bonds can be established, for example, between animal activists and those with competing interests.

In his book *Ecology, community and lifestyle,* Arne Naess, a Norwegian environmental philosopher, writes that " . . .moral harping . . . may be considered ineffective . . . (and) nature magazines and associations should be kept largely free of . . . moral propaganda. Without a change in consciousness, the ecological movement is experienced as a never-ending list of reminders: 'shame, you mustn't do that' and 'remember, you're not allowed to . . .' With a change in mentality, we can say 'think how wonderful it would be, if and when . . .', 'look there! what a pity that we haven't enjoyed that before . . .'"[225]

One may contend that it is more expedient to hurl moral outrage at one's opponents than adhere to the more scientific and less divisive approach presented in this text. For example, if an AR activist stumbles upon a person at a shopping center locking her dog in a hot car, some might think it is best to yell at the person, "Shame on you. That is evil." The AR activist may believe that calling someone a sinner will garner fast results. I argue it is more powerful—and less alienating—to say calmly, "I'm sure you're unaware, but it's illegal to lock dogs in cars," perhaps even insinuating that a bystander might call law enforcement.

Threatening legal action is more effective than slinging moral stones because laws are concrete and factual, whereas many people are hazy about what qualifies as a truth of the universe—if they subscribe to ethical absolutes at all. When individuals are assaulted with a moralistic tone, they are likely to become defensive, doubling down and searching for a way to counterattack—perhaps by asking the activist if her shoes are leather or if she has ever eaten a steak. The battle will likely escalate from there, with verbal punches flying back and forth while the helpless canine is still locked in the vehicle. We see this sort of scenario regularly, and it is one reason why anti-animal folks have come to tune out AR advocates, calling them "shrill." It is also the reason many animal defenders have rage toward their adversaries.

You may ask about the best course of action when the abuse

of an animal is sanctioned by society. After all, laws rarely protect nonhumans. Let us assume that someone is about to mutilate a chicken. Farm animals have virtually no rights in America today, thus the killer would probably not face legal peril. Would it make sense for an activist to call the perpetrator "evil" or "barbaric" or use the S word: "shame?" I argue that it would be more powerful to appeal to the feelings and needs of the chicken without leaning on "morality."

The activist might want to use words such as *pain*, *suffering*, and *agony* or ask the question, "How would you feel if you were that poor hen?" It is wholly rational (and indeed more scientific) to pluck language out of the moral sphere and place it within the realm of compassion. The animal abuser would be less inclined to become indignant or hypersensitive, get riled up, or stand her ground. The abuser would be less likely to become more vicious or cruel toward the chicken. The abuser might even have a change of heart. A modification in tone can instigate a modification of behavior.

Members of the animal movement have not found success with moralistic rhetoric. Shrillness has not worked. Moral hatred has not worked. Strident accusations have led only to more conflict. In fact, they often prompt anti-animal folks to get puffed up with pride, tout "I'm entitled to do what I want," and cling to a belief in human superiority. In the short term and in particular situations, hurtling moral bullets might produce a quick result; it might stop objectionable behavior at that moment. But over the long term, this strategy is likely to fail—as it arguably has in the past. Perhaps it is time for the AR movement to try a new tactic. The omniocratic suggestions offered in this book could be the answer.

As an aside, you may wonder whether this text supports direct action, defined as illegal activism, such as destroying vivisection equipment or rescuing distressed animals from factory farms. Would an omniocracy and the definitional good support the actions of an AR activist who, for example, snatches the distressed chicken from the would-be killer and transports the creature to safety? The short answer is yes, as long as this action aligns with the activist's leastality and creative essence and as long as the activist understands that she could receive jail time for failing to follow the law.

It would be legal to rescue protectable living beings in Bioland[226] (the human-occupied areas of an omniocracy) due to the foundational tenets of the government: that nonhumans are of equal value to people and worthy of equal consideration. Today it is lawful to save an abused human baby from her sadistic mother, so by the same reasoning, it would have to be legal to rescue an abused animal. Note that there are forms of direct action that would likely not be permissible in an omniocracy, such as burning down an objectionable building (i.e., a fur salon, butcher shop, vivisection lab, or factory farm). Fire could—and probably would—result in harm to thousands of living beings (insects, mice, etc.), even if it did not spread to large vertebrates.

I would like to touch on a couple of things related to the sado-moral and free will before delving into the maso-moral. First, you may wonder how compliments can exist in a determined society. Do feelings of love and admiration diminish when one sees a friend or neighbor not as the instigator of an altruistic or heroic act but as a product of causal forces? Is the dedicated animal activist hard-pressed to bestow praise upon those who adhere to a vegan diet and refuse to go to the zoo?

The answer is "not really," because hatred, anger, and other negative feelings are much more forceful and all-consuming than positive ones. Loving emotions are less likely to be weakened by a belief in determinism. Praise and acceptance contribute to overall human happiness, so they are more likely to prevail despite the slippery foundation upon which they rest.

With negative thoughts, a person may recognize the act of judging and alter her behavior. She can stop, take a breath, and curb biting words. She can abstain from angry stares or withdraw from a fight. When it comes to positive emotions, there is no need to "catch oneself," reconsider, or change direction because the comments are warm and welcoming. In fact, people do not "catch themselves" now. Parents are applauded for a newborn's beauty, although they did nothing but give birth. Those with beautiful eyes or a perfectly symmetrical face are praised for their pulchritude, yet these attributes stem from good fortune or more precisely "biological luck."

Secondly, one might wonder if tempering hostile emotions would transform people into zombies, indifferent and robotic, devoid of humanity. This would not be the case, because some positive and negative feelings will automatically emerge from one's creative essence and leastality and impact behavior. A dedicated animal rights advocate may disagree with the killing of shelter dogs. She may feel upset and angry and hope to change public policy, but it makes no sense to call the shelter staff "evil" because they are a product of nature and nurture. The advocate can only loathe their behavior while aiming to influence them toward her way of thinking. She can also work to implement no-kill laws or fight against the system by taking direct action.

Let us look at this issue using an inanimate object. Peggy detests snow. When she sees it—or, God forbid, stands in it—she gets a feeling of dread, claustrophobia, anxiety, and even anger. But her negative feelings are likely tempered because she knows the ice crystals and frigid weather are not evil or anyone's fault. They just *are*. Morality is irrelevant in this circumstance. Peggy understands that blame and righteous outrage are nonsensical reactions. The snow merely qualifies as an unpleasant situation. In an omniocratic world, the same holds true when the cause of anguish is another person because it is understood that humans are as determined as snow.

All people—including AR activists and their detractors—could use determinism as a bridge between competing interests, a bridge that could, in the end, foster dialogue, cooperation, connectedness, and warmth. This technique is wholly consistent with moving toward the definitional good and building an omniocracy.

Maso-Morality

If people are addicted to hatred of the other,[227] as journalist Dero Saunders claims, and if "each culture chooses an enemy on which to blame a goodly portion of the earth's evil . . . turn[ing] hatred of that group into a virtue,"[228] what about the apparent hatred of the self, such as when monks once wore bristly hair shirts and flagellated themselves in the streets and when Martin Luther chained himself to his bed to remind himself of his sins? Is it true, as Nietzsche writes, that "under peaceful conditions, a warlike man sets upon himself?"[229] One could argue that the guilt produced by moral absolutes turns a person against herself. It matters not whether she subscribes to mainstream values and has a lapse in thought, word, or deed or whether she rejects the community's values in the first place. The fear of social ostracism and the sour taste associated with self-reproach can be oppressive and damaging. It can curtail creativity and free speech, and it can result in emotional pain, anxiety, and self-loathing.

The "maso-moral" is, in a word, masochistic. It relates to self-condemnation, overriding guilt, or hatred of the self. It is the mental equivalent of whipping one's own flesh. It amounts to an inner rebellion against one's own character, one's own personality, one's own beliefs, or one's own behavior. Physical self-flagellation is still common today in the Philippines and Latin America. Some religions and spiritual assemblages embark upon sleep deprivation, starvation, and beating the body in an attempt to achieve an altered state of mind or to induce discipline. To restore conformity, social ostracism is sometimes used by groups and institutions—religious or otherwise—as a manipulative force to turn an individual against herself.

The "moral" could be likened to a cult, kidnapping the essence or value system of a wanderer or dissenter and bringing her under its firm and unrelenting rule, requiring a sacrifice, demanding loyalty and service, brainwashing her into believing its maxims, isolating her from that which it opposes, teaching her to hate its enemies, and sending her into the world to preach its message. It uses the unique maso-weapons of guilt and shame to punish for noncompliance in thought, word, and deed.

To express it another way, "morality" initially plants its bundle of seeds deep inside the individual. It nourishes and sustains these budding kernels through repetition by echoing its goals and ideals until little "moral" voices fully blossom inside the head. These voices in the conscience become an internal vehicle for expressing "moral" outrage and disapproval toward the self, thus creating a situation where an animal activist, for example, may feel guilty for eating at a table with carnivores or for failing to rescue (steal) an enslaved fish from a tiny bowl.

Whenever the activist does not live up to the "moral" ideal that has been implanted in her head, she feels bad, inadequate, and sinful and cannot shed this guilt because, after all, she deems herself free to have done otherwise. She needs to understand that practical limitations exist (as will be discussed in a later chapter), and she need not blame herself since she is a determined creature and moral truth is illusory. She can relax and be more forgiving of herself while embracing her leastality and creative essence—and while striving to protect nonhumans and move society toward the definitional good.

Attacking oneself for being evil is, of course, illogical in an amoral and determined universe. It makes no sense to think one could have done otherwise and feel bad about it. It is silly to feel guilty about taking one path in lieu of another. However, the American masses tend to accept the myths regarding the moral and the free, thus often fall into a state of self-blame and self-loathing.

It is rare for people to stand by their convictions and declare, "Society is incorrect. Plus, I could not have done otherwise." It is more common for them to be contrite, turn blame inward, and promise to change their errant ways. But in so doing, they are donning an itchy hair shirt and enslaving themselves with ideological chains.

Philosopher Baruch Spinoza suggests that "self-castigation and repentance is a sign of malcontedness,"[230] as well as a glaring indication that one does not subscribe to determinism, but instead surrenders to the illusion of moral rule. He notes that remorse is an irrational feeling.

By its very nature, determinism combats the maso-moral; it alleviates feelings of regret and self-blame. It makes the habit of automatically deferring to society's grand inquisitors seem foolish. This is not to say that a person cannot change. One can be propelled to alter behavior going forward, but it is illogical and unproductive to look back and beat oneself up for doing something over which one had no control.

The idea of being maneuvered into silence by the maso-moral and sado-moral is touched upon by philosopher John

Stuart Mill in his discussion about the need for a marketplace of ideas. He writes, "There is a very real evil consequent on ascribing a supernatural origin to the received maxims of morality. That origin consecrates the whole of them and protects them from being discussed or criticized."[231]

Although Mill examines this idea in the context of religion, he identifies the dangerous and inhibitive nature of absolutism. He recognizes "the coercive power of public opinion"[232] and argues that a person must be encouraged to express her uniqueness. This is a boon not only to the individual[233] but to all. A multiplicity of voices can improve society by introducing original ideas that would otherwise be lost to conformity. Mill argues that a dissenter may have a true opinion while a majority holds a false one, yet the true opinion may be tragically quelled by conscience.

Mill's "conscience" sounds a lot like the "maso-moral," as expressed in this book. In *Utilitarianism*, the philosopher says that conscience results from "internalizing the sanctions imposed on us from outside . . . becom[ing] mentally enslaved . . . [and] coming in effect to side with public opinion against ourselves.[234]

The maso-moral contorts the essence, dries creative juices, and causes a person to deny herself in favor of a publicly stated ideal. The external forces sneak into the individual, into her psyche, thereby creating the unfortunate reactions of guilt, shame, remorse, and a stifling conformity. These forces convince her that she "should" obey, even in thought, the now internal (but formerly external) command. When a person is muzzled by these suffocating forces, she cannot fully contribute to the marketplace of ideas. Her freedom of opinion is contorted. Her freedom of speech is quelled. She is blocked from new ideas and from forging a better direction for her life and crusade.

There are a few final matters to consider in relation to this topic. First, one might question how one can discuss the maso-moral (or assert a distaste for it) when this concept seems to conflict with psychological hedonism (the theory that says a person automatically does that which brings her the greatest expected utility). Even pain can become enjoyment within this context. That which appears to be altruistic, such as devoting one's life to helping the ill, actually expresses a deeper pleasure for the self.

Although the theory of psychological hedonism states that a person will unconsciously do that which brings her the most perceived happiness, this is not to say that she is faced with the best of all possible scenarios when making this decision.

For example, if society adopts a "moral" hatred of homosexuality, a woman named Madge who is attracted to other women will be in a quandary, unsure whether to hide the truth or "come out of the closet." With the former, Madge experiences the maso-moral, stifling her essence, being manipulated by public opinion, and feeling inferior or sinful. With the latter, Madge openly counters society's heterosexual norm but receives stares and sado-moral condemnation for her "deviant" status. She may then internalize this negativity, feeling guilt and embarrassment—in other words, once again falling victim to the maso-moral. No matter what, Madge loses, despite the fact that she has made the best of the situation and has "chosen" the option that will provide her with the greatest expected happiness.

If the "moral" imperative to be heterosexual had never existed or was replaced with something less detrimental—such as a lessality or a multiplicity of leastalities—Madge could confront better alternatives and expect a more favorable outcome. She would not have to fear public ridicule for expressing her sexual orientation. She would not shudder at the notion of being silenced. She would not be the target of "moral" hatred, and she would not fault herself for being unable to escape from her predicament. She (and society) would understand that everyone is determined, and thus not at fault.

This takes us to a second question. Can one draw a contrast between true beliefs and the manipulative, outside forces? It could be argued that external influences are often internalized and become indistinguishable from the self, such as when a person willingly adopts societal norms and calls them her own. A child may, for example, listen to her parents preach about gun control, then embrace this ideological rhetoric as her own, unaware as to whether it was forced upon her or voluntarily welcomed.

The obvious haziness between the "real self" and the "self who has imported ideas from the environment" would be problematic but for the postmodern technique of devising a creative essence. This postmodern exercise involves self-definition, thus allows a person to decide who she is and what she believes. As stated earlier, this is an ever-changing process. The creative essence is a tool for differentiating between one's core beliefs and the pushy maso-moral, between the true self and the society-made self, and between the individual's value system and unwanted intrusion.

This takes us to a final issue. There is an irony in criticizing "the moral" because even though it is a harmful myth, it arguably bolsters freedom of expression. "It is wrong to eat meat," or "You will go to hell if you wear fur," or "It is immoral to go to the greyhound races" are messages that afford the utterer an opportunity to express her point of view despite the fact that they may assault the message recipient in so doing.

In an omniocratic society, morally absolutist phrases are transformed into something less offensive and more accurate, such as, "I personally do not support meat-eating," or "We have a new law that has outlawed fur," or "I feel greyhound races should be abolished because they harm animals."

One might argue that softening the message stifles the communicator from full expression. If either the speaker must be partially restrained or the target of the message must be assaulted, why side with one over the other? I would argue that a person is not silenced when absolutizing words are diluted into a lessality or leastality. A lessality or leastality can be adequately communicated in lieu of morality without significantly jeopardizing the content of the message. It does not make sense to perpetuate fairy tales about "the moral and the free" due to a bizarre notion that mean-spirited, absolutist comments are important to preserve.

Abandoning the maso-moral and sado-moral—which happens naturally when accepting an amoral and determined universe—is pragmatic. It advances "the good life" and fosters an omniocratic society.

Chapter Seven

THE FORTRESS ON THE HILL

Hierarchy is a central component within Western culture, religion, philosophy, and language. It is commonly used to crown humans as mini-kings, anointing them with the nectar of distinctiveness and vindicating their aggressive behavior toward the powerless subjects of their kingdom: nonhuman animals and nature. Although Charles Darwin's findings in the mid-1800s stressed the nonhierarchical, evolutionary continuum between humans and nonhumans, his theory has been repeatedly modified by others into a platform aimed at illustrating the complexity and superiority of *Homo sapiens*. George Romanes, for example, published a book soon after *The Origin of Species*, tinkering with Darwin's data and outlining fifty levels of development in which those at the top excel as "capable of reflection and self-conscious thought . . . [and] indefinite morality,"[235] and thus have greater value than those lower on the scale.

Even today, some researchers and writers within the social sciences are disturbed by the full implications of Darwinian theory and fight to preserve the entrenched view of humans as "the top animals, separated from the rest [of nature] . . . by . . . man's noble qualities and godlike intellect."[236] Some claim natural selection "cannot [completely] be taken seriously,"[237] whereas others say their opponents are complicit in "a diabolical plot."[238]

Most theologians agree with the notion that humans are a superior life form because it is usually part of religious doctrine. For example, Karl Barth puts forth the traditional view that humans are an end in themselves and that "God is for man."[239] Theological ethicist James Gustafson, however, expresses a rare perspective: He calls for uniting with nature, ending the reign of human beings as deities, and shifting the emphasis away from "man [as] the moral measure of all things . . .."[240]

The Great Chain of Being expresses an order of intrinsic worth from the deficient to the perfect, with humans occupying a post near the top, second only to God. According to a 1993 article written by Ken Wilber, most people endorse this "overwhelmingly widespread [notion of hierarchy, making it] . . . either the single greatest intellectual error to appear in humankind's history—an error so colossally widespread as to literally stagger the mind—or . . . the single most accurate reflection of reality yet to appear."[241] Science unambiguously informs us that it is the former.

Flattering words and optimistic images describe the notion of "freedom." Masterful, omnipotence, control, salvation, scope, latitude, autonomy, noninterference, emancipation, authority, rights, privileges, absolute, preference, self-direction, spontaneity, sovereignty, choice, option, alternative, and self-determination are but a few. American ideals include freeing the enslaved, liberating those deprived of free speech, being a free thinker, and living in a free country. In virtually every shape and form, freedom is an enticing and patriotic notion.

On the other hand, determinism or a lack of freedom evokes bleak images of shackles and limitations. Its negative implications are revealed in adjectives such as *chained, controlled, silenced, restricted, stifled, enslaved, obstructed, hindered, captured, hampered, muzzled, repressed, inhibited, mindless,* and *manipulated,* and in such nouns as *stockade, prison, addiction, finitude, dependence,* and *confinement.* Gloomy feelings are often associated with the idea of a determined self; there is a perceived helplessness and dejectedness. We are taught that pain accompanies non-freedom and that an individual loses "human dignity" if she forfeits the idea of superiority over those considered determined, such as trees, insects, many animals, and inanimate objects like rocks.

Free will is defined as "a theory in which human beings have the *power* [emphasis added] to make their own choices about what they will do."[242] Power is correlated with energy, force, and strength. According to Nietzsche, it is the ultimate goal of existence, but he is not alone in assigning extraordinary value to it. Former secretary of state Henry Kissinger calls power "the great aphrodisiac."[243] Today, the president of the United States is celebrated as "the most powerful man in the world," an office so alluring that political contenders risk character assassination, and the winner faces an astounding 9 percent chance of being shot dead while in office.[244] For the most part, Americans view "lack of freedom" as a cancer, infecting both individuals—such as those who plead insanity in court—and repressive societies, such as Cuba, China, and the former Soviet Union.

When a person sees freedom as a treasure, as a spiritual goal, as a foundation for moral perfection, as a fundamental human right, or as a basic principle underlying the best form of government, she cannot overlook (on some level) the notion of supremacy and elitism that accompanies it. She reinforces her deity-like stature when she assigns free will to herself and withholds it from other species. It is, of course, especially problematic when animal rights advocates do this because it derails their aim to convince the world that all sentient beings have equal value. Although their outward message is "equality," the underlying foundation of their theory—which relies upon the "moral" and the "free"—implicitly supports hierarchy and attributes inferior status to (at least some) nonhumans.

"Morality" is much like "freedom." "Moral agency" is code for preferential status, unique power, and quintessential worth. It implies that one has the ability to move toward perfection. Romanes, mentioned earlier, misconstrues Darwinian natural selection, suggesting that one significant and differentiating characteristic is the ability to be an unhampered moral agent. Like freedom, "morality" connotes power and status and is consistently linked with formidable and uplifting words such as *ethical, righteous, just, good, fair, honest, high-minded, decent, correct, integrity, virtue, standards, ideals, scruples, principles, good faith,* and *correctness.*

Although "amoral" is not the opposite of "moral," and it is not a synonym for "immoral," those unfamiliar with philosophy may find themselves confused, assuming amoral acts to be evil, wrong, or bad and the perpetrators of these acts to be rogues, villains, or devils. In fact, the word *amoral* immediately brings to mind the prefix "without," suggesting a deficiency or defect—although it actually means "neither good nor bad." The dictionary describes it as "without a sense of moral responsibility"[245] and "having no moral standards, restraints or principles,"[246] wording that could be interpreted in a less-than-flattering way.

Even those who fully comprehend the meaning of "amoral" may connect it with negative ideas. Calling animals "amoral" while calling humans "moral agents" arguably vilifies the former, a tactic that was once employed against so-called subhuman people. Blacks, for example, have been compared with irrational wild beasts, mad dogs,[247] and half-wits, and Native Americans have been branded "treacherous . . . savages without souls."[248]

Asserting that specific groups or species lack access to the moral and the free (as is certainly the case for those labeled irrational half-wits or savages) is a surefire way to denigrate and further marginalize powerless members of society. When animal activists plead with human "moral agents" to alter their behavior toward (these poor) amoral beings, they contradict their request, stalling their moral vehicle—crashing it into a wall.

Long ago, the "civilized" mindset included a moral imperative to conquer the "savage" Indians and Blacks and compel them to live in the White world. This was ostensibly done for their own sake so that the inferior could have the benefit of being ruled and directed by those who were rational, moral, and who had complete access to freedom of the will. As author R.R. Cobb said in 1858, "In a state of bondage . . . [the Negro] enjoys the greatest amount of happiness,"[249] a perspective that (often) prevails today with respect to animals. Some maintain that nonhumans must be governed, dominated, or manipulated "for their own good," such as when hunters claim to balance the wildlife population or when someone keeps a pigeon captive, allegedly to protect the creature from predators. In this view, the "amoral" and "determined" are not capable of regulating themselves, surviving, or doing what is best. They must rely upon the "superior human" to step in and handle the situation.

Throughout the ages, the view that humans must conquer nature has been widespread. Although we are in the twenty-first century and the struggle for survival is not what it once was, the "Wild West" mindset continues to pervade our culture.

Many Americans are reluctant to give up their rifles and set aside their traditional cowboy heritage. There lingers a yearning to dominate nature, to modernize, to civilize, to mechanize, to put everything into human terms for the benefit of humans, and to exaggerate the need for self-defense against the natural world.

In addition, the "amoral" is associated with the earthly rather than the preferred heavenly state. It is the psychopathic killer rather than the Good Samaritan, it is selfishness rather than altruism, and it reflects the nonhuman as opposed to the human. Words such as *treacherous, barbaric, sadistic, ruthless, wanton, heartless, cruel, wild,* and *uncivilized* are used to describe the amoral forces.[250] A rugged cliff is treacherous. A snarling tiger, hungry wolf, or man-eating lion is barbaric, feral, or sadistic. A powerful hurricane is ruthless or wanton. Connotations of immorality imbue the language of the amoral, recasting nonhumans and nature as criminals to be jailed, constrained, thwarted, quelled, fought like a foe, or shoved further down the hierarchical chain. Even when the amoral is not publicly decried, it is relegated to society's dungeon. It lingers in the dark pits of people's minds.

"Moral authority" is a commanding idea reserved for those at the helm of the hierarchy who have expertise rivaled by none. "Moral" has an otherworldly, impenetrable strength to it, just as "authority is a word that has an aura about it, a mystique."[251] A moral authority has influence, an almost God-like ability to know truth, and an unfettered right to sentence like a judge. It is a distinction reserved specifically for humans and deities. Not only are animals assumed to lack this omnipotence, but they cannot even be credited with "amoral authority" because this term is nonsensical. These two words clash; they contradict each other. "Amoral" implies that there is no authority. It suggests equality and describes the disinterested and swirling universe.

In light of these arguments, how can nonhumans and nature truly compete for equal status within a society of, by, and for the moral and the free? How can they be taken seriously when even their defenders—the animal advocates—use language secretly derailing their fight for recognition, acceptance, and legal representation? Most animal rights philosophers and activists believe that bringing sentient nonhumans up to the level of humans is the answer, but it is clear that if one wishes for (any semblance of) equality, the reverse must be done: humans must be toppled from their thrones and seen for what they are: amoral and determined creatures. *Homo sapiens* is not significantly different from any other species. There is a metaphysical connectedness, a bond that, if acknowledged and fostered, could lead to omniocratic peace and a happier existence for all.

Tom Regan is an example of an animal rights philosopher who errs by sustaining the myth between "higher humans" and "lower animals." In fact, he makes an explicit distinction between "moral agents" and "moral patients,"[252] defining the former as "those individuals who have a variety of sophisticated abilities, including in particular the ability to bring about impartial moral principles to bear on the determination of what, all considered, morally ought to be done and, having made this determination, to freely choose or fail to choose to act as morality, as they conceive it, requires."[253] On the other hand, he says moral patients are those beings who cannot do what is right or wrong because "they lack the prerequisites that would enable them to control their own behavior in ways that would make them morally accountable for what they do."[254] Despite Regan's desire to support the AR movement, this contrast places the latter grouping (who are usually nonhumans) in an inferior position.

In everyday terminology, "agents" are viewed as robust, active, healthy, and productive, while "patients" are regarded as sickly, weak, bedridden, delicate, paralytic, crippled, vulnerable, contaminated, confined, withered, decrepit, deteriorated, and in need of assistance. A patient cries out for help or mercy, while an agent has the power to ignore the crisis or bandage the wounds. The patient looks up from the emergency room table while the agent looks down from her fortress on the hill. The patient begs, "Be kind to me. I'm dependent," while the agent retorts, "I have control and you need to revere me." The patient is unable to ever recover due to her determined and amoral state; she cannot escape the label of inferiority that plagues her. She is forever at a disadvantage because everyone—including the traditional animal activist—never really stitches up her lacerations but inadvertently deepens them.

The common perception is that humans are moral agents and animals are moral patients. Tom Regan does not automatically accept this simple dichotomy, asserting instead that very young children and the mentally incapacitated may qualify as amoral while some nonhumans may fall into the moral category. Regan goes on to admit that animals who are aware and sentient and who have cognitive and volitional talents, such as belief and memory, are moral agents. Yet later in his book, he seems to refute this argument, stating that "wolves are not moral agents [because] they cannot bring impartial reasons to bear on their decision making—cannot, that is, apply the formal principle of justice or any of its normative interpretations."[255] Dogs seem to fail the test as well, according to philosophers Daisie and Michael Radner in their book *Animal Consciousness*; they describe an attacking, rabid dog as an "innocent . . . moral patient."[256] If wolves and dogs fail the "moral agent" test, would any nonhuman group pass? It seems unlikely.

Human newborns cannot see, hear, smell, or taste until becoming accustomed to the environment. They are defenseless compared with the young of most other species. Many people in society would argue that Regan is correct in labeling these babies "moral patients"—a sentiment that coincides with the following passage from the *World Book Encyclopedia*: For the infant, all activities "are merely reflex actions . . . . He presents a physically helpless and weak picture . . . . He acts instinctively and repeats whatever brings him satisfaction."[257] A normal human baby may, of course, blossom into an adult with abilities that far exceed those of her caretaker. Those who support the delusion of human superiority tend to argue that a baby should be included within the umbrella of concern because she will eventually transform from a moral patient into a moral agent. She has that important quality: *potential.*

Potential is a popular talking point or buzzword used by speciesists who want to deny intrinsic worth and legal rights to nonhumans while protecting human babies within the moral and legal realm.

Potential is a precious commodity. The word is upbeat and hopeful. It instills warm and fuzzy feelings. A modest retirement account, if fostered, can eventually grow into an enormous sum. A tiny seedling may seem inconsequential, but it can sprout into a luscious orange tree. A cheap piece of land in the middle of the desert could someday be situated in a bustling, highly valued metropolis. It has that all-important potential. An acquaintance may initially be of little significance, but this connection could ultimately bring personal success and wealth. Potential does not connote inferiority. It is "a latent excellence or ability that may . . . be developed."[258] It is also defined as that which is "capable of being or becoming,"[259] while its root, "potent" (tucked away inside), means powerful, mighty, influential, and capable. Just as being a free, moral agent confers a confident impression of strength and vitality, so, too, does "potential."

The mentally incapacitated could be listed as "moral patients." They lack that all-important potential yet are routinely included within the parameters of moral concern. The reason for this has nothing to do with science or philosophical consistency. It has to do with bias. The justifications run the gamut from "There are people who care about them" or "They are part of our species" to the assertion "Most humans in the world are moral agents with free will, and what matters is the abilities of the majority. The outliers are irrelevant"—arguments explored in an earlier chapter. All of these justifications are speciesist.

Nonhumans can never gain equal status in a society of, by, and for the moral and the free. Humans have raised themselves vertically toward the heavens, but this is only part of the problem. There is also a vicious chasm at work, which creates a horizontal divide, alienating people from other living beings.

The Chasm

A chasm or lateral divide obstructs the natural continuum between humans and other living beings. It alienates. It disallows unity and sabotages the AR movement's message of equal value and equal consideration for all sentient creatures. Zoologist David Suzuki says, "By encouraging a distancing between us and other species, we diminish the sense of awe and respect that is needed to temper our attack on them."[260] Philosopher Baruch Spinoza insists that one cannot truly understand oneself and the universe if one ignores the interconnectedness of all living things because "we [people] are part of the whole of Nature."[261] Alexander von Humbolt, an eighteenth-century geographer who is often labeled the "father of ecology," has called nature "an interconnected living web."[262]

Due to this problematic gulf, the "haves" (those who are said to have access to the moral and the free) and the "have-nots" (those who are said to lack access) cannot be equals, friends, colleagues, or allies but instead experience a disconnect, an estrangement, a disparity, and an inequality. The "haves" include human infants with their massive "potential" and the severely mentally incapacitated because, after all, they are members of the revered species, *Homo sapiens*. Because anthropocentrism and speciesism are embedded in today's culture, even people who are considered "moral patients" are positioned in the human camp, on the preferred side of the great abyss.

Humans are celebrated as the lucky winners, the chosen, the victors. They are the select ones invited to join the exclusive club, which bars outsiders. Members must sever bonds with other living organisms, philosophically speaking; that is part of the pact, the sacred pledge, the perk of having dominion. And if you dare peep outside the carefully crafted bubble and express that other living beings are of equal value to people, you will likely be shunned or called "a traitor, . . . [a] defector . . . to [the human] tribe"[263]—an experience that animal advocates know all too well. Many who tout the supremacy of *Homo sapiens* consider it blasphemous to propose that nonhumans are of comparable value to people.

In the beginning, there was no elite club. Although people hunted and ate meat, they were physically, emotionally, and mystically intertwined with the natural world. They were attuned to nature's rhythmic lullabies. Early peoples believed that elements of the landscape—rocks, streams, trees—had special energies and certain spirits. Nature was something to revere, to honor, to coalesce with, and to cherish. People measured days by sunrise and sunset. Months and years were measured by bird flights and weather changes. Time was dictated by the natural surroundings.

Then came violent interruptions: traditional religion, Western philosophy, the Industrial Revolution, the field of economics, big agriculture, a larger and larger human population, rampant consumerism, and urbanization. Nonhumans became collateral damage, casualties, and commodities. They were assaulted, made subordinate, and viewed as inconsequential and spiritless. The human imperative was bellowed loud and clear, stamped with the public seal of approval: It was deemed "good and rational" to bring nature under control, to manipulate nonhumans for the benefit of "man." Democracy was not the only thing that was of, by, and for the people. The world had become of, by, and for the people. Changes were advertised as "advancement." In truth, these changes were leading to deforestation, pollution, climate change, land degradation, water scarcity, the acidification of oceans, and species extinction "at a rate not seen in 10 million years."[264]

The communities that once belonged to nonhumans were rapidly disappearing. For example, a tree arguably has a citizenry of its own—a full-fledged society. It is filled with all sorts of life forms: termites, ants, spiders, butterflies, beetles, lichen, and spider mites. There may be raccoons, frogs, squirrels, iguanas, and birds. The tree is not just a future kitchen table for a Beverly Hills family in a sterile, smart home. It is much more. But people are estranged from this intricate brotherhood and sisterhood of living creatures because humans tend to only see their "own." For most people living in the twenty-first century, other beings do not count. They are invisible, subjugated, and written off as mere instruments for a human end.

A series of interesting experiments were conducted by plant

ecologist Frederic Clement in the late 1890s. He created something called the quadrat method, in which he learned that there is logic involved in the existence of plants, grasses, shrubs, and trees. Certain species would pop up next to other species like clockwork—even after being removed and relocated—while other types of flora would not survive in that location, no matter how many times they were replanted.

The testing was predictable, repeatable, and thus scientific. Clement's experiments led to the realization that plants are not a "mere collection of atomistic individuals . . . . [They] were not merely co-existing. Rather, they had formed a community of organisms that arises, grows, matures and dies."[265] His findings fueled the theory of interconnectedness, the idea "that humans and nature are fundamentally one and the same."[266]

In an earlier chapter, I listed animals with extraordinary skills with respect to communication and intelligence. I would like to expand on that information by investigating a broader array of talents, abilities, and attributes in order to put forth another reason why it does not make sense to relegate nonhumans to the forsaken side of the chasm. Acute sensory perception, speed, beauty, durability, and muscular vitality are positive and powerful attributes, but most people today believe these qualities cannot compete with the sacredness and potency of the "moral" and the "free." I hope people will shift their mindset, embark upon postmodern deconstruction, and take a deep look at their prejudices. They will likely realize that the talents and abilities of nonhuman species put them on equal par with *Homo sapiens*—a "truth" supported by the scientific evidence found within our amoral and determined universe. Recognizing this equality is the first step in patching up the chasm. Embracing unity is an all-important move in terminating the disconnect between humans and other species.

Scientist Terry Erwin states that there may be as many as 30 million species on earth—although people have thus far only identified 1.7 million—and many have skills and capabilities far exceeding those of *Homo sapiens*. For example, humans are sensorially limited compared with whales who listen to each other sing over distances of hundreds of miles and dogs who "can hear a wristwatch ticking from thirty feet away . . . [and have a] sense of smell . . . forty times sharper than a human's."[267] According to the *LA Times*, water fleas are at "the top of the evolutionary chain" when it comes to the length of their genome,[268] and another article touts chimps as more genetically evolved than humans.[269]

Raccoons have a keener sense of hearing than virtually any mammal, elephants make sounds too low for people to discern, and bats make noises pitched at about five thousand vibrations per second, well beyond the scope of human hearing. There are other facts about bats: "500 plant species rely on [them] to pollinate their flowers, including species of mango, banana, and cocoa."[270] Additionally, bats have internal radar enabling them to maneuver in the dark, a fact that seems to prompt Dr. James Fullard, a researcher from the University of Toronto, to express astonishment and respect for the " . . .profound neurological decisions handled by both bats and moths. [These creatures] exhibit a degree of economy and sophistication that could be the envy of human aerial warfare strategists."[271]

Homing pigeons demonstrate talents ranging from sensory superiority to intelligence. When traveling over thousands of miles, these birds use the position of the sun, Earth's geomagnetism, their memory for topographical detail, and their keen sense of smell and vision as a compass, in addition to their sharp auditory faculties; the latter permits them to detect sounds at a very low frequency of less than 0.1 hertz, a level inaccessible to the human ear.[272] In fact, compared with homing pigeons, humans are not only inferior in the area of sense perception but have almost no inborn ability to navigate and must suffer laborious training and numerous drills to compensate for this deficiency.[273]

Honeybees are often singled out for their aptitude;[274] one such example involves what is called the waggle dance, as mentioned earlier, requiring computational abilities that are much too difficult for any human to master. Bees navigate complicated routes and convey complex and detailed information to other bees in symbolic codes that emerge in the form of a patterned dance. The number of waggles signifies the distance and route to a chosen site.

Numerous species of nonhumans have physical prowess, such as fleas who can jump 130 times their body length, up to six hundred times an hour for seventy-two hours without stopping. Mice demonstrate their contortionist flair by squeezing their supple bodies through openings no larger than a thimble, and cats, both large and small, are much more agile than human beings. Some species of chameleons can change color in response to temperature, light, or a particular emotional state, just as Pacific tree frogs can alter their color by expanding or contracting the pigment cells of their skin.

If durability and length of time on Earth are taken to be criteria worthy of superior status, the cockroach would be the winning candidate, most certainly honored as a higher life form than the fragile and less-adaptable human. As many as six hundred species of cockroaches have existed for at least 340 million years on this planet, prior to the appearance of dinosaurs and well before the development of primates from which *Homo sapiens* would eventually evolve.[275]

On the other hand, if the "superiority award" is granted to the most indispensable living thing—whose existence sustains all other life forms and without which the world as we know it could not exist—plants or microbes might take the prize for they "produce up to half of the atmosphere's oxygen, . . . help digest food, produce essential vitamins, . . . protect us from organisms that cause disease, . . . break down dead plants and animals, . . . and recycle life-sustaining sulfur, nitrogen, carbon, and other nutrients and minerals that keep the planet running."[276] In fact, the article providing this information is appropriately subtitled "Microbes, not Man, are the Real Powers on Earth."

If one prefers to give the title to a more mobile creature, the worm would be a fine choice, since this invertebrate ensures the continuation of aerated soil that is integral for sustaining plant growth and other life. The human would, of course, fail this competition because she does not further the existence of, or benefit the lives of, any species beyond her own (perhaps except for a few companion animals). If altruism is the measure of greatness, ants might win the prize because they often sacrifice their lives for the good of their colony. If not harming others is the measure, rabbits might prevail, as they are strict and gentle vegetarians. And the list goes on.

All of these creatures—worms, cockroaches, chimps, bacteria, bees, mice, bats, pigeons, frogs, lizards, moths, fleas, ants, rabbits, dogs, cats, whales, and elephants—have one thing in common. They are generally perceived as lesser beings despite whatever impressive talents they may possess, a perception largely attributable to the alienating chasm. The divide between nonhumans and humans is arguably nothing more than a contrast between so-called instinct and the perceived freedom to choose. No talent or ability can compete with the colossal power of free will. And free will is, of course, the prerequisite for morality.

Instinct is code for "not free." Animals are typically saddled with this word *instinct*, even when they do that which appears mind-blowing or praiseworthy. They are said to operate out of blind and mechanical impulses. Animal rights advocate

Bernard Rollin reinforces this widely accepted label by implying that humans are higher creatures because they can access the moral and the free. He reinforces hierarchy and the toxic chasm. He states, "As moral agents, we make moral choices according to principles of right and wrong and need not operate simply by instinct . . . . It is the animal's nature to kill by predation . . . . We can shape our natures according to right and wrong . . ."[277]

Rollins's perspective is not unusual. Animal rights advocates typically use the free will/moral versus instinct/amoral distinction to delineate predatory creatures from humans—with hopes that the latter will become vegan. They think it is the only way to counter the question "If animals kill for food, why is it wrong for people?" But there is another way to respond: One can accept that the world is amoral and determined, as science demonstrates. One can accept leastalities and lessalities while basing laws and public policy on the definitional good, and improving the lives of as many creatures as possible. In later chapters, I will explore how to implement governmental and societal guidelines within an omniocracy.

As a final exploration of the word *instinct*, I would like to draw on a hypothetical case. Let us assume that an intellectually superior, sentient robot materializes from outer space. She can jump 130 times her body's height like the flea, do waggle dance calculations like the bumblebee, hear noises hundreds of miles away like the whale, compute data better than any living person, and make communicative sounds that are inaudible to the human ear (like bats and elephants can). Despite these amazing talents, this visitor would most likely be tagged with inferior status, labeled "not fully human," "an automaton," or "only a machine."

The actual reasons for this subjugation might be hazy and not consciously understood by most people. But it would be visible on a deconstructed level. It would be because the robot lacks the two essential components for human-like superiority: morality and free will. The majority of people would likely argue that the robot's data must have been imputed by someone (human), that it resides in a predetermined state, that it reacts rather than creates, that it merely consists of wires and circuits, and that it is programmed rather than free to decide. Being programmed is the technological equivalent of instinct. It would be an "it," not a "he" or "she." (*It* is a word used to subjugate animals.) The robot would likely be relegated to the far side of the chasm, quarantined in a distant land.

Animal rights advocates have good intentions and truly want to help nonhumans. However, rather than acknowledge people as determined and amoral beings (like the rest of nature), they throw down a rickety bridge and try to guide sentient beings—one by one and species by species—over the abyss. This tactic may temporarily help a lucky few, such as some dogs and cats, but in the end, it fails.

Not all living beings can make it across the perilous ravine. Some will fall in. Many are not easily transported. Fish need to be in the water at all times. Birds might have to migrate when the weather changes. Caribou, wildebeests, and other roaming breeds might be displeased with the confinement necessary to make it over the wobbly bridge. Trees are too heavy and cumbersome to move, and insects and microorganisms are too hard to locate. Of course, animal activists do not even attempt to rescue so-called insentients. It is hard enough to get people to have concern for dogs and cats. (The American Society for the Prevention of Cruelty to Animals estimates that more than 920,000 shelter animals are killed each year in the United States.[278])

Animal advocates would be wise to change their strategy. Merely saving a few animals here and there is nothing more than a "quick fix," especially considering the huge number of species on Earth. It makes more sense to compassionately guide *Homo sapiens* over the bridge to where the nonhumans reside, to live among equals on the lush, picturesque side of the chasm. By joining our nonhuman brothers and sisters, people can experience unity, kinship, and joy. Determinism and an amoral universe are not really about powerlessness. They are the epitome of freedom from hatred, alienation, self-judgment, and hierarchy. They are the quintessence of connectedness, equality, contentment, and love.

Chapter Eight

SENTIENTISM

Although the disconnects outlined in the previous chapter may have initially seemed harmless, they were later found—through postmodern deconstruction and other analyses—to distance humans who are said to have access to morality and free will from nonhumans (who are said to lack access), and to raise the status of the former while lowering the status of the latter. In addition, there is the ever-present foe: the prejudice called speciesism, a bias not so very different from the human-directed forms of oppression (racism, sexism, etc.) experienced by, or affixed to, those on the perimeters of society. Speciesism is a fundamental enemy of the animal rights movement.

There is another debilitating "ism" that is overlooked: sentientism. I define "sentientism" as discrimination by an individual, society, or institution against an individual (or a community of individuals) based on whether she (or they) can feel pleasure and pain. Questions about self-awareness and consciousness also factor into the equation. The victims of this bias are always nonhuman living beings because incapacitated people (i.e., those who are comatose) are protected under the umbrella of being a member of the treasured group: *Homo sapiens*. AR activists and the general public often argue that they do not need to consider the interests of "insentients" because of their (supposed) inability to feel pain. Few people consider the fact that these beings have interests and want to survive and flourish, as evidenced by their behavior. Instead, they are treated as if they are worthless.

The animal rights activist methodically and convincingly disassembles the species barrier but then purchases a fresh tub of mortar and a new pile of bricks and erects another alienating blockade rather than delighting in the open space and the prospect of unity with all living things. The sentients (or those believed to feel pleasure and pain) are lifted away from the great crevice and toted over the movement's sentient wall where they are united with *Homo sapiens*. This is a worthy goal of sorts, but unfortunately one with drawbacks.

It is true that the new barrier is better placed. It makes room for many who were previously unwelcome. It allows the dog, chicken, and cheetah to join the human on the elite side of the divide. However, it ignores others who likewise have interests:[279] the (supposed) insentients. While sentencing the latter group to death, or at least banishment, it sequesters humans and their sentient cousins. It keeps them imprisoned in the dark, alienated from the rest of nature.

Alienation has no single meaning but is often interpreted as "to make inimical . . . to estrange [and is associated with] mental derangement; insanity,"[280] the first part of this definition referring to a distancing that may be deleterious to the Other and the second part describing the damaging effect this act can have upon the self.

A significant number of thinkers and writers focus on the

concept of alienation, such as the young Karl Marx, G.W.F. Hegel, Herbert Marcuse, Jean-Paul Sartre, Martin Heidegger, Paul Tillich, and Erich Fromm. Fromm perhaps makes the strongest case against alienation by saying it is "the equivalent of what in theistic language would be called 'sin'"[281] and likening it to an all-pervasive "failure" or "sickness." He argues that as man embarks upon the process of detaching himself from the natural world, he experiences a lack of oneness,[282] for "to transcend nature, to be alienated from nature . . . finds man naked, ashamed."[283] Author Rebecca Hall emphasizes the need for a communion with nature, which "we have forgotten, which we ignore to the detriment of ourselves and all that lives."[284]

Others equate this distancing with "an avoidable discontent or lack of satisfaction,"[285] a self-destructive experience,[286] or a loss of a good or desirable relationship.[287] Author Arne Naess states that a split from the natural world hinders the self from realizing essence and true fulfillment. He says that " . . .with maturity, human beings will experience joy when other life forms experience joy and sorrow when other life forms experience sorrow. Not only will we feel sad when our brother or a dog or a cat feels sad, but we will grieve when living beings, including landscapes, are destroyed . . ."[288]

Segregation, withdrawal, isolation, disjunction, sequestering, disaffection, and estrangement characterize the process of extracting oneself from the whole—a process that leaves people with the false notion that they are not part of the natural world. Author Ariel Salleh says, " . . .Overcoming the division between humanity and nature promises a release from alienation."[289]

Alienation can emerge in many different forms, from homophobia to xenophobia, from anthropocentrism to androcentrism, from racism to sexism. It arguably punishes both the oppressed and the oppressor. When it surfaces as patriarchy, feminist Mary Daly calls it "a disease attacking the core of consciousness in females as well as males,"[290] and when it parades as racism, it paradoxically transforms both the so-called inferior and superior beings into slaves.

Centuries ago, slaveholding laws, initially meant to keep the vassal in check, in the end disciplined the White man, placing additional burdens upon him by "requir[ing] him to punish his runaways, prevent assemblages of slaves, enforce the curfews, sit on special courts, and ride the patrols."[291] In Nazi Germany, it was argued that the mass genocide of the " . . .absolutely and unredeemably evil [Jews] . . ."[292] required a significant personal sacrifice by the Nordic who had to carry out the extermination orders and " . . .see a hundred corpses lie side by side, or five hundred, or a thousand."[293] It seems absurd to even draw these comparisons, but the argument is that oppression and prejudice destroy tyrants just as they do the victims of persecution.

This is also the case for adherents of the AR movement who hinge their philosophy solely on the concerns of sentient, conscious (subject-of-a-life) creatures while negating the value of those whom they proclaim to be insentient (i.e., plants and insects). The activist who builds an ideology upon this rickety foundation not only derails her project—implicitly, if not explicitly—but is likely to detect philosophical inconsistencies on some level and become bothered by them. The unease can be especially noticeable when the animal advocate is bombarded with tough questions about whether insects, plants, and (even) microorganisms deserve moral protection. She might be challenged by someone like J. Baird Callicott, who asserts that "meat eating . . . may be more ecologically responsible than a wholly vegetarian diet"[294]—a claim that is factually false and which will be addressed later.

Sentientism creates its own chasm, hoisting the preferential group above the "mediocre," in this case, trees, grasses, insects, pond scum, and others who might be said to lack access to conscious sensation. According to a significant number of AR philosophers, only those who are aware and can suffer pain are worthy of inclusion within the moral sphere. This has been a common thread in the animal rights literature of the past. Only recently have some AR philosophers decided to embrace a different strategy.

British utilitarian philosopher Jeremy Bentham holds that moral inclusion should be extended to those capable of feeling pain, and adhering to this premise, Peter Singer writes in *Animal Liberation*—the accepted bible of the Animal Rights Movement—that "the capacity for suffering and enjoyment is a prerequisite for having interests at all, a condition that must be satisfied before we can speak of interests in a meaningful way. It would be nonsense to say that it was not in the interests of a stone to be kicked along the road by a schoolboy. A stone does not have interests because it cannot suffer."[295] It is noteworthy that Singer elects to compare a sentient being, about which he feels there can be no question of intrinsic value, with an inanimate object that has no apparent interests, rather than grapple with perplexing and more controversial examples, such as how one should treat an insect or plant.

Largely agreeing with Singer's stance, William Frankena says that he is unable to understand "from the moral point of view, why we should respect something that is alive but has no conscious sentiency and so can experience no pleasure or pain, joy or suffering, unless perhaps it is potentially a consciously sentient being, as in the case of a fetus."[296] Philosopher Joel Feinberg also relies upon a consciousness-like argument, maintaining that interests must "presuppose at least rudimentary cognitive ability."[297] He says it is a bit of a stretch to assign interests to plants.

AR philosopher Bernard Rollin uses "awareness" as the all-important measure for determining whether a being has interests. He says, "Although plants, bacteria, viruses, and cells in culture are alive and may be said to have needs, there is no reason to believe that they have interests . . . any more than getting oil matters to a car."[298] Spence Carlton argues, "To see this enslavement [of non-humans] for what it is, and to comprehend the *suffering* [emphasis added] that it causes, is the first step toward understanding the meaning of animals' rights—that is, the rights that are possessed by human and non-human animals alike."[299] Carlton is like the others in that he places emphasis on "suffering."

There are AR advocates, however, who do not draw this overt and arguably prejudicial distinction between sentients and insentients, consciousness and unconsciousness, or needs and interests, yet these very same people rarely scrutinize the difficulties involved with—and the importance of—embracing all living things within the movement's ideology. This "blunder" may include making overly generalized comments that appear to intentionally obscure the issue, failing to sufficiently designate which species qualify as sentient, ignoring how to incorporate the interests of all beings who have interests into the AR equation, or tottering on the brink of some other glaring omission.

Philosopher Tom Regan, for example, confers moral rights upon only one group, namely, " . . .those who are the experiencing subjects of a life,"[300] while omitting concerns outside this sphere. Yet, he does not find this problematic since he does not demean the Others but merely chooses not to address their situation. He admits, " . . .whether natural objects (trees or sagebrush, for example) possess rights remains an open question . . .,"[301] and he intimates that his "rights view" may someday need to be revised to take new findings into account.

Is Tom Regan successfully doing what the aforementioned feminists did when concentrating their efforts on helping females in Afghanistan rather than extending their activism to women in all parts of the world? Is Regan reinforcing his message by limiting the group owed respect? Or is he impeding the cause by ignoring those on the so-called insentient side of the chasm? I think he is doing the latter. In addition, it is not at all clear that a speciesist who utilizes an identical argument—namely, that she merely wishes to focus on humans—would escape the animal rights movement's criticism for this seemingly narrow-minded and elitist view.

Michael W. Fox, a former executive with the Humane Society of the United States, says that "animals of obviously similar sentience should be accorded the right to equal and fair treatment."[302] But unlike Regan, he makes outward reference to the predicament of worms, moths, mosquitoes, and flies, submitting that "we should recognize their right not to be harmed or killed and their will to live."[303] Despite Fox's worthy attempt to include other living things, his recommendations are hazy and brief. In fact, his comments on this matter cover only a few paragraphs in his 253-page book, *Inhumane Society.* He merely asks the reader to " . . .feel for flies and other insects struggling to be free from sticky fly paper . . . and . . . think twice about going fishing, putting worms on hooks, and other unthinkable acts of cruelty . . .."[304] His ideas are never sufficiently incorporated into the whole of his theory.

AR philosopher Steven Sapontzis does not criticize Regan, Singer, or the proponents of sentientism but, in fact, supports their exclusionary tactics, thereby disagreeing with the omniocratic theory in this book. He discounts the importance of "'Where do you draw the line?' questions [because they are, in his view] irrelevant to the current, major, practical concerns of the animal liberation movement . . . . [He adds that] once the questions currently being raised concerning how we ought (morally) to treat these [sentient] animals have been settled, it may be time to wonder whether insects have moral rights, need to be liberated, and what form such an enlightened morality should take."[305]

This does not seem correct, for if where-do-you-draw-the-line questions are inconsequential, why not draw the line at the species barrier? In addition, if one liberation movement either outwardly or suggestively crushes another, the credibility of the first is damaged, especially when its supporters constantly cry "prejudice," utilizing this charge—or slur—as a platform for their activism. For example, if Person A fights for racial equality and labels White supremacists as "bigoted" but then criticizes another's effort to abolish anti-Semitism, somehow Person A seems hypocritical, reckless, and foolish. She has defeated her own cause, undercut her anti-xenophobic platform, and made herself seem just as intolerant as the one she rebukes. Of course, those of "like mind" may not see the absurdity, but it remains nonetheless, and will no doubt repel those who are a bit more perceptive.

All oppression is woven together like a patchwork quilt. Thus, an activist who removes one square ultimately derails her own project, whether she fights for people or animals. The resulting hole hurts the whole, lessens the impact. The quilt no longer emits warmth but chills her message. It paralyzes her authority on the cause she so robustly supports. This is the problem for the AR activist who insists on placing the dividing line at the "ability to feel pain," while assuming small beings and plants are insentient and lack value.

In the 1800s, the prominent Anna Kingsford recognized this notion of derailment, of being hypocritical, of damaging one's cause in just this way. Pointing to the advocates of freedom for women, of which she was one, she remarked, " . . .I always feel that such of these who are not abstainers from flesh-food have unstable ground beneath their feet . . . [for] the Vegetarian movement is the bottom and basis of all other movements towards Purity, Freedom, Justice, and Happiness."[306] Martin Luther King, Jr. says, "Injustice anywhere is a threat to justice everywhere . . . [and] whatever affects one directly affects all indirectly"[307]—a sentiment that highlights the link between various justice movements and their fundamental dependency on one another.

Kingsford's and King's advice also applies to the AR activist who discounts other liberation movements or outwardly encourages, in word or deed, the domination of "subordinates" or an atmosphere of intolerance. This is no less the case when the "subordinates" are deemed insentient.

As explored in an earlier chapter, the animal rights advocate chides those who rely upon essentialist criteria, such as intelligence, communication skills, and species membership, in order to differentiate between those who are worthy of moral consideration and those who are not. She may brand them "speciesists," the worst "four-letter word" in the AR handbook, equating them with Nazi tormentors and brutal slaveholders. Yet the AR activist who clings to sentientism is likewise making an essentialist distinction no less problematic. She is forfeiting consistency and sabotaging her mandate for equality. How can the animal rights movement hope to have its message adopted if it is marred by foundational flaws and contradiction?

Let us examine this issue in the context of the feminist movement. Those who contest the subjugation of women but ignore the exploitation of nonhumans are routinely admonished by many—both within and outside—feminist circles. This condemnation does not simply emerge because females have been derogatorily associated with animals and nature for centuries; it surfaces because oppression comes in many flavors and should be recognized as such. As scholar Karen Warren says, "Transformative feminism . . . [must] develop a more expansive and complete feminism, one which ties the liberation of women to the elimination of all systems of oppression,"[308] including the domination of nature, and " . . .any feminist theory and any environmental ethic which fails to take seriously the twin and interconnected dominations of women and nature is as best incomplete and at worst simply inadequate."[309]

Several decades ago, it was virtually impossible to find a feminist text that alluded to the subordination of nonhumans. It is more commonplace today, as evidenced by the advent of ecofeminism. Ecofeminism regards social oppression and environmental exploitation as intricately linked through historical, theoretical, conceptual, empirical, ethical, and symbolic connections. It should, however, be noted that there are factions of the feminist movement that cling to human supremacy; they may argue that supporting legal rights for animals would dehumanize women. And a huge swath of feminists fails to mention the plight of nonhumans at all. Victoria Lee Erickson advances the " . . .full liberation of human beings . . ."[310] but does not directly address the liberation of animals, and renowned feminist Rosemary Radford Ruether calls women the "oppressed of the oppressed"[311] rather than pointing out the more obvious example of nonhumans who are experimented on, butchered, and electrocuted by the billions each year.

It should also be acknowledged that ecofeminism does not necessarily translate into a concern for individual animals as the AR movement requires. A 1993 feminist anthology, however, attempts to expand the idea of "nature" to include specific nonhumans, especially those held captive or domesticated. One contributor to this work argues that by ignoring individual animals, " . . .ecofeminism . . . run[s] the risk of engaging in the sort of exclusionary theorizing that it ostensibly rejects."[312]

Piggybacking off this idea is Carol J. Adams's trailblazing critique. Like the aforementioned Kingsford, Adams emphasizes the need for supporters of the feminist movement to conform to a vegetarian diet. In her book, *The Sexual Politics of Meat,* Adams writes, "I am dismayed by the failure of feminists to recognize the gender issues embedded in the eating of meat"[313] for "meat eating is to animals what white racism is to people of color, anti-Semitism is to Jewish people, homophobia is to gay men and lesbians, and women hating is to women . . . . Meat-eating offers the grounds for subjugating animals . . ."[314]

Adams then describes a poem written by the late Pat Parker that encourages the ingesting of chitterlings, neckbones, and other flesh products that were consumed by ancestor slaves in order to help the diner feel more connected to her long-lost relatives. Adams retorts that "the vegetarian body of literature demonstrates that . . . knowledge of enslaved and oppressed ancestors need not be at the expense of the enslaved oppressed animals."[315]

A message delivered by a feminist who exploits others might be justifiably ignored. If this close-minded woman has been the target of sexist attacks, there may be no desire to come to her aid. It can be difficult to feel sympathy for the victim of any "ism" who overtly contributes to the subjugation of others. She is arguably an oppressor rather than a member of the oppressed group.

The book *Dumping in Dixie* is objectionable for this very reason. The author, Robert Bullock, complains in chapter after chapter about the "evil" perpetrated upon humans due to environmental racism. However, he does not once exhibit concern for the animals and plants who are likewise affected by toxins in the air and water. This omission is especially noticeable because environmental organizations, such as Greenpeace and the Sierra Club, offer their time, money, and assistance to the human victims in the area.[316] It would only seem reasonable for Bullock to have *some* consideration for the other oppressed members of their community: the nonhumans.

There is an enormous difference between focusing on only one cause due to a lack of energy and resources and limiting the scope of one's concern to a select minority due to the chauvinistic parameters of one's belief system. If a feminist were to assert that only tall women, White women, or blue-eyed women were worthy of concern, there would be outrage. Qualifying and limiting adjectives can be inherently problematic. For example, rather than saying "All women deserve equal consideration," our feminist might inject the restrictive adjective *White* into the sentence so that the revised statement reads, "All White women deserve equal consideration." The word *White* would rapidly become a topic for scrutiny and postmodern analysis, raising questions about those who are not White. Was this adjective inserted to secretly exclude people of color? The answer must be yes, for this word silently, but clearly promotes exclusivity.

In the same way, it is problematic for an animal activist to transform the phrase "Nonhumans are worthy of equal consideration" into "Sentient nonhumans are worthy of equal consideration." The underlying message is that insentients are unworthy of concern. The emphasis on sentience arguably represents an elite and intolerant position, one that is especially problematic for those who claim to abhor bias and rely upon the notion of equality.

There is little difference between being outwardly devalued and being overlooked in the first place. For centuries, women were omitted from history (his story) books. They were invisible, voiceless, forgotten, bypassed, dismissed, without presence, excluded from the conversation, and denied opportunities because of their femaleness—at least beyond the sphere of family and home. Silence has been an effective weapon used against women. It has crippled opportunities for them throughout the world.

Sentientism hangs over those deemed insentient in a similar way. Sometimes this prejudice is boldly embraced. Sometimes it lurks on a deconstructed level. Sometimes it is communicated through silence and omission. Regardless, it clashes with the goal of equality and unity. Sentientism capsizes the animal rights platform, shattering the impact of its generally captivating message.

Collecting Interest

Now that the sentient wall has fallen, how do we advise the AR movement to proceed? I argue that animal advocates—and decision-makers within the omniocracy—become collectors of interest, seekers, investigators, and scouts, always open to further inquiry and passionate about evidence. Interests are not always visible or readily definable but may lurk under a rock in the postmodern realm, exposed only by a subjective eye and a resolute hand. As philosopher H. J. McCloskey notes, "The concept of interests . . . is an obscure and elusive one."[317]

Our definition of "interests" does not rely upon awareness, cognitive capacity, sentience, or the ability to qualify as "a subject of a life." Instead, it broadly represents the active or passive "quest" for happiness; life; pleasure; freedom; nourishment; flourishing; relief from physical, mental, or spiritual pain; the passing on of one's genes; the propagation of one's species; or other possible "goals." It coincides with the well-being of a living thing. The terms "needs," "desires," "interests," "wants," and "wishes" are being used interchangeably in this book to convey the same thing—the potential for having a stake in something. The word *potential* illustrates that this is largely a subjective enterprise; interests can never be objectively determined. They are always a little elusive.

Success, power, fame, financial security, intellectual accomplishment, remaining alive, being happy, finding love, passing on one's genes, and making a meaningful contribution to the world are some of the interests attributed to humans. Although most people can communicate their desires, this is not to say we necessarily believe them. There is always a component of guesswork, hypothesis making, evidence building, and evaluating the totality of the situation. The "other minds problem" is always at play,[318] just as it is when straddling the species divide.

There will be different opinions about what is in the best interest of a human or nonhuman. For example, in April 2000, some said that Elian Gonzalez—the six-year-old who was found floating in an inner tube off the coast of Florida—should not be returned to Cuba because it was not in his best interest to reside under a Communist regime. Others stated that it was in the boy's best interest to be with his father regardless of where he had to live. What Elian had to say about the matter may or may not have had a bearing.

We may tell a suicidal friend that it is not in her best interest to take her own life, yet we may argue that it is in the best interest of our terminally ill grandmother to die. A battered wife may maintain that she should remain married to her abusive husband, although others may disagree. Even relatively trivial issues do not escape unnoticed, for we may convince our spouse that it is not in her best interest to buy a new car, change jobs, or have a fattening piece of chocolate cake. We decipher data, weigh issues, and make "interest" evaluations all the time, aware that they may conflict with what the person in question has to say about the matter.

The "other minds problem" adds complexity. This can make it difficult to access data and intention, even with so-called normal people. If we are evaluating "what is best" for not-fully-communicative humans or nonhuman living beings (with whom it can be difficult to converse), there are additional hurdles. An individual in a "permanent" coma is without access to consciousness and sentience but arguably still has interests. We may decide that she does not "want" to be killed, that she "wants" to be intravenously fed, that she "wants" to be turned over periodically so as not to develop bedsores, and that she "does not want" to be dissected in the medical school practice lab.

On the other hand, we may conclude that it is in her best interest to be immediately euthanized since she is not expected to recover. Whatever our opinion, we can credit her with having interests, although she lacks awareness and may not have relatives to speak on her behalf. Indeed, we are merely attributing these interests to her, and our decision is partly conjecture. But this judgment also rests upon empirical factors, such as medical data about her condition, psychological information about people in general, avowals by those who knew her prior to her comatose state, and assumptions about how we would feel if we were in her situation.

We evaluate the interests of animals just as we do those of humans, despite the fact that we lack the ability to communicate in their language, and they in ours. We may readily concede that our dog "does not want" to be in physical pain, "does not want" to starve, "wants" affection, "wants" a bone, "wants" to take a walk, "wants" to sleep on the pillow next to us, and "wants" to be alive. It is true that our inferences cannot be fully verified, but neither can our inferences about other humans. This lack of certainty does not preclude us from compiling evidence, forming postulates, and arriving at an educated guess. It does not prevent us from attempting to interpret and satisfy the perceived "desires" of our dog.

The AR activist must do the same with those deemed insentient if she wants to be inclusive of all living things. She must recognize every being who may have something at stake. This is the process of moving toward the definitional good within an omniocracy. When evaluating the interests of Others, the picture may sometimes seem unclear. There may be a worry that it is too onerous to assign these interests. But the activist must plunge ahead because recognizing the equal value of—and equal consideration due—those labeled as "insentient" is necessary if she hopes to maintain philosophical consistency and dodge the dreaded curse of the "ism."

The activist could transform herself into an impartial observer or position herself behind a Rawlsian-type veil of ignorance in order to reflect upon the "needs" of insentients. (This tactic works equally well when interpreting the needs of sentients.) The activist might reasonably conclude that a tree "wants" to thrive because it expands in size, "wants" nourishment since its branches stretch toward the sun and its roots extend toward groundwater, and "wants" to propagate its species because it disseminates its seeds with the help of the wind and other natural forces. Of course, she could instead conclude that death is a tree's "goal" because this is its ultimate fate, but this is absurd unless she is also willing to concede that death is in the best interest of the human who also finds it to be her destiny.

This position leads to a paradox because if death is best for humans and trees, it is certainly best for all living things since they, too, eventually perish. If dying is best for all living things, it follows that all living things should perish as soon as possible. Of course, when all living things are dead, there remain no interests whatsoever—a consequence that is wholly nonsensical. Thus, it must be concluded that being alive is in the interest of all living beings (unless there is an extenuating circumstance such as extreme pain).

When applying her theory, the AR activist might look to the lowest common denominator (LCD). This is required for any resulting decision to be considered impartial. This LCD represents the most basic quality that applies to all in a particular group. It must be expansive to avoid an arbitrary or prejudicial outcome. Sentience is the LCD for sentient beings, whereas communicative ability is not. Being gay or lesbian is the LCD for homosexuals whereas having brown hair is not. Being female is the LCD for women, whereas being White is not. In each case, the LCD represents all who must be included in the category, whereas the second description (i.e., being communicative, brown-haired, or White) limits and discriminates. If one were to apply a theory, for example, to only brown-haired homosexuals, one would be irrationally or unfairly excluding those with black, red, or blonde hair. The latter are bona fide members of the group with interests.

The same pertains to insentients. The LCD for all living beings is that they are living, not sentient. Because all living things potentially have interests, restricting one's leastality—or laws and policy—to only a small segment of this population is no less problematic than harboring a theory about sexual orientation and restricting it to those who are brown-haired. Being alive implies that one may have an immediate interest in at least remaining alive, even if there are no other discernable needs.

The 1973 book *The Secret Life of Plants* offers that even "plants . . . are capable of intent"[319] and have interests. This was one of the first texts to assert this controversial (and viewed by many as "kooky") thesis. Today (in the mid-2020s), science has caught up with *The Secret Life of Plants* and learned that some of the assertions in this book were not so ludicrous after all. Recent studies also suggest that insects and other tiny life forms are conscious and sentient.

New Scientific Evidence: Small Beings and Plants Are Likely Sentient

Two decades ago, there was an assumption that insects could not feel pleasure or pain, and most individuals—including many animal activists—still believe this today, despite the fact that recent research indicates otherwise.

In April 2024, philosophy professor Jonathon Birch said, "This has been a very exciting 10 years for the study of animal minds."[320] Scientists and philosophers all over the world now contend that it is likely most creatures on the planet are sentient; they have the ability to feel . . . and have an internal experience."[321] This includes worms, flies, bees, crayfish, squid, lobster, ants, mollusks, mosquitoes, beetles, termites, cockroaches, grasshoppers, butterflies, and moths.[322] No insect failed the rigorous testing. Concerning worms, their neurons and behavior have been studied extensively, proving they are "sensitive to vibrations . . . [and they have] rational intelligence."[323] Scholar Tam Hunt and psychology professor Jonathan Schooler have proposed a theory "based on the observed behavior of the entities that surround us, from electrons to atoms to molecules, to bacteria to mice, bats and on . . . [that] suggests all things may be viewed as [at least] a little conscious. [This is called] . . . panpsychism [which is] an increasingly accepted position."[324]

Biologist Marc Bekoff says, "It's time to stop wondering if nonhuman animals are sentient—they are. Abundant science tells us so."[325] He adds that 32 countries have officially recognized broad animal sentience, including Austria, Chile, Croatia, Germany, Hungary, Lithuania, Poland, Sweden, and the United Kingdom.[326] The United States is not on the exhaustive list. Despite the official declaration about the sentience of nonhumans, nations around the world—including America—are not so very kind to so-called lower creatures (i.e., mice, guinea pigs, insects). They are routinely and abundantly used, abused, and killed in research labs—not to mention their deplorable treatment in ordinary society. This is partly because many "think it's impossible that they are sentient beings or . . . casually write them off as so-called pests."[327]

In recent years, scientists have uncovered a considerable amount of interesting data. A study reveals that bumblebees roll balls around just for fun, and the cleaner wrasse fish reacts to her image in the mirror in ways that are similar to a person preparing for a date.[328] Professor Jonathon Birch says "No one in a million years would have expected a tiny fish to pass the test."[329] This was only a fraction of the information presented in April 2024 by The New York Declaration on Animal Consciousness. The declaration—which was signed by 40 researchers—states that a huge host of creatures are likely, or possibly, conscious.

Kristen Andrews, a philosophy professor at York University, suggests that the new data could end boiling lobsters alive or intentionally stepping on ants, adding that "the recognition that so many creatures have feelings offers everyone the possibility of a wider, deeper connection to the natural world around them."[330]

The results of this research are, in my view, commonsensical. If my theory, "the body protection theory"—which argues that consciousness, including the ability to feel sensation, is a by-product of the need to protect one's body—holds, it would also apply to insects. Any being who moves "on its own accord" or has "the ability to change significantly when under stress" would need consciousness as a self-defense measure. It could face peril from fire, flood, predators, or other threats in the natural world.

This theory could even apply to plants, although it is less clear. A tree's branches may move because of the wind or a squirrel scurrying about, but this is not moving "on its own accord." The tree has roots and branches that grow toward moisture and leaves that stretch toward the sun, but this is very slow movement. Although it is uncertain as to whether a minor amount of movement would be significant enough to comport with the "body protection theory," plants have "the ability to change behavior when under stress," as evidenced by ground-breaking research. They "scream" when hurt or uprooted—a sound beyond the reach of human ears, and they can apparently communicate with other plants and insects. They can let off certain smells and alter their color and shape when under duress. These changes and sounds can "signal danger to other plants nearby, which in response, boost their defenses; or attract animals to deal with the pests that may be harming the plant."[331]

In short, a growing number of scientists claim that plants do indeed "feel pain . . . have intelligence . . . and perceive and interact with their environment in sophisticated ways."[332] Cleve Backster (a CIA agent and polygraph test expert) hooked up a Dracaena plant to a lie-detector device and found increased levels of stress when a flame was lit near it. He concluded that plants communicate telepathically—research later confirmed by a study in the *Biomed Central Ecology Journal*. The study demonstrated that "plants can indeed communicate with each other, and they do so by using nano-mechanical sound waves."[333] Other research has shown that plants are affected by anesthetics to the point in which they will go to sleep.[334] The test is scientific in that the trick of putting plants to sleep has been repeated over and over with the same result.

It is not uncommon for mainstream media outlets today to discuss how plants are aware, feel pain, or respond to stress. A journalist for *The Atlantic* writes about a lab in Wisconsin where the veins of plants are forcefully squeezed; it is found that the greenery is aware of being touched in an unpleasant way. The article states, "Consciousness was once seen as belonging solely to humans and a short list of nonhuman animals . . . . Some scientists now posit that plants should likewise be considered intelligent. Plants have been found to show sensitivity to sound, store information to be accessed later, and communicate among their kind."[335] A *New Scientist* article reads, "It's a wild idea, but recent experiments suggest plants may have the ability to learn and make decisions."[336] In short, it is becoming accepted by many within the sciences that plants have subjective internal experiences and enjoy a kind of sentience.[337]

In his 1972 essay "Should Trees Have Standing? Toward Legal Rights for Natural Objects," legal scholar Christopher D. Stone reasons that if the court system can grant legal standing to corporations, trusts, joint ventures, and municipalities, it should be able to bestow legal rights to trees. (This essay was written many decades before scientific findings about the probable sentience and consciousness of plants). Stone seems to grasp the idea of insentient interests when he writes, "Natural objects can communicate their wants (needs) to us, and in ways that are not terribly ambiguous. I am sure I can judge with more certainty and meaningfulness whether and when my lawn wants (needs) water, than the Attorney General can judge whether or when the United States wants (needs) to take an appeal from an adverse judgment by a lower court."[338]

Philosopher Steven Sapontzis—who had earlier argued that the animal movement should set aside concerns about bugs, trees, and greenery due to pragmatism—seems to change his tune in a separate passage. He writes, "If animal liberationists are to be consistent . . . all those who can meet the interest requirement . . . [such as possibly] insects and plants . . . must be included in the concerns of this movement."[339] Although he is writing prior to the astounding research related to "small beings" and vegetation, he insightfully suggests that—when in doubt—the movement should strive to be inclusive.

Despite the argument that plants may be conscious and sentient, most people (including many animal activists) hold to the old paradigm that they are not. This mindset may partly emanate from a lack of knowledge about recent discoveries. However, a more likely reason pertains to the inconvenience that would arise from embracing moral rights for insects and plants. In their view, it would complicate daily living and make it more difficult to convince others what it means to be a good person. Black-and-white would morph into gray and hazy—a calamitous situation for today's AR movement since their philosophy is based on good versus evil.

AR activists are routinely confronted by adversaries, such as angry carnivores, who argue that nonhuman lives do not matter. A detractor may bring up the "small beings problem," asking, for example, "Are you saying I'm supposed to care about every tiny insect?" Traditionally, the activist has replied, "No. Insects are not sentient"—a statement she likely believed since she was (and probably still is) unaware of the groundbreaking new research. It was an easy way to avoid getting into the weeds with an intellectual discussion that could derail the mission at hand: to protect those animals who are fairly easy to protect.

There are other questions that the AR activist might encounter, such as "Is it wrong to eat plants since they may be sentient?" and "Aren't more small beings killed with plant eating than with eating cows?"

The first question is best answered by pointing out that plants rejuvenate themselves. The proper way to obtain leaves of lettuce, for example, is to remove them piece by piece. This does not kill the vegetable; it allows for continued growth. Plucking fruit, such as apples and oranges, does not harm the tree; it remains intact. Even potatoes are not a problem. They die back naturally at the end of the growing season and can be harvested without causing death to the plant.[340]

With respect to the question of whether a vegan kills more animals than a carnivore, research indicates that an entirely plant-based diet protects more life forms than a meat-eating one. This is because animals eat a whopping 36 percent of the world's crop calories.[341] In other words, farm animals are fed a tremendous amount of plant life before they are butchered for human consumption. Thus, with a vegan diet, fewer insects (and field mice, rabbits, etc.) will die.

Some countries are working to preserve the bugs and wildlife affected by plant agriculture. For example, the Netherlands has "diversionary fields and refuge sites for birds, as well as indoor agriculture."[342] If the United States truly wants to move toward the definitional good, technology should be targeted toward finding solutions to the harm done by crop production. It goes without saying that animal agriculture would be eliminated.

The above responses (and others like them) might help today's animal advocate who is trying to defend current AR philosophy. But these rebuttals are not a perfect remedy. This is because the animal rights movement relies upon the "moral" and the "free." Morality is firm, unmalleable, and in the end undercuts the cause. It communicates that behavior is either right or wrong. One cannot argue that it is wicked to kill two thousand people but not one thousand. One cannot argue that it is evil to kill two thousand chickens but not one thousand. And one cannot say it is immoral to kill two thousand spiders but not one thousand.

Per morality, killing is either wrong in a particular situation or not. So, when an AR activist tells a carnivore that she kills fewer beings by being vegan, this is like saying it is okay to kill some but not too many. This contradicts current AR ideology, which puts forth an absolute theory of right versus wrong. It would be like saying, "I don't kill as many people when I bomb single-family homes as when I blow up crowded apartment buildings. So, I am moral."

The detractor's response would be, "Why are you blowing up anything? I thought you said it was immoral to kill people."

The philosophy discussed in this book—which promotes an omniocracy within a determined and amoral universe—eliminates the need for answers to these controversial questions. It changes the conversation. Morality and free will are no longer relevant. Sentience is immaterial because all living beings are treated with value and viewed as having interests within this new structure. The traditional AR conversation is recast into one that focuses on policy, law, pragmatism, the definitional good, and how to organize protection for as many beings as possible within the geographical designations that I call Bioland and Ecoland (a topic that will be discussed later).

In conclusion, it is important that AR activists err on the side of inclusion. They are well advised to abandon their black-and-white philosophy that demarcates sentience from insentience and accept that all living beings have interests—or as an alternative, simply assume all living beings are sentient as science is beginning to confirm. The next step will be to develop a strategy for implementing this new AR theory—a subject that will be explored in the next few chapters.

Chapter Nine

THE JAIN DIFFICULTY

I have argued that the animal rights movement is wise to discard "the moral" and "the free" and instead rest its tenets upon a lessality, or better yet, a collection of leastalities. "Morality" and "free will" promote—if only on a deconstructed level—the supremacy of *Homo sapiens* over other life forms. These myths reign as sacred cows, influencing the thoughts and behavior of individuals as well as dictating the direction of legislation, mores, and the judiciary. They stifle the marketplace of ideas, provoke hatred against the self and others, and discipline society toward an anthropocentric end.

In the next chapter, I will discuss how a shift away from Tom Regan's (moral) rights theory and Peter Singer's (moral) utilitarianism is required. In their stead, I will propose a system that relies upon a nonmoral utilitarian guideline, which will then be used to move the society in Bioland (where humans reside) toward the definitional good. But first, I would like to focus on pragmatism and the "small-beings problem." A devil's advocate could argue that building a society around consideration for all living things is onerous, even utopian. I respond by examining Jainism.

Jainism is an influential religion with rigorous precepts and a reported ten million followers worldwide.[343] Most adherents live in India, but there are temples in 28 U.S. states with thousands of members.[344] Jainism promotes admirable but arduous standards, which arguably lead to what one might call the "Jain difficulty." Complications stem from the religion's core precept: ahimsa, or noninjury to all living beings. Followers are supposed to be vegetarian or vegan, abstain from violence in word, thought, and deed, and set an example for others. Mahatma Gandhi was deeply influenced by Jain thought.[345]

Lord Mahavira (599–529 BCE), the founder of modern Jainism, spent his life as a wandering ascetic, endeavoring to protect all living things. The legend is that "many sorts of beings gathered on his body, crawled about it, and caused pain there. (He did not scratch himself.) Without ceasing in his reflections . . . [he] slowly wandered about, and, killing no creatures, he begged for his food."[346]

Jains revere nature. They do not support the notion of a transcendent, anthropomorphic God; a man-centered universe; or a human existence disconnected or alienated from other living things.[347] Harmony with all species and a love for the environment are critical components of the religion. Jains consider the interests of all beings who may have a stake in a particular state of affairs and acknowledge that these creatures "want" to avoid pain. Additionally, Jains espouse that a person's behavior toward both individuals and the whole planet ultimately impacts the self. Acts of violence are, for example, to be avoided because they "will result in injury to oneself at some future time, even perhaps in another embodiment [Karma]."[348]

Jainism blends nicely with a world of lessalities and leastalities rather than a world that salutes "morality." In fact, the Jain religion does not advance "a two-prong, right or wrong analysis of arguments in the style of Aristotle . . . . It disallows the holding of any extreme views . . . [or] absolutes . . . [and] it does not condemn alternate views as incorrect."[349] In other words, tolerance is a central theme within Jainism,[350] and the religion gels with perspectivalism.[351]

Despite this open-mindedness, Jain texts often use phrases that sound a lot like moral absolutism because of the limitations of human language. Jains may advise that "nonviolence is . . . the highest religion,"[352] "to impose suffering is to impose evil,"[353] and people have "the responsibility to protect . . . every living organism in the galaxy."[354] In spite of forceful comments like these, Jainism outwardly condemns building one's philosophy on absolutes and even opposes the use of hurtful, assaulting, or absolutist speech[355]—a recommendation that parallels the arguments made in this book about the manipulativeness and offensiveness inherent in "the moral." Jain texts also recommend that "words . . . be uttered not for inflicting harm on creatures but [only] for their benefit."[356] Peacefulness, balance, and empathy are valued.

In addition to admonishing violent speech, the religion discourages other more obvious "forms of violence,"[357] such as "careless[ly] . . . crush[ing] . . . a tiny living creature . . . under the foot,"[358] owning property (other than necessary items) because it causes suffering to other living things,[359] and eating anything other than very specific plant foods since "even . . . organisms, like soy [and vegetables], want to live, want not to be eaten."[360] In fact, Jainism pinpoints meat eating as the basis for many vices.[361] Followers may take spiders outside rather than kill them, refrain from building fires while on camping trips (so as not to harm flying insects), and abstain from eating after sunset to avoid inadvertently hurting tiny life forms.[362]

Naturally, the religion is opposed to the military and

capital punishment. However, it also disapproves of working in professions that intentionally or accidentally injure living creatures—such as agriculture, timber, and pharmaceuticals—and it discourages wearing fabrics connected with the death or abuse of living beings. Orthodox Jains may go to extreme lengths to comply with what they believe to be the duties of ahimsa. They may be celibate because ejaculation "kills, on average, seventy-five million spermatozoa,"[363] and they may deprive themselves of some plant-based food—such as alcohol and certain kinds of figs—because these products are likely to harbor microorganisms,[364] who also "want" to live.

It should be noted that the majority of Jains do not follow the most demanding precepts of the religion because doing so would be impractical. These duties are generally observed only by monks and the ultra-devoted. Ordinary people may adhere to strict non-injury practices from time to time to experience asceticism. This is usually done on a limited basis, such as on weekend retreats. Author Michael Tobias writes, "Jainism can work, and must work, anywhere, everywhere,"[365] but is this indeed true? Ahimsa, when loosely applied, is integral to omniocracy, and it harmonizes beautifully with the journey toward the definitional good. But could strict ahimsa work on a national or worldwide scale? Or would compliance by all lead to a paradox?

One could argue that *orthodox Jainism* is unworkable if extended beyond a small segment of the population because it makes unrealistic demands. First, a devout Jain is instructed not to obtain her own food because even gathering vegetable products (often) qualifies as a violent act.[366] Thus, she must depend upon others for her sustenance. She relies upon the "unsavory" acts of others or, more accurately, the acts of others that run counter to the leastalities to which they subscribe, that is, if they are also Jains. Not only would there be no one to acquire food (or any agriculturalists to grow it) in what Jainism would call a "perfect world," but there would be no one to work in the many other "corrupt" professions that foster human life.

Secondly, if all people were to emulate Jain monks by remaining celibate, *Homo sapiens* would become extinct within a short time. There would be no one to practice the religion or assist living beings who are in pain or who face death. This brings us to the third point: Jain texts seem to require the rescue of living beings, including the imperative to save them from predators.[367] This is not only a monumental undertaking but an impossible one. Fourthly, devout Jains are supposed to live in the desert[368] so as to damage fewer life forms. But there is no water and a scarcity of vegetarian food in arid regions, and even if some Jains are permitted to gather fruits or vegetables in other locations, how would they transport the food to the desert? Orthodox Jains are not allowed to drive cars because vehicles could inadvertently kill or injure creatures on the roadway. In short, the hurdles are considerable. It is hard to imagine how the obligations of strict ahimsa could be expanded to include an entire city, an entire region, or an entire world.

Now, let us examine this topic in relation to the animal rights crusade. *Orthodox Jainism* would obviously be impractical, as delineated above. But what about a more relaxed Jain attitude? Would it be problematic if the AR movement adjusted its philosophy to require consideration for all living beings rather than just the sentient ones? The answer would be yes due to the movement's reliance upon "morality." There is no wiggle room within the crusade as it currently stands. Actions are endorsed as either right or wrong, as good or shameful, as compassionate or evil. The movement promotes rigidity and a black-and-white philosophy.

Let us assume everyone became vegan and no longer wore leather or fur; industries halted the practice of animal agriculture, vivisection, and trapping; shelters solved the problem of "pet" overpopulation; horse racing and dog racing venues shut down; and zoos, aquariums, and animal circuses closed their doors for good. There would still be other practices that would negatively impact—even kill—various life forms. Nonhumans are routinely the victims of so-called collateral damage. Possums are killed by traffic, sea life die tangled in plastic debris, forest dwellers perish when trees are cut and roads are built, gophers drown in backyard pools, rats die of starvation in attics, birds are killed by airplane propellers, mice die during plant harvesting, and rabbits perish by ingesting fertilized grass and artificial turf (which has unfortunately become a popular but toxic trend). In addition, there are hazards related to wind turbines, arson, fossil fuel operations, and nuclear power plants, to name a few. In other words, there are and will forever be conflicts of interest between *Homo sapiens* and other life forms, just as there are and will forever be conflicts of interest between humans and other humans. Clashes will multiply as human society expands—as more people inhabit the planet.

Is there a way to hold to the basic tenets of the animal rights movement while escaping the impracticalities and paradoxes that stem from the Jain difficulty? The answer is yes, if and only if the movement deviates from "the moral" and instead patterns its philosophy off lessalities and leastalities. As discussed earlier, moral principles are not malleable, subjective, or open to compromise. They demand and expect obedience. Perhaps Mahavira and other Jain leaders understood the difficulties that would emerge if ahimsa were presented as a nonnegotiable precept. Perhaps this is why they rejected the you-are-evil-if-you-do-such-and-such maxim and instead opted for a nonjudgmental path, a welcoming vision, a paradise that could ostensibly be achieved if the community wished to be gentle and loving toward all of creation.

Practitioners of ahimsa seem to recognize that "it is not possible to act in this world without hurting other living beings (stepping on them, killing them with the body, etc.) . . . . Awareness of causing pain [is] the nature of existence,"[369] and with this in mind, they embrace the notion that "one can only do one's best"—a slogan that could be adopted by animal rights advocates as well. John Robbins, author of *Diet for a New America*,[370] has been known to express this sentiment during interviews and public appearances, but he is an anomaly.

Rather than claim to be "morally" pure or flawless in conduct, as they sometimes do, animal advocates might be better off admitting that they do their best by working toward the definitional good. They need not become defensive or concoct elaborate justifications for seemingly faulty behavior. Nobody is perfect. Nobody can escape her flesh-and-blood predicament. Even the most noble-minded Jains cannot avoid causing harm. Author Swati Sharma writes that animal activists must "shed the fixation on personal purity that has prevented the movement from shaping policy and regulation. Animal advocates should have a seat at the table in rooms where decisions are made about how animals live and die"[371]—a topic that will be discussed at length later.

AR activists may also want to accept that campaigns are routinely geared toward a utopian end. Perfection is often unachievable. For example, true equality cannot be attained, even within human-to-human relations, but this in no way discounts the importance of this goal for the individuals and societies who pursue it. It is not possible to eradicate every scintilla of sexism, but this does not diminish the urge to strive for a sexist-free society. The same holds true for racism, anti-Semitism, *speciesism*, and so on. The goals of an omniocratic AR movement are not invalid or reduced in importance simply because they are not wholly (and easily) achievable.

With a relaxed and confident attitude rather than with morally shrill rhetoric and a guarded demeanor, AR advocates can overturn the often-negative perception that their adversaries have of them. An animal activist who is inclusive of all living things and insists that she is only expressing a leastality instead of a morality cannot legitimately be called a hypocrite by her opponents. She is theoretically consistent yet realistic enough to understand that her mission toward equal value and equal consideration for all living things is only a goal in a certain direction, an evolving and never-ending project. When bombarded with questions meant to throw her off course, she can answer, "I abide by my personal value system as best as I can." Who can fault her for that? She can be forgiving of herself and others while marching forward in her own unique way.

Chapter Ten

AN OMNIOCRATIC DECISION-MAKING MODEL

A political system is comprised of institutions and interest groups, decision-makers and constituents, governing documents, and potentially lobbyists, parties, special factions, and alliances. Those in charge design rules for maintaining order in society and often rely upon compromise, fairness, and consistency. It is generally assumed that there are great disparities between democracies, communist regimes, monarchies, republics, fascist systems, aristocracies, and the other types of government that operate today or once did. However, the disparities are inconsequential compared to one resounding similarity: they are all of, by, and for the human. They routinely ignore the interests of Others (nonhuman animals and nature). If owls, cats, cows, rats, ladybugs, trees, and so forth, could communicate in one voice, they would surely come together to denounce all political systems, past and present; they would admonish those institutions as bigoted, cruel, tyrannical, and complicit in the heartless treatment of nonhumans throughout the world.

Democracy is described as "an ideal, an aspiration, really, intimately connected to and dependent upon a picture of what it is to be human,"[372] and its two premier characteristics are listed as equality and justice.[373] It is held by many to be the optimal form of government because it is said to give the most vulnerable a voice in matters that affect their lives. But this is false. The truly defenseless—nonhuman animals and nature—have no say in the matter. Their fundamental interests are cavalierly ignored, and their lives are routinely snuffed out in favor of human profit, convenience, and luxury.

People—regardless of whether they are elderly, female, disabled, LGTBQ+, an ethnic minority, or defined as some other human group—are not disadvantaged compared to nonhuman animals. Even poverty-stricken people in undeveloped countries have great power and influence over their nonhuman brothers and sisters.

International alliances and foreign nations regularly use political pressure, economic sanctions, and sometimes armed combat to assist *Homo sapiens*, but this is never the case for other species. There is no such thing as a war crime against a dog, chicken, or pigeon. There has never been a Geneva Convention for the animals. No government has imposed trade sanctions or instigated military action to end cockfights, crush films, deforestation, dog-eating, or seal hunts.

Democracy is a totalitarian regime in which the powerful (humans) use, abuse, manipulate, and murder the powerless (nonhumans) for the former's own perceived gain. This system of government ignores the truly voiceless, powerless, marginalized, and oppressed: animals and Earth. In the United States, nonhumans have no standing in court, no legal rights, and no constitutional protections; they are viewed as property or a mere means to a human end. When a law is passed to protect the interests of a nonhuman species—which happens on rare occasions—it is usually watered down later or quickly subordinated to commercial profits or other anthropocentric aims.

It is generally considered desirable to be aligned with or operate under a democracy. But when the root word *demos*—which means "people" or "populace"—is used to describe a country's political system, it reduces those who are nonhuman to a lesser status. Could African Americans expect equality in a White-ocracy? How would women feel living under a man-ocracy? Would gays accept rule by a straight-ocracy? As stated earlier in this book, omniocracy (*omni* means "all") is a form of government that provides representation for *all* living beings. Decision-makers must consider the interests of every species in Bioland. Each living being is a constituent: dogs, bulls, horses, trees, humans, and so on. All are designated as part of society and are worthy of equal consideration.

Unlike oppressed human groups, animals cannot resist cruelty and exploitation with civil disobedience or direct action. They cannot picket, refuse to sit at the back of the bus, hold sit-ins, throw tea overboard, go on a hunger strike, form underground railroads, or embark upon other forms of protest. They cannot sneak into factory farms or vivisection labs to rescue their distressed friends. They must rely on compassionate animal activists to come to their aid. These activists face overwhelming hurdles because, in this world, being human is not everything; it is the *only* thing. An activist may be sidelined for her opinions, marginalized as a "terrorist," fired via "cancel culture," or called a traitor to her species. She may be subjected to verbal warfare by mainstream media and other societal leaders who don their "pretend psychiatrist hats" and brand her an aberration, a sociopath, or a nutcase.

Some countries and cities are gesturing toward what I call

"omniocratic guidelines." Germany, Ecuador, Brazil, Bolivia, India, Austria, Egypt, and Switzerland have inserted provisions protecting nonhumans or the Earth into their constitutions. In recent years, Turkey's parliament passed a bill stating that animals can no longer be classified as "commodities."[374] Unfortunately, the changes have largely been all talk and no substance.[375]

A few local governments have shifted in an omniocratic direction. There is a town in a predominantly Jain area of India called Palitana,[376] where meat-eating is illegal. Several cities in Italy—Rome, Turin, and Reggio Emilia—have ratified laws that protect other beings.[377] For example, the city council in Reggio Emilia passed a bundle of laws in 2004 that ostensibly give animals "equal rights to man."[378] They banned boiling lobsters alive and keeping goldfish in glass bowls. They also hired a full-time city employee to care for stray cats.

Despite a handful of pro-animal city charters and constitutions, nonhumans are generally treated as a means to a human end. Meat-eating—which arguably causes more animal suffering and death than any other human activity—is a case in point. In 2002, people averaged 180 pounds of meat per person in Germany, 160 in Switzerland, and 99 in Ecuador.[379] The average in the U.S. was a massive 275 pounds per person. According to the USDA, the number of birds (chickens, turkeys, etc.) slaughtered each year in America is a staggering nine billion.[380] This number does not include fish, pigs, cows, and other victims of the human dinner plate. Even the countries with amended constitutions do not mandate, or recommend, an end to carnivorous behavior, and it is unclear how one can give respect to nonhumans and treat them with equal consideration while confining them inside squalid and crowded factory farms, slicing off their heads, and stuffing their lifeless flesh down people's throats.

In Search of a Decision-Making Model

A model is a framework that serves as a tool for establishing policy. It can assist a sole decision-maker, activists within a movement, and the leaders of society—especially if they wish to maintain a semblance of consistency, fairness, impartiality, or coherence. When facing a dilemma, one will select a particular model, input relevant factors, compute the data, and arrive at a potential resolution. This will be the task later: I will create a model for the definitional good. But first, I explore whether some of the traditional models could be of assistance to an omniocracy.

Author Carol Gilligan promotes a "female care" decision-making model[381] because women, in her view, frame problems in a different way from men. She claims the former focus on relationships, communication, and an ethic of responsibility, whereas the latter operate from a structure of detachment, autonomy, and an ethic of rights. She feels that the male justice model is alienating, such as the one offered by psychologist Lawrence Kohlberg. Kohlberg stresses the "equality of human rights, respect for the dignity of human beings as individual persons . . . [and Immanuel Kant's idea that] persons are ends in themselves and must be treated as such."[382] He makes no mention of nonhumans and, in fact, emphasizes the social contract, thus must exclude those who are not (believed to be) moral agents. Kohlberg's human-centered model does not provide adequate grounding for an omniocracy.

Although a model may translate across human cultures, this in no way suggests that it will translate across species. In fact, the models presented by Gilligan and Kohlberg are quite useless for bestowing value on those who are not human; they are anthropocentric. They disregard nonhumans from concern. As mentioned, Gilligan's model stresses the importance of relationship, reciprocity, communication, and the "special ties we feel for others." It dovetails with Deborah Slicer's feminist theory discussed earlier in this book. Focusing on communication and relationship means excluding those, such as animals and plants, with whom it is more difficult to communicate and with whom it is, in some cases, challenging to establish a relationship. Additionally, the feminist model can lead to prejudice against those humans with whom one does not feel a "special tie." Its subjective elements provide an inadequate basis for policy; it can too easily lead to racism, sexism, and other biases (as I noted earlier when evaluating Slicer).

In an essay titled "The Generalized and Concrete Other: The Kohlberg-Gilligan Controversy and Moral Theory," professor Seyla Benhabib argues that a decision-making model must include both rights and needs, both justice and all possible modes of the good life. She deems it important to analyze how "gender sex systems have contributed to the oppression and exploitation of women,"[383] but she, like Kohlberg and Gilligan, fails to recognize that animals and nature have been, and continue to be, exploited. Benhabib says that actual dialogue is the sole fair and viable option, for only what "all could consensually agree to be in the best interest of each could be accepted as the outcome of this dialogic process."[384] Nonhumans obviously cannot participate in this sort of communicative enterprise thus their interests remain unprotected. Benhabib is interested in eradicating that which is "racist, sexist, cultural[ly] relativist, [and] discriminatory."[385] Yet, she is blind to the fact that her theory harbors an inherent bias against nonhuman living beings.

Is there such a thing as a "male model," and do females use a different framework from males when arriving at decisions? Author Susan Moller thinks not and says, "The implication drawn from [Gilligan] . . . that women tend to be more particularistic and contextual, appears to be unfounded."[386]

The arguments that Benhabib and Gilligan make against the "male model" seem to be targeted at deontological theory. However, they would probably maintain that utilitarianism is equally male, faceless, and rational, thus no less dubious. Act utilitarianism focuses on the specific and the personal; a decision-maker reviews the intricate factors of a situation before calculating utility. She must consider the interests of all, even oppressed females. Nonhumans could be included in the calculation, as evidenced by the more inclusive philosophy of Jeremy Bentham. The utilitarian model has another benefit: it does not grant greater concern for those with whom one feels closest or with whom there is an ease of communication. Biases can theoretically be avoided.

Renowned philosopher John Rawls argues against utilitarianism. He says it fails to respect individuality, citing how the interests of one can be superseded to satisfy the interests of the majority. To compensate for the perceived inadequacy of utilitarianism, Rawls devises what he calls the original position and his two principles of justice: 1) "each person is to have an equal right to the most extensive basic liberty compatible with a similar liberty for others. 2) social and economic inequities are to be arranged so that they are both, a) reasonably expected to be to everybody's advantage, and, b) attached to positions and offices open to all."[387] Because "person" applies only to humans, mistreatment of animals is permissible.

Rawls admits that his theory covers only "our relationships with other persons and [does not consider] how we are to conduct ourselves toward animals and the rest of nature."[388] He adds that "it does seem that we are not required to give strict justice to creatures lacking this capacity [for having a sense of justice]."[389] He notes that animals may have "some protection certainly, but their status is not that of human beings."[390] Rawls says that people have a duty not to be "cruel" to animals, but he never defines what this term means or how he arrives at this directive.

He does allow for a degree of environmental protection to accommodate future generations of persons;[391] however, he does not recognize the innate value of the natural world as an omniocracy requires. Rawls's "difference principle" focuses on the least advantaged person and seeks to maximize the long-term expectations of this least advantaged person. Although nonhumans arguably qualify as the "least advantaged," they are omitted from concern.

Is Rawls's theory inherently speciesist, as many contend, or could it be revised to accommodate Others? One could pretend, for example, that those in the original position (behind the veil of ignorance) face the possibility of being born as a bird, a pig, a butterfly, or a tree; they must problem-solve with this assumption in mind.

Author Lilly-Marlene Russow says that "the original position already has in place mechanisms by which the interests of animals could be considered in the same way as those of humans . . . but any attempt to force an expansion of the original position fails."[392]

Professor Donald VanDeVeer, on the other hand, thinks a complete revision of Rawls's theory is feasible. He says that although people in the original position are rational and able to understand complicated economic calculations such as the maximin,[393] their task is to devise a policy that presupposes they could be born simple-minded, thus unable to understand philosophy. VanDeVeer concludes that "it seems equally legitimate to insist that [the contractors] . . . be allowed . . . [to assume] that they [might not be] . . . moral persons at all."[394] With this revision, he contends that nonhumans could be equally protected.

Lilly Marlene-Russow, at first, seems to agree with

VanDeVeer. She suggests that Rawls's theory cannot necessarily be dubbed speciesist because it might allow for the rights of some nonhumans, such as those with "moral" capacities. She continues that this "will not save the veal calf or the laboratory rat . . . [but it could include] a few nonhumans, perhaps dolphins or gorillas."[395] But then she seems to shift her perspective, conceding that Rawls's theory could be called speciesist and inconsistent due to its appraisal of "marginal cases" (i.e., humans who cannot make rational choices and have no realistic chance of ever acquiring these abilities). "Marginal" humans are "clearly less able to construct or follow a life-plan than a pig or a hamster, yet Rawls still accords them protection[s] that he does not extend to nonhuman animals."[396]

Russow concludes that Rawls can only escape charges of inconsistency if he excludes "marginal" humans from protection. This is a conceivable option, for Rawls openly admits that "those more or less permanently deprived of moral personality may present a difficulty [for his theory]."[397] However, this alteration would not open the gate to legal rights for animals and nature, thus failing to satisfy the needs of an omniocracy.

Another option for Rawls might be to devise a supplemental policy that provides for the protection of nonhumans and "marginal" people. Russow states that Rawls does not view his philosophy as "a complete moral theory;"[398] therefore, she thinks it might be possible to extend concern to Others in this way. Yet Rawls does not devise this secondary policy in his books, and it is unclear what this approach might entail. Plus, one could still criticize him for excluding those without "reasoning abilities" from his primary theory. It could be argued that justice, fairness, or consistency is achieved only when all are initially included. It would be objectionable, for example, to devise a policy for males and then add a footnote later that one should be kind to females. It would be equally unsatisfactory to provide rights for Whites with an addendum, drafted later, suggesting one should not be cruel to African Americans.

Setting aside the decision-making models of Rawls, Kohlberg, Gilligan, and Benhabib, some prototypes rely upon virtue and/or character. "Character" focuses on the moral attributes in a person that predispose him toward the good. "Virtue" speaks to the attributes of individuals and communities that enable them to attain high standards. These frameworks place significance on community, tradition, and moral ability and require "communication, or perhaps more specifically a conversation among all the relevant actors in the moral environment in which a decision is being made."[399] In other words, these models butt up against the same problems as the aforementioned ones. Those who are unable to easily interact with people and who are deemed unable to access "morality" and virtue are omitted from the conversation and consideration.

In a nutshell, the reliance upon past stories, tradition, virtue, communication, morality, and/or narrative—as well as any reliance upon the previously explored formulations of the "female" care model and the "male" justice model—are not well equipped for informing a biocentric lessality or leastality or becoming a tool that could aid decision-makers when moving toward the definitional good. These frameworks exclude nonhumans from concern, and thus are ill-suited for an omniocracy. However, this does not mean the so-called male/rational model cannot provide a suitable structure for decision-making if it is pried away from the "moral" and deontological—and reimagined as a nonmoral, utilitarian guideline.

The rational model is not inherently biased in favor of humans, males, Whites, or any privileged group, despite the fact that it has historically been applied in a discriminatory manner. It could comfortably proceed from an assumption that all living things are of equal value and worthy of equal consideration. It could even be based on a variety of other concepts, such as pantheism, the connectedness of the nature/essence/spirit of all living things, philosophical materialism, the belief that all things are made by a Creator and therefore deserve equal consideration, the fact that all living beings are necessarily determined, or some other principle altogether. When prejudices that favor humans are eliminated from the grounding of a theory, a biocentric policy is free to emerge.

The seven-step decision-making model—as formulated by Dr. Michael Davis—spells out a rational framework that could operate within an omniocracy.[400] It provides a concrete way for arriving at decisions, harbors no inherent prejudices against nonhuman living beings, and could easily "be appropriated by all users, without prior philosophical knowledge."[401] It simply asks the decision-makers to (a) illustrate the problem; (b) determine the facts; (c) identify the stakeholders; (d) make a list of options; (e) test the options with respect to pragmatism, professional duties, the amount of harm that could emerge, and other previously defined measures; (f) make a tentative choice by comparing alternatives; and (g) arrive at a final decision.[402]

Although the seven-step model might be appealing, one could argue that the framework for decision-making within an omniocracy must explicitly and directly include the interests of animals and nature. Therefore, one might prefer to adopt the model of the definitional good or what I call the "Good Model."

The Good Model

To briefly rehash that which was explained earlier, the definitional good involves taking the interests of all living things into account to arrive at a happier world or a more favorable state of affairs. The DG has nothing to do with "morality" but is instead based on the definition of a "good world," in much the same way someone might be described as a "good piano player" or a "good criminal." It is descriptive rather than prescriptive.

Due to the inborn mechanism of psychological hedonism/egoism, every living being naturally strives toward what it "deems" to be pleasurable or beneficial (to itself) and away from that which it "concludes" is disadvantageous. Because these interests can be assumed to be subjectively important to these individuals, a world that creates more satisfaction can be called definitionally better than one that does not. Some might say that *deeming* and *concluding* are inappropriate words for describing the movement of plants and microorganisms, but language has been created by and for humans thus, applying it to Others may have peculiar consequences. Despite this imprecision, the general idea should be clear.

A person or a group of people—such as the political leaders in an omniocracy—might apply the model of the definitional good or what I call the "Good Model" to develop public policy and law. The Good Model provides a guideline, structure, or roadmap for decision-making within society.[403] Due to the Jain difficulty, as discussed in the previous chapter, courses of action must make practical sense. It is for this reason that *size matters.* In most cases, it would be impractical, indeed inconceivable, to legally provide for extremely small living beings in society (or Bioland). A person who attempts to do so would be incapacitated, unable to sustain her own existence or satisfy the needs of larger creatures.

Laws could not be so demanding as to punish those who negatively affect or incidentally kill "the tiny"—such as insects, small plants, or microorganisms—by moving, breathing, or merely surviving. Implementation of laws restricting basic movement would be futile and absurd. Philosopher Baruch Spinoza wisely concludes, "It is best to grant that which cannot be abolished, even though it be in itself harmful."[404] Laws must be created around those things that can, on some level, be controlled and that are, at the same time, deemed beneficial for individuals within the whole.

In some instances, very small living things can be collectively protected if society makes such a decision, plus the tiny can be recipients of compassion campaigns or lessality-affiliated crusades. Some individuals might promote calls to action, such as "Please take insects outside rather than kill them" or "Give plants water if they look dry." Communication of this sort can change hearts and minds and ultimately influence behavior. Larger beings, such as trees, dogs, squirrels, cows, coyotes, birds, and people, can realistically be considered for legal protection within Bioland—an issue explored in the next chapter.

What follows is a brief description of the Good Model—a ten-step framework that embodies the concept of the DG. It is based on "the good" and "the practical." It amounts to a nonmoral utilitarian guideline. First, as with many models, the problem must be broadly defined, and secondly, those impacted must be identified. Because the interests of all living things are to be taken into account, the list of those impacted could include humans, animals, trees—and in rare cases, "the small" (plants, insects, et al.) or groups or collections of these individuals.

The third step would harbor traces of the Rawlsian theory in that the decision-makers would place themselves behind a veil of ignorance or imagine themselves as impartial observers. They would be required to pretend they are each of those affected by the policy—whether a tree, pig, bear, whale, and so on—and envision how they might feel and what their needs might entail. A tree might conceivably have an interest in living, flourishing, and perpetuating its species, whereas a pig might want to be free from pain, to survive, to have other pigs with whom to socialize, to be able to roam, and to propagate his or her species.

The impartial observers would assume that all living things have equal intrinsic value and are worthy of equal consideration, but they would also give weight to practical considerations. Determining the definition of "equal, "practical," and other such terms is a subjective enterprise, as is the bulk of this utilitarian-like exercise, but that should not dissuade the decision-makers from completing their task. Even traditional utilitarianism cannot escape these types of difficulties.

Relevant information about society, science, economics, psychology, law, and history, among other disciplines, would be available to help with discerning interests or any other factors involved with this model. The decision-makers would be able to use past or present data except for anything pertaining to their own identities. They would ask themselves questions such as, "Is there any unknown information that could affect the situation? If so, where do I obtain this information?" and "Has a decision like this been made in the past, and if so, what was the outcome?"

Fourthly, the impartial observers would detail the conflicting or controversial issue(s), asking who are the interest-bearing parties and what are the central claims they make (or might make). The fifth step would involve listing the possible solutions to the dilemma, and the sixth would require evaluating both the immediate and the long-term consequences and benefits of each of the possible solutions.

The seventh stage would entail assigning hedon (positive) and dolor (negative) values to each solution. The observers would pinpoint the solution that indicates the greatest possible good—the maximax—and that which indicates the least possible harm—the maximin. The eighth step would be similar, except the emphasis would be on evaluating how practical or impractical each solution might be. The observers would ask themselves questions, such as "Are there practical concessions that have been made in the past that could potentially affect this decision?" "Are there any practical concessions that could be made in the future so as to compensate any of those whose interests are overlooked in this situation?" "How difficult is it to implement this rule?" and "Can those who do not comply be easily punished?"

The ninth step would entail determining whether the maximax and maximin coincide. If so, this would be the decision. If not, the decision-makers would go to the tenth step, and each would vote on the solution that he or she feels provides for the greatest good and the least harm. There would be a tallying of the votes; the solution with the most votes would determine the course of action or the decision.

One might contend that emphasizing "the practical" in this exercise is merely a way to deprive some living beings of legal rights. I disagree, for being of equal value and worthy of equal consideration does not necessarily mean that one's life or interests will be protected under the law. It merely means that one's needs and desires will not be automatically overlooked.

One could consider the following analogy. In some countries, such as England, if one is elderly and diagnosed with a particular severe illness or complication, one is not entitled to government-paid medical care. It is said to be impractical to earmark billions of dollars for those over a certain age and who have a meager chance for full recovery. This is not to say that these individuals have less innate worth than healthy young people or that the former are unworthy of equal consideration. The allocation of medical resources reflects practical concerns. There are circumstances unrelated to age in which medical pragmatism weighs heavily in decision-making, such as in the case of transplant patients who may have to participate in an organ lottery or wait for donors on a "first come, first serve" basis.

There are also examples of practical decisions made outside of the medical arena, such as in the case of war. Who will be drafted? Do we take all men and women over 18 years of age? Do we have a lottery? Who will be on the front line? Whose life will be risked? Regardless of who is chosen, the recruit or person on the front line is not of less value than, or unworthy of the same consideration as, a civilian. Choosing someone for a sacrificial task merely represents a difficult but pragmatic decision—much like that which results from the negotiation of conflicts of interest between all living things.

It should be noted that the Good Model is merely a tool that can assist or inform decision-makers. The process will often require hard conversations and compromise, which is no different from what happens under a democratic republic. The solutions are not absolutes. They are flexible. Results can vary—from time to time, from month to month, from year to year. The Good Model allows a society to drive toward an ideal while being wholly pragmatic. It is not utopian yet conveys hope, fuels optimism, and fosters connectedness. It enables an omniocracy to be propelled in a better direction for all who may be affected.

Chapter Eleven

ECOLAND AND BIOLAND

Beyond providing legal and political consideration for all living beings, an omniocracy has an added benefit: It coalesces two movements that have long been at odds—animal rights and environmentalism. To a layperson, the discord may seem surprising. These social movements appear to be homogenous. Both are brimming with committed activists who implore the world to give up luxuries and consumer-driven habits that harm other species. But, in reality, these groups have fundamentally different ideologies and contrasting goals. This often results in friction, even conflict. An omniocracy provides a way to unite these two movements, allowing animal rights and environmentalism to forge a mutually beneficial partnership—a partnership that emerges within policy.

To end the ideological battle, animal activists and environmentalists should first abandon their embrace of democracy because a system that is exclusively for people cannot advance the interests of nonhuman living beings or the planet. Secondly, they should champion omniocracy, which allows for both the protection of individual animals and the earth. Thirdly, they should eliminate the language of hierarchy, discarding the divisive fictions of "morality" and "free will"—and disposing of the anthropocentric models and theories that arise from these concepts. Fourthly, they should synthesize their missions under the banner of the mutually fruitful system of Bioland and Ecoland—a "carving up" within omniocracy that is both pragmatic and in accordance with the aims of the definitional good. I will clarify what this means after exploring the long-standing strife between animal rights activists and environmentalists.

It is common for environmentalists to focus on the whole, on habitats, on the diversity of species, on the land, on nature's processes, and on the ecological management of resources. They seek to protect the natural environment and may ask people to reassess their relationship with the earth. Although there are nuances of opinion, there are two primary categories within environmentalism. The first is *deep ecology* or *radical environmentalism*. Adherents of this mindset identify their goal as protecting the planet apart from its usefulness to *Homo sapiens*. They have a nature-centered view. In some measure, they are sympathetic to animal rights philosophy, although many deep ecologists stress that "it is indeed the complex interrelated whole that is of supreme value . . . [while] sensitivity to the suffering and killing of individual animals is an anthropomorphic mistake."[405] Deep ecology promotes ecocentrism[406] and may suggest as its central theme: diversity, stability of ecosystems, overturning industrial society, returning to a hunting/gathering type of existence, or moving toward a decentralization of power.[407]

The second and larger category in the environmental world consists of advocates known as *conservationists, mainstream environmentalists,* or *shallow ecologists.* They hold an anthropocentric perspective, maintaining that the environs must be protected for the benefit of people—often future generations of *Homo sapiens*. They may focus on environmental clean-up, climate change, pollution control, clean water, or conserving resources—all important, in their view, to benefit human health and well-being. Most environmental organizations fall into this grouping.

Animal rights advocates or *animal liberationists* have a different outlook. They value each sentient being (rather than simply focusing on the whole) because it is the individual who suffers in agony—not the forest, species, or ecosystem. Although hundreds, even thousands, of sentient beings, may exist within a cluster, such as an ecosystem, overlooking their status as individuals means that each is insignificant or disposable—a result that is abhorrent to AR activists.

Within animal advocacy, there are naturally an array of opinions. Some advocates rely upon a deontological grounding, while others prefer utilitarianism. Some focus on saving the lives of dogs and cats, while others target the abuse at factory farms and vivisection labs. Some protest in the streets. Some circulate petitions. Others engage in illegal, underground activities. Despite their different approaches, all hardcore animal activists decry speciesism and argue that animals are of equal value to people and worthy of equal consideration. They strive to eradicate the notion that animals are mere tools for a human end.

Animal welfarists differ from hardcore animal advocates. They do not fight for an end to animal exploitation but instead hope to improve conditions for those sentient creatures who are imprisoned, victimized, oppressed, or churned into a product for human consumption. They are similar to shallow ecologists in that both reinforce the status quo; they accept a human-centric society. Animal welfarists think people take precedence over other living beings. They may argue that people are entitled to use animals as long as these beings are treated "properly" or "decently" before being killed—often prior to decapitation, electrocution, being ground up alive, or some other kind of excruciating death.

Conflicts emerge between animal rights advocates and welfarists in the same way that there are disagreements between deep ecologists and conservationists—and these core disagreements can be compared with the differences of opinion that have existed (and still exist) within other social movements. For example, in the 1800s certain abolitionists called for an end to slavery in the South, but others (essentially welfarists) advocated for compromise and merely sought better conditions for slaves. Abolitionists—regardless of whether they are involved in animal, environmental, or other justice causes—claim that incremental improvements are not only "immoral" but impair the overall struggle. On the other hand, proponents of compromise may allege that abolition is unrealistic and that "extremist positions" alienate those with different views.

Let us circle back to the foundational chasm between animal advocates and environmentalists, which has arguably proved damaging to both movements. As mentioned earlier, the dissension rests in the fact that environmentalists look at the macro level (ecosystems, species, natural processes), while animal advocates focus on the well-being of each creature. Author Aldo Leopold—considered the father of wildlife ecology—highlights this divide when he writes that his theory, "the land ethic," fails to address the "management and use of . . .. 'resources.'"[408] For Leopold, the term "resources" is code for "individual animals."

Leopold's land ethic (and the environmental movement in general) deems it acceptable to exploit individual animals, irrespective of whether these beings live in a city, in a suburb, or in the wilderness. Leopold and most other mainstream environmentalists ignore the plight of farm animals—such as cows, chickens, and pigs—and domestic creatures—such as dogs and cats. Their confinement, suffering, and death are inconsequential to the cause. Environmentalists focus on the natural landscape and processes connected to it, often glorifying wild creatures and the wondrous ecosystems that bustle with life. They may harbor a spiritual reverence for uncultivated nature.

Leopold says that "a thing is right when it tends to preserve the integrity, stability, and beauty of the biotic community. It is wrong when it tends otherwise."[409] This statement demonstrates the environmentalist's emphasis on the whole rather than the parts, in effect, declaring the belief that the fate of an individual animal is irrelevant as long as the species does not go extinct. It is immaterial to Leopold whether a specific nonhuman animal writhes in agony, endures a poor quality of life, or suffers a grueling death. AR philosopher Tom Regan calls this way of thinking "environmental fascism" because it implies the individual can be sacrificed for the greater biotic good."[410]

Author J. Baird Callicott holds that "to hunt and kill a white-tailed deer . . . may not only be ethically permissible [to Leopold], it might actually be a moral requirement, necessary to protect the local environment, taken as a whole."[411] Environmental ethics—which is in lockstep with many environmental organizations, such as the Sierra Club (whose members may hunt and/or fish[412])—could require that particular animals and plants be killed in order to conserve those animals and plants deemed "rare" or "special."

The friction between environmentalists and AR advocates can impact real-world situations—usually to the detriment of individual animals. For example, Janet Albrechtsen, an author in *The Australian,* asserts that fur is an ecologically and politically viable option because synthetic fur is composed of "19 litres of petroleum, a non-renewable resource."[413] She assumes an either-or proposition; she promotes wearing real pelts without even entertaining the option of swearing off all fur—real and synthetic. This is the sort of argument that gets co-opted by fur manufacturers who then claim their product is environmental—which can, in turn, lead to a renewed public interest in wearing dead animal skin.

There are other examples of how environmental campaigns can hurt the animal rights movement. In 2009, 400 kangaroos were killed in a so-called ecological endeavor to protect a grassland that housed rare plants and animals.[414] Now, there is a regular schedule for culling kangaroos in that region. The 2024 program "targets [killing] 1336 kangaroos across seven priority reserves."[415] Plus, some ecologists endorse replacing red meat with kangaroo meat in order to "help save the world from global warming."[416] There is no suggestion that it would be better to refrain from animal products altogether. As mentioned in an earlier chapter, most environmental nonprofits say nothing about meat-eating because a large number of their members and donors are carnivores and have no desire to alter their lifestyle.

On the topic of food, some environmentalists advocate ingesting chickens rather than beef to preserve the land and biosphere. But for animal advocates, swapping out one life for another is unacceptable, plus the suffering that humans impose on chickens is hideous. They suffer more at the hands of humans—and in larger numbers—than any other creature on the planet. It takes a significant number of dead hens to equal the amount of flesh in one dead cow. Thus, an animal advocate might say it is worse to eat chickens than cattle.

One environmentalist, Arne Naess, has attempted to combine "respect for all individuals with respect for ecosystems,"[417] although he admits that his suggestions cannot be viewed as a "finished philosophical system."[418] Many thinkers agree that the clash between these two divergent ideologies presents an insoluble problem. Professor Eugene C. Hargrove writes, "It is difficult, if not impossible, for animal liberationists and environmental ethicists to find a common starting point for a debate."[419]

The New Landscape: Ecoland

The animal rights movement and environmentalism cannot be ideologically reconciled, but they *can* find common ground within omniocratic policy. They can forge an alliance on procedure and strategy and secure an equitable framework for achieving each of their goals. This can happen via Ecoland and Bioland. Within an omniocracy, the landmass is divided into two sections to protect the environment, as well as to provide humans and other individual living beings with a fulfilling existence. I call these areas Ecoland and Bioland. Ecoland is off-limits to people and encompasses vast untouched regions, whereas Bioland is the place humans and some nonhumans live, work, and play. There is a perception of "fairness" and "equality" in this partitioning, which both animal advocates and environmentalists should be able to appreciate.

Ecoland is ecocentric; it is focused on the whole, the biosphere, species, populations, land, natural processes, and all that encompasses the passion of environmentalists. It operates in accordance with the principle of non-interference with nature. It allows the wilderness to remain unharnessed; it permits streams and lakes to remain untainted by man's manipulative hands. There are no campsites, hunters, or park rangers in Ecoland. There is no human footprint. It is of, by, and for the natural systems. It is also a place where small beings, such as those who compose an ecosystem, can interact and flourish.

In 1842, Henry David Thoreau said, "In society, you will not find health, but in nature. Society is always diseased, and the best is most so."[420] Justice William O. Douglas stated in 1970 that "virgin stands of timber are virtually gone . . . . The wilderness disappears each year under the ravages of bulldozers, highway builders, and men in search of metals that will make them rich."[421] Of course, the situation is considerably more dire today than in 1842 or even 1970. But both men seemed to recognize the need for untarnished lands out of human reach.

The elected officials in an omniocracy would likely approve the use of satellites, drones, or other unmanned aerial vehicles for the surveillance of Ecoland.[422] These technological tools could be called upon to make sure the area remains untainted, monitor the environs, and ensure humans do not interfere with the wild animals, plants, and natural systems. These devices would be able to detect human threats, identify intruders, and aid law enforcement with arrests. They would be equipped to inspect inaccessible or hard-to-reach locations, and would provide crucial and continuous information—such as aerial images and real-time footage. It would be too risky to allow humans to enter Ecoland, even those with good intentions,[423] because when people try to make things better, they often make things worse. As the Jesuit priest Balthasar Gracian says, "Know how to leave things alone."[424]

Untouched natural areas around the world are dwindling as humans decimate forests to create grazing land for cattle and to build new roads, parking lots, pipelines, and structures to accommodate the ever-growing human population. If current levels of deforestation continue, the United States "will be stripped completely bare of all its forests in 50 years . . . . [This country has] converted approximately 260 million acres of forest into land which is now needed to produce the wasteful [meat-based] diet . . . [that] most Americans take for granted."[425]

Forests contribute to the health of the planet. They hold "more than half of the world's land-based plants and animals, and three quarters of all birds . . . . Trees absorb and store carbon dioxide and other greenhouse gases . . . . There's simply no way we can fight the climate crisis if we don't stop deforestation."[426] Allowing Ecoland to remain untouched would be good news for the entire planet. In the end, vast, pristine terrain would also benefit the human-populated areas.

Only 5 percent of the land in the U.S. is currently protected as wilderness.[427] It is for this reason that uninhabited areas would need to be enlarged beyond what we see today. The parcels would need to be adjacent to each other because safeguarding small pieces of land here and there would be onerous and ultimately not beneficial to those species of wildlife who naturally are inclined to wander. An ambitious, privately-funded project is currently underway, which aims to "return to nature" an area encompassing approximately nine trillion square feet.[428]

Donating land to nature is a form of "passive rewilding." It is an affordable method for instigating a recovery of ecological processes, and in Ecoland, this happens without human management. It might be important to remove fences and dams between land parcels so as to facilitate the ease of movement for the residents of Ecoland, and it could be essential, on rare occasions, to drop water from helicopters on an out-of-control forest fire that threatens Bioland. But, in general, tampering with Ecoland would be unacceptable in much the same way as states are discouraged from meddling in governments on Native American reservations.

Although alienating and prejudicial chasms were criticized in an earlier chapter, the delineation between Bioland and Ecoland is not harmful, since humans are not permitted to have contact with residents of the ecocentric areas. Any attempt to physically subdue the "uncivilized" land, or those beings who inhabit it, will not affect the latter. Although the goal is not to disturb or alter Ecoland in any way, admittedly, pollution from Bioland could drift down streams or through the air into those otherwise pristine territories. Thus, monitoring for contamination and periodic cleanup on the outskirts of Bioland might be necessary. These are the kinds of decisions that will fall on the leaders within an omniocracy.

Many so-called emergencies, such as floods, hurricanes, and earthquakes, are natural. They have transpired since the beginning of time, and they will no doubt continue to occur—and they should be allowed to persist in Ecoland. If humans were to justify preventing these catastrophes, what would stop them from interceding in non-emergency situations? Thus, the general goal in Ecoland is to allow the natural processes to move "to and fro" unhampered.

As mentioned above, out-of-control forest fires may be an exception to this rule, especially when the flames threaten Bioland. Today, approximately 90 percent of all forest fires are caused by people.[429] The blazes that occur are often related to discarded cigarettes, powerlines, unattended campfires, intentionally burning debris, equipment malfunctions, car accidents, fireworks, and acts of arson, to name a few. Fires would likely be rare in Ecoland due to the absence of humans but also because diverse ecosystems are more resilient to extreme weather events. (Remote territory would probably be more heterogeneous without human interference.) It should be noted that there can be a restorative power in fire, and some tree species use it for propagation. When flames emerge, wildlife tends to flee, and birds fly away. Small creatures may hide under rocks or burrow in the ground, while other animals scurry into rivers or lakes. The soil can become more fertile after a low-intensity fire. In short, forest fires are not all "dolors" and no "hedons." They can have some long-term benefits for the environment.

To increase the quantity of untouched land in Ecoland, private parties could be encouraged to donate real property through financial incentives and other inducements. There is already a mechanism in place in many states that could be expanded. Donors receive tax credits when they gift acreage for conservation purposes.[430] The states currently participating in these sorts of projects are Arkansas, California, Connecticut, Delaware, Iowa, Maryland, Georgia, New Mexico, South Carolina, and Virginia.[431] There could also be a program that allows the less affluent to donate by pooling their money. The combined sum would preserve a parcel of land in Ecoland. Many average citizens would no doubt feel good knowing their money will help lifeforms survive, flourish, and experience freedom in the splendor of the natural terrain.

Ecoland might also be expanded via eminent domain—a method that has been used in the past for environmental protection and conservation. Eminent domain refers to the governmental power to expropriate private land for public use. Property owners are financially compensated as part of the process. The term "public use" does not only pertain to humans under the omniocratic banner. It pertains to the residents of Ecoland—plants, wildlife, insects, microorganisms, and so forth—because these beings are also constituents or citizens within an omniocracy. Many national parks in the U.S. exist due to eminent domain, such as Rock Creek National Park and the Great Smoky Mountains National Parks.

The notion of establishing a division between humans and untouched nature is championed by Jainism. Earlier, it was noted that Jains advocate living in the desert. However, as a second choice, they recommend living together in cities to reduce the calamitous effect of industrial exploitation and human civilization on the natural world. This indeed seems to be a better approach than allowing decentralized units of people to be scattered throughout the land. In fact, many economists argue against the bioregionalism that some deep ecologists promote. Economists say that small groups of people living in a back-to-nature way will ultimately fail because all territories do not have ample resources. Therefore, trade will occur, and before long, capitalism as it currently exists will be ubiquitous. Animals and nature will once again become commodities, subdued and exploited for human gain.

As an aside, it should be noted that omniocratic policy would not require hiking trails to be eliminated or people to be jammed into high-rises in congested cities: campgrounds, parks, nature walks, suburbs, and rural-like neighborhoods would still be available. Today, 56 percent of people in the world live in urban areas, and the green spaces in these communities are in decline.[432] In an omniocracy, natural gardens and parklands would need to be reestablished for human and nonhuman residents alike.

Although this is a controversial idea—especially in our world which reveres humans above all other creatures and promotes an "entitlement mentality"—the leaders in an omniocracy might want to incentivize people—financially or otherwise—to have fewer offspring. Humans take much more than their "fair" share of land and resources, which worsens every year with the uptick in human population. Today, there are 8 billion people on the planet and quintillions of other living beings.

Elected officials virtually never urge the citizenry to have fewer children, partly because they are focused on one thing: money. Within a democracy, there is an obsession with garnering campaign donations and tax revenue. Politicians want to stay in office, and a winning campaign can cost millions of dollars. Plus, they seek tax dollars to pay for essential services, government salaries, and "pet projects." More people mean . . .

more money. This is why politicians tend to complain when residents flee their city, county, or state. Numerous articles and political speeches decry the notion of a reduction in humans on the planet.[433] Although fewer people amount to a clear "win" for nature, most politicians—including those who claim to be environmentalists—care more about the economy than other living beings and creating a sustainable world.

The New Landscape: Bioland

Bioland spotlights individuals; it is biocentric or "centered in life."[434] It harmonizes quite well with animal rights ideology and the Enlightenment principles of tolerance, liberalism, and freedom, as lauded in the U.S. today. It is focused on the legal rights and interests of individual creatures. According to philosopher Paul W. Taylor, the main components of biocentrism—and what this book calls "Bioland"—are that (a) humans are equal to other life forms and, in fact, any suggestion to the contrary is groundless and biased, (b) all things are interconnected, and (c) individual organisms pursue their own good in their own way.[435]

The government of Bioland mirrors a democratic republic in structure but is blessed with one major difference: constituents are expanded exponentially to include dogs, cows, frogs, squirrels, pigs, coyotes, birds, fish, trees, and so on—in effect, all living beings. Each and every creature is cherished. The elected leaders of society have a professional duty to represent the interests of all constituents, not just *Homo sapiens*. Due to the similarities between democracy and omniocracy, the transition will be smoother and more straightforward than implementation for a wholly unfamiliar governing structure.

Omniocracy is the underlying political system in Bioland, and the Good Model—with the goal of moving toward the definitional good—serves as the process by which legislators reach decisions. The system operates off an alternative economy rather than the dominant and conventional system we have today. Although all living beings are of equal value, and their interests are worthy of equal consideration, practicalities must be considered. First, policies should be enforceable; secondly, laws will rarely protect very small beings, such as microorganisms, insects, and tiny plants, due to the Jain difficulty. There may be special situations in which society finds a way to assist "the pint-sized," such as when sterile insects are released into an existing population, supplanting any plans to exterminate.

During decision-making, Bioland's elected leaders become impartial observers or place themselves behind a veil of ignorance. They engage in empathetic understanding for all living beings. They are similar to lawyers in that their job requires them to represent the interests of these individuals, regardless of whether they like them or not. It is a matter of professional duty and an obligation of the job. This is an exercise with which political leaders are already well-acquainted. Their task in a democracy involves making decisions that require them to assess the subjective desires of their constituents with the goal of bettering the community as a whole. They keep the interests of the "silent"—babies and the severely mentally incapacitated—in mind. The omniocratic decision-making process largely resembles that of a democratic one, except the "silent" constituents are increased considerably. All living beings are stakeholders and deemed part of society. They are essentially citizens.

An omniocracy is not based on absolutes, such as "morality." It is, instead, malleable. Laws can be reconsidered, readjusted, revamped, or improved. Experimentation or pilot programs can be implemented; they can be valuable tools which can later be abandoned, expanded, or signed into law. The pliant nature of the system allows politicians to make modifications or draft amendments based on new information. Absolutes have no place in statecraft because politics is about change, negotiating conflicts, compromise, and continually tinkering with legislation in an effort to improve society as a whole.

As mentioned earlier, introducing practical considerations into the decision-making process is not meant to negate or lessen the value of some living beings or deprive them of legal rights. But funds are limited. Challenging decisions about resources—and who or what will be protected—are routinely and painstakingly made within society. As mentioned earlier, the elderly may be deprived of costly medical treatments, and there are often lotteries for organ transplants. This is not to say that sick or older patients have less value than healthy or young patients, but when resources are scarce, there will always be winners and losers.

Traffic regulation is another case in point. Numerous studies associate an increased number of deaths with a higher speed limit and a lower number of traffic signals. However, society's leaders may purposely ignore the fatalities because they do not deem it practical to keep traffic at 10 mph despite the lives it may save. Plus, a single stop light can cost a whopping $500,000, excluding maintenance fees.[436] With tight city, county, state, and federal budgets and limited revenues, some sacrifices must always be made. The same is true in an omniocratic system.

In an omniocracy (like in a democracy), the majority may not always get their way, and decisions will not always involve a "numbers game." Politicians might support the legalization of gay marriage and wheelchair ramps for the disabled—despite objections from a plurality of protestors—because such legislation leads to greater satisfaction of interests for the community as a whole. In an omniocracy, the same logic applies to sheep, pigs, oak trees, mice, and so on. There will always be competing interests and tough decisions to be made, and the majority cannot expect to prevail on every issue.

As touched on earlier, a looming problem in our democracy involves the emphasis on money. Political decisions are often slanted or weighted in such a way as to favor the rich and well-connected. There is a crippling problem of influence by moneyed interests. Hefty campaign contributions can lead to biased legislation. Corporations, unions, and the ultra-affluent are often advantaged over less powerful constituents, such as middle-class taxpayers. This situation would worsen when nonhuman living beings—who are financially impotent—are added to the mix. Thus, clean money elections (or removing private money from politics) would most likely be necessary in an omniocracy. This would lessen the chance of fundamental bias. The system must be capable of dispassionately considering the interests of all, including the most disadvantaged members of society.

Science has historically focused on improving life for people. This would change in an omniocracy. There would be an impetus for—and a significant uptick in—technological advances that benefit nonhumans, as well as a greater embrace of the few pro-animal inventions that have already been developed. For example, today there are viable alternatives to vivisection, such as 3D printed organelles, in vitro testing, microdosing, human organs-on-chips, advanced simulators, computer models, and cell cultures, to name a few. But it has been an uphill battle trying to convince scientists—and university administrators—who receive millions of dollars in research grants to move away from the outmoded tradition of animal models. It is difficult to get people to change a habit, even when such a habit has no usefulness. Approximately 115 million living beings, including dogs, cats, rabbits, horses, monkeys, birds, and mice, endure excruciating lab tests in the U.S. each year,[437] and the results of these experiments "rarely extrapolate to humans."[438] Animal tests do not accurately represent how the human body and human illness will respond to drugs and treatments. In fact, the safety and effectiveness of interventions are mostly just guesswork.[439]

To zero in on another area of scientific achievement, American society offers the option of plant-based "meat" and the promise of cultivated meat (which is still in the development phase), but there are politicians who seem to care nothing about the suffering of factory farm animals because they have taken it upon themselves to ban—or vow to ban—lab-grown meat (which is derived from animal cells).[440]

Congressional representative Ronnie Jackson from Texas, tweeted on the social media platform X, "I will NEVER eat one of those FAKE burgers made in a LAB. Eat too many and you'll turn into a SOCIALIST DEMOCRAT. Real BEEF for me!"[441]

Some politicians do not even want to give consumers a choice. They are clearly married to the tradition of human exceptionalism and the practice of treating nonhumans like disposable objects. Plus, it is common for politicians to receive huge campaign contributions from animal agriculture.[442] This callous, human-centered attitude would be unlikely to prevail in an omniocracy due to the legal (and lessality-related) shift in giving equal consideration to all constituents, including nonhumans. In fact, political leaders might establish a "call to action" for the research community—a request for innovations that specifically save the lives of, or improve the experiences of, nonhumans. There is truth in the mantra: "If you seek it, it will come."

Scientists (and inventors of technology) might focus on finding ways to keep animals away from busy highways—perhaps using particular sounds or smells—to limit the chance of these creatures coming into contact with vehicles.

Four high school students in Colorado recently developed artificial intelligence that can detect deer on a roadway. The device sends information to drivers so they can avoid clashes with wildlife; it has already influenced automakers, who are "working on a mandate that would require vehicles to be able to detect animals and automatically brake to avoid collisions by 2029."[443] Residents in Agoura Hills, California, have been working on a different type of solution: A wildlife crossing is being constructed to provide mountain lions and other creatures with a safe way to traverse the freeway.[444] Colorado is already a leader in this area. In the past ten years, the state has constructed twenty-eight large game-crossing structures over roadways.[445]

Scientists might find innovative and less harmful ways to keep rats out of attics, birds and bats away from wind turbines, ants away from structures, and pigeons off roofs. They might be able to devise less damaging building materials for homes, furniture, and household objects (to protect trees). They could come up with animal-friendly packaging for products. In fact, there is a recent development: Edible and biodegradable six-pack beer rings have been created to replace the traditional plastic beer can holders. They comprise wheat and barley.[446] The possibilities are limitless. If science and technology can invent satellites, the internet, and spaceships, they can surely come up with ingenious solutions for mediating some of the everyday clashes between humans and nonhumans.

An omniocracy would also encourage recycling, the manufacture of long-lasting goods, a neighborhood exchange of household items, and resale shops. America today countenances, even promotes, the reverse. Cheap, discardable, foreign-made products dominate big-box stores. Plastics fill the oceans. Appliances that used to last 15 or 20 years may last 5,[447] a predicament that has made many consumers wish "they had held on to their clunky '90s-era appliances."[448] Landfills are almost full.[449] In fact, piles of refuse "belch methane . . . [which is a major factor in global warming]. The EPA estimates that landfills are the third largest source of human-caused methane emissions in the United States."[450] In short, America is a throw-away society that—implicitly and explicitly—promotes overconsumption, indifference to waste, convenience, disposability, consumer patriotism, and a gluttonous lifestyle. All of these negatively impact nonhuman animals and the environment.

An omniocracy would encourage the resale of used items and community-based giveaways, such as Facebook's "Buy Nothing" groups. In the case of the latter, items are gifted at no cost to neighbors, a practice that aids with local waste reduction. In addition, the government might incentivize manufacturers to construct durable appliances (like those of yesteryear), or as an alternative, it might mandate long-term warranties. If a company is required to repair at no cost every refrigerator, water heater, and air conditioner that breaks before, for example, a 20-year mark, a company would be inclined to construct long-lasting goods. There will always be friction between lining pockets and protecting nonhumans, but within an omniocracy, the economy would no longer automatically prevail.

Despite the firm hold that tradition can have—on vivisection labs, grocery store options, political ideologies, and everyday life—it is likely that the embrace of an omniocratic government would prompt a new and more inclusive outlook by the masses. Caring for Others would likely become the norm, not the exception. Hearts and minds would open. Leastalities would be revamped. Empathy would surface. There would be a marked shift in how most people perceive the world. For example, today, when there is a natural disaster—such as a forest fire or tornado—the media might report, "Ten homes have been damaged. It amounts to five million dollars in damage." There tends to be an emphasis only on that which affects humans. Even killed or injured companion animals might not be mentioned in news reports. But under an omniocracy, a broadcaster might note, "One thousand trees have been burned, and an estimated two hundred thousand animals have died," in addition to reporting the lost human lives, deaths of companion animals, and toll on property. Omniocracy would allow public awareness to emerge. It would become clear that all living things have needs, interests, and desires.

Chapter Twelve

PROGRESSING TOWARD AN OMNIOCRACY

How does a dedicated animal advocate nudge America's government and political system to be inclusive of all living beings? For obvious reasons, it cannot happen overnight; it is a process that must be eased into or incrementally implemented.

The first step is to stop advocating for democracy and to publicly promote an omniocracy. Thousands of voices within the animal movement (and the environmental movement) should thunderously endorse the notion of nonhumans as constituents, stakeholders, worthy of political representation. There must be a deafening call to change all branches of government—legislative, executive, and judicial—and make them friendly to all species, not just *Homo sapiens*. AR advocates should cast votes only for those candidates who have shed the antiquated notion that nonhumans are "commodities"—or, in many instances, "trash" to be discarded when they are no longer useful to people.

Even though the majority of today's politicians eat meat and participate in institutional violence against nonhumans, there are a handful who claim to be vegan or vegetarian. Some have made public comments about the need to love and respect other creatures. These folks come from different frequencies on the political spectrum: left, right, and independent. Although there are statistically more progressive or left-leaning supporters of AR, there is no black-and-white "party-related" dividing line that leads one to differentiate between those who might be persuaded to move toward omniocracy and those who would be likely to remain in the "racist," we-prefer-to-exploit-animals camp (caring only about the human race).

The Republican lane has Dr. Ben Carson (vegetarian), Tulsi Gabbard (vegan), and Vivek Ramaswamy (vegetarian).[451] The Democratic side of the aisle has Senator Cory Booker (vegan), Congressman Jamie Raskin (vegetarian), Congressman Adam Schiff (vegan), and President Bill Clinton (vegan after he left the White House). There are also independents: Mayor Eric Adams (vegan)[452] and Dennis Kucinich (vegan).[453] Kucinich has publicly announced his concern for other species on various occasions. Although Republican senator Rand Paul eats meat, he has recently put a great deal of effort into ending a mandatory animal experimentation rule[454] by sponsoring the FDA Modernization Act (along with Senator Cory Booker). This is an important law that could save thousands of nonhumans' lives. It took years to get passed because instituting change is tough, both in the U.S. and abroad.

Some of the pro-animal efforts in Europe over the past couple of decades relate to the formation of political parties. In Holland, there is a political party called the "Dutch Party for the Animals," which was founded in 2002 and embraces the mission of "providing representation for nonhuman animals."[455] It has garnered some success within the multi-party system in that country, winning a few seats here and there. It inspired similar parties in other European nations: "The Animal Welfare Party" in the United Kingdom (established in 2006) and the "Action Party for Animal Welfare" in Germany (founded in 2017). The latter two receive about 1 percent of the vote in most elections.

In the United States, there is the Green Party, which generally receives a modest chunk of support; it focuses on preserving the environment but also speaks out on a menu of issues. It backs single-payer health care, tuition-free college, reparations to the African American community, cancellation of student debt, eradication of the death penalty, cutting aid to Israel, and support for the International Criminal Court.

There is also a Humane Party in the U.S., which was founded in 2009. It promotes veganism and "peace, nonviolence, and rights for all animals, human and otherwise . . . . It [endeavors] to abolish animal slavery, cruelty, and killing through existing political and legal systems . . . [and aims to] pass legislation that protects the rights of sentient beings."[456] Their website displays a laundry list of public policy positions, and to be fair, most are related to ending the use, abuse, and murder of nonhumans. However, some fall outside that realm. For example, the platform recommends replacing the electoral college with the democratic election of the U.S. president, granting free access to contraceptives, replacing "non-emergency" fossil fuels, providing tuition-free education, ending the so-called Three Strikes laws, and guaranteeing universal health care.

There are problems with the "Greens" and the Humane Party—a criticism that also applies to the aforementioned animal parties in Europe. First, they outwardly endorse democracy. This topples their message, derails their ecocentric and/or biocentric goals, and exposes a core inconsistency. They want legal rights for nonhumans and/or the environment but sabotage any hope for establishing these rights by supporting a human-centric system. As an analogy, this would be the same as a "Civil Rights Party" seeking acceptance within a "White-ocracy" and going so far as to endorse the White supremacist principles of the existing government—a government that is of, by, and for Caucasians.

There is a second problem. By expanding their platforms beyond issues related to animals and/or the environment, the Green Party and the Humane Party paint themselves into a progressive, far-left box, decreasing their chance of securing support from moderates, conservatives, independents, and even old-school liberals. If they were to limit their platforms to their primary areas of concern—while allowing individual candidates to craft their own promises and objectives—they might find greater appeal across the political spectrum.

As mentioned earlier, all types of people support the animal movement. Some might call themselves "liberals" or "progressives," such as actors Alec Baldwin, Joaquin Phoenix, and Ed Begley Jr., while others might identify as staunch "conservatives"—such as Matthew Scully (a former speechwriter to George W. Bush and the author of the AR book *Dominion*) and Alan Clark (a one-time Conservative member of Parliament in the UK). Plus, there are self-described independents, such as the aforementioned Dennis Kucinich, who not only "walks the talk" but has spoken out repeatedly about protecting animals.

A YouGov poll found that 35% of the people who are vegan or vegetarian, or who make an effort to reduce their intake of meat are Democrats, whereas 21% are Republicans.[457] However, an article in *The Economist* (that analyzes this poll) hypothesizes that meat consumption may be unrelated to political affiliation but instead correspond to other factors, such as age, sex, and whether a person lives in the city. Democrats tend to be younger, be female, and reside in urban areas . . . just like vegetarians and vegans.

President George Washington was not a fan of political parties, arguing that they would "divide and destroy" the country.[458] Here in America, the duopoly—the Democratic and Republican Parties— have a stranglehold on the system. They want to retain power and, in effect, crush alternative views—as well as the views of their own candidates who may be afraid to speak out against their party's platform and the interests of its donor base.

The Democrats and Republicans make the election process less competitive and more divisive. They frighten citizens into thinking they have only two options, and if a "wrong" vote is cast, the so-called bad guy (their opponent) might win. They erect a blockade, or more accurately a toll booth that can cost millions of dollars to pass through. They make it virtually impossible for an independent candidate or third party, such as the Greens or Humane Party, to get their foot in the door. Nonpartisan elections are arguably a better option; they work quite well for the states, counties, and cities that implement them, such as San Francisco, Chicago, Nebraska, and Minnesota. An omniocratic government would be well advised to do away with political parties, which hurt nonhumans; they should instead establish nonpartisan, "clean money" elections.

Can a U.S. politician today confidently confess to being vegan or vegetarian and promise to tackle animal rights issues? According to 2023 research,[459] this confession could damage her chance of winning an election. She could face what the experts call "voter backlash," especially if she is a Republican. For Democrats, it may not be as bad, but mentioning this subject does not help. The meat lobby in the U.S. is centralized and powerful. It dishes out millions of dollars to its favorite politicians, such as the ones on key congressional committees who can sway legislation in its favor.

In addition, many voters are married to the myth that people are superior to other life forms and know that genuine legal protections for animals could require a lifestyle shift. There are even folks who go so far as to claim that eating less meat (or no meat) is "un-American" or "not manly." In other words, there are relatively few independent thinkers in society who have done research and soul-searching to come to a more scientific and compassionate conclusion. It is for these reasons that the experts in political circles say that "animal issues" are "vote losers." Some election consultants might go so far as to classify these topics as "taboo."

The reluctance to discuss animal issues not only hurts non-humans but also impacts public discourse on global warming. Meat is "synonymous with unsustainability,"[460] and "most scientists now agree that our climate change goals will not be met without addressing food, particularly animal products . . . . A dietary shift to plant-based foods has the potential to reduce food's emissions by 61 – 73% due to American over-consumption of meat . . . . [In addition,] 83% of the world's farmland is used to produce meat, aquaculture, eggs, and dairy, yet these outputs provide just 18% of all calories and 37% of all protein globally produced."[461]

Although most people in the U.S. are, on some level, aware of this correlation, "per capita meat consumption has steadily risen [for much of the past century] . . . . American consumers are blasting their way through chicken wings at a faster rate than poultry producers can supply."[462] The uptick in carnivorous behavior is somewhat surprising because a hefty 5 percent of Americans identify as vegan or vegetarian.[463] A 2015 Gallup poll found that 33 percent of people in the U.S. think nonhuman animals should receive "the same rights as people to be free from harm and exploitation."[464]

Although meat-eating is one of the main causes of global warming, even the progressive left—which purports to care about this issue—rarely mentions it. This is partly due to identity politics—a fear that caring about nonhumans might hurt or trivialize the struggle of minority groups[465]—a topic that was examined in an earlier chapter. The Green New Deal, which was introduced by progressives, does not even outwardly address meat or animal agriculture.[466] Apart from the left, the public, in general, may be disinterested in hearing about veganism or animal rights because these topics do not align with self-interest in the way that the economy, inflation, crime, jobs, healthcare, the influx of migrants, and education do. Voters do not want to alter their lifestyles or feel guilty. They prefer to place the blame for global-warming on the big, bad corporations that emit toxic chemicals and contribute to greenhouse gases. By shaming faceless corporations, John and Jane Doe can distance themselves from the problem and congratulate themselves for being "good people."

Despite the aforementioned poll results and warnings about "voter backlash," it is critical that the animal rights movement—and political candidates—plunge forward, placing fear in the rearview mirror. They must be brave, dynamic, and forceful. They must be a billboard, not a tiny note slipped to a classmate behind the teacher's back. They must confidently roll down the freeway like a tanker, not be shoved under the sofa like a plastic toy truck. They must stand tall like Niagara Falls, not allow themselves to be stepped on like a puddle in the driveway. In other words, dedicated AR activists—as well as politicians who embrace the cause—must be calm, confident, noticed, persistent, reasoned, and dedicated.

Voter backlash occurs at the start of every new movement—or

any old one that has not yet gained traction, such as animal rights. Take revenge porn (or image-based sexual abuse)—a topic with which I am an expert.[467] In 2012, when I began pushing for legislation to protect victims, virtually everyone was against the cause: the public, the media, law enforcement, and most politicians. It was considered the victim's fault if someone hacked into her computer, stole her nude photo, and posted it online. Luckily, there were a few bold "electeds" who were willing to go out on a limb and ignore the prospect of voter backlash. Together, we fought the naysayers, the resistant legislators, and even the ACLU—and eventually prevailed. It took time for the public (and the media, law enforcement, and the majority of politicians) to catch up or start caring about victims. Today, almost everyone is on board with the crusade. There are anti-revenge porn laws in all 50 states, and President Trump signed the federal Take It Down Act into law on May 19, 2025.

If you cannot relate to the above example, consider the suffrage movement and civil rights. It was once considered preposterous to give rights to women or Blacks. It required courageous leaders—both elected officials and dedicated activists—who were willing to face ridicule, verbal backlash, and sometimes physical violence. After much struggle and many years, they were able to change society and get much-needed laws in place. Social and political metamorphosis can be—and usually is—sluggish. There will always be hurdles, challenges, and occasional setbacks, but with a steady effort, collaboration, and perseverance, the goal can often be achieved. As the *Economic Times* says, "Many good ideas now canonized as revolutions took decades to have impact."[468]

Change can happen at a grassroots level, then move up the ladder to become legislation. The reverse can also occur; it can start with official government decisions and trickle down to everyone else. The animal rights movement should work to accomplish their mission from both ends. Establishing an omniocracy should be a two-pronged campaign. For a movement to take hold from the bottom up, it needs to hit a tipping point or fall into something called the Overton Window (aka the Window of Discourse).

The Overton Window essentially means that a topic or policy has crawled into an opening in which it (finally) enjoys a high degree of public support. In other words, the issue has become mainstream. Same-sex marriage was outside the Overton Window back in 2004 when only 25 percent of the public endorsed it. But boundaries can get redefined, and public opinion can evolve. Today, 71 percent of Americans support it.[469] The same can happen with veganism and animal advocacy. Today's "voter backlash" can be tomorrow's accepted vision for a better world.

An animal advocate who wants to get elected to political office in a locale that has partisan elections should join either the Democratic or Republican Party—not the Greens or Humane Party. This is because the duopoly has a tight vice on elections, maintaining all control. The system is organized to hurt outsiders, to keep them away from victory. The AR candidate should consult her leastality and creative essence to see which political persuasion fits best with who she is. If she has no obvious preference, she should go with the Republicans. Why? Because she can likely make a greater impact. If elected, she will stand out as an animal rights Republican. She will bring more media attention to herself and, by default, to the issues at hand—including the need for animal protection and an omniocratic government. Plus, she may be able to get backing from her conservative colleagues on the bills she sponsors (simply by being one of their own) while garnering support from some Democrats (because they may feel guilty voting against an animal protection bill that is brought forth by a Republican).

Animal issues are up for political grabs. Neither party has laid claim. This can be seen as a positive. The subject has not been coopted; there is no "issue ownership." In other words, one side has not tainted "AR goals" to make the other side fight against them with all their might. Unfortunately, animosity toward political opponents—as well as a reactionary hatred of the issues they support—is commonplace in today's polarized America.

Although animal issues are rarely covered by mainstream media, a few liberal and conservative outlets run pro-AR pieces from time to time. *Vox* and the *Guardian* do so on the left, and there has been a surprising uptick of pro-animal segments on right-leaning Fox News over the past few years. *Jesse Watters Primetime*, *Hannity*, and *Tucker Carlson Tonight*,[470] among others, have aired numerous segments on the cruel and unnecessary lab testing on animals, the merits of veganism, and the U.S. government's refusal to rescue the dogs and cats (the companion animals of American contractors) from Afghanistan. These animals were left behind when the troops pulled out in 2021. Despite a widespread online campaign that targeted the U.S. government, the Biden Administration refused to budge, leaving the animals' fates in the hands of the Taliban. India and the UK (under Boris Johnson) did the opposite: they rescued their dogs and cats. The bottom line is this: both the left and the right are ripe for embracing the AR cause. Establishing an omniocracy should be a "more the merrier" proposition.

In addition to supporting omniocratic candidates, AR advocates should step into the political arena themselves. This is the most straightforward and powerful way to effect change. Many activists feel comfortable in faded blue jeans, running through the streets with placards, and shouting at passing cars, but donning a business suit and nabbing a seat at the negotiating table can make a lasting difference. There is respect for those in elected office, and politics is where power is.

As an "elected," there is a greater chance your voice will be heard by the media and the masses, as well as other politicians. When you get a pro-animal bill or measure passed, you are transforming the system. Compromise is a central component of politics; therefore, your elected colleagues (who may not care about nonhumans) will want to support your legislation if they think you might support theirs. This may sound like tit for tat or "you scratch my back and I'll scratch yours"—and it might explain why members of Congress are rated lower than car salespeople on the "most hated professions" scale[471]—but this *is* how the system works.

I know from personal experience. I had no training or background in government, but on a whim, I decided to run for political office in the early 2000s. I was already an animal rights advocate who endorsed "omniocracy." (I invented this term in the mid-1990s while obtaining my doctorate in Social Ethics from the University of Southern California.) I ran for a seat on the Greater Valley Glen Council—one of the 86 local councils in the Los Angeles region. This was a nonpartisan election (just as it is when running for a position on the Los Angeles City Council). In other words, political parties were not involved; thus, I was not pressured to conform to an onerous platform—one to which I would surely disagree.

I campaigned on the platform that I would represent all living beings in my district—not just the humans who are the elite. Miraculously, I prevailed. I served eight years on that council until "termed out" and was able to assist nonhumans on numerous measures—and yes, sometimes with the tit-for-tat help of my anti-animal colleagues. I also helped other AR activists get elected to councils in the region, and I started a political organization called the Directors of Animal Welfare (DAW), which was endorsed by the city of Los Angeles. The idea behind DAW was to give nonhumans an official representative in every area of Southern California, thus providing them with political representation. Although I was an abolitionist on animal issues, I welcomed both AR activists and welfarists as DAWs. These people had "official" status because they had been appointed by an elected body: either a city council or a neighborhood council. They had credibility, legitimacy, and the authority to change the system. The councils that had DAWs ranged from Lancaster and Acton, north of Los Angeles, down to San Diego in the south; most councils were in and around L.A. County.

During that time, I was also appointed by the mayor of Los Angeles, Antonio Villaraigosa, to be a city commissioner on the 912 Commission. One of our tasks was to decide who qualified as a stakeholder within Los Angeles. We were asked to come up with an official definition. Due to my presence on the commission, I was able to make sure nonhumans were included (or, more accurately, not excluded) in that definition.

After our wording was passed by the Los Angeles City Council, animals, in effect, became constituents. The city of Los Angeles had become perhaps the first place in the world that entitled nonhumans to governmental representation—at least on paper or in theory. Admittedly, practice is tough under a democratic system.

Let us assume you have decided to give politics a whirl . . . for the animals. I have compiled a list of recommendations that might aid with your pursuit: (a) attend Toastmasters to fine-tune your public-speaking skills and then deliver speeches whenever possible, (b) take political training courses (they are offered by both the Democrats and Republicans), (c) network with everyone you meet, (d) dress and act professionally, (e) volunteer on political campaigns, (f) be well rounded, informed on current events, and involved in multiple issues, (g) get to know influential people, (h) do not criticize others in the animal movement, (i) speak calmly, rationally, and intelligently, and try not to be shrill, (j) write articles and seek media interviews because awareness of the issues is critical, (k) pre-orchestrate answers so you can respond smoothly to the standard anti-animal objections leveled by your ideological opponents, and (l) speak during public comment at city council meetings, commission meetings, and so on, to gain experience and put forth your opinion.

In conclusion, an omniocratic animal advocate may further her leastality—and the movement as a whole—in ways that a traditional AR activist cannot. She who despises inconsistency can be consistent. She who abhors speciesism can avoid charges of sentientism. She who embraces equality and unity can escape hierarchy, dualism, and alienation. In addition, she who is confronted with tough questions from those who seek to derail the movement can reply with poise and persuasion, and she who wants to unite with environmentalists in a common goal can finally do so. With the assistance of the omniocratic model, the animal rights proponent can focus on the whole and the part, seek truth but be practical, and find both optimistic and realistic resolutions to the animal rights dilemmas of the twenty-first century.

Appendix

DETERMINISM AND CRIME

This appendix provides a continuation of the scientific evidence that deals a blow to arguments in favor of free will. The data below is largely presented in a rapid-fire manner, and it pertains to how biology and environment can, in effect, turn a person into a criminal.

The typical lawbreaker today is a young male between fifteen and twenty-four. Although a one-time offender is not necessarily predisposed to continue with a life of crime, this is more the case than not, according to sociological studies. Some people might attribute this to a self-fulfilling prophesy, in which the "deviant" takes this label to heart, believing that illegal or "immoral" behavior is thereafter unavoidable. Others might advance the argument that successive arrests anchor this person within an "aberrant" subculture where the likelihood of future arrest is heightened. But now, in the twenty-first century, investigating inherited factors, such as IQ and personality, is more common.[472]

Childhood aggression, as early as age one, and low IQ,

as early as age four,[473] are predictive of "deviant" or criminal adult behavior. In fact, "more serious or more chronic offenders generally have lower (IQ) scores than more casual offenders"[474] (although not so low as to preclude them from carrying out a crime), and these scores often correspond to verbal ability.[475] In a longitudinal study in Sweden, a strong correlation between low IQ and crime was determined from a sample of more than five hundred boys.[476] In research conducted in Hawaii, it was found that adult criminals were identifiable at the age of ten by their low IQs, ill temper, belligerence, and lack of honesty.[477]

Two other studies reveal similar results. The Cambridge Study of Delinquent Development researched 411 English boys and found that "the signs of [aggressiveness and] chronic adult criminal behavior were already in evidence before the boys reached the age of ten."[478] In another study of over 200 American boys, the males "who were hard to raise when they were toddlers were more than four times as likely to be multiple [criminal] offenders as boys who were easy to raise."[479] The first study found that inconsistent parenting, low intelligence, economic hardship, and parents with criminal records were predictive factors, whereas the latter study found no correlation between parenting skills and the child's "deviant" behavior. Avshalom Caspi says criminal deviance seems to be "part of a more general disposition toward unsociable or actively antisocial behavior that, in many cases, begins to emerge in the pre-toddler stage."[480]

How can one assert that "immoral" behavior is freely chosen and embarked upon if it seems so powerfully determined at such a young age, before one is considered a "moral" agent and held accountable to the law? In addition, research suggests that one's birth date contributes to the chance of exhibiting criminal or "deviant" behavior later in life. Children who were approximately five years of age during World War I, World War II, or the Great Depression were found to be statistically more prone to crime than those born at less stressful times. The researchers of this study conclude that wartime and economic depression could have negatively affected toddlers at a time when "social communication was beginning to be effective."[481]

Perinatal and neurodevelopmental factors can alter the developments of a fetus's brain and are believed to be related to a "deviant" result. The frontal lobes and the (frontal and temporal) regions of the left hemisphere of the brain are perhaps the most susceptible to criminal outcome. People who are injured in the frontal lobes often suffer from "argumentativeness, lack of concern for consequences of behavior, impulsivity, distractibility, emotional lability (volatility), and aggression,"[482] whereas those who have left hemisphere dysfunction experience verbal IQ deficits.[483] Like the other studies, this provides evidence in favor of determinism.

Free will has become a topic in the courtroom. Some attorneys have made arguments that revolve around inherited criminal tendencies or genetic defects, such as those associated with MAO-A.[484] A lawyer representing a convicted killer in Georgia pointed to his client's family tree and said, "His actions may not have been a product of totally free will."[485] The felon's family was littered with crimes: murder, rape, and robbery. Although these sorts of arguments often fail in court, they succeeded in 2009 when a judge in Trieste, Italy, reduced a prison sentence after it was discovered the offender had gene variants linked with aggression.[486] (It should be noted that the revelation about a defective gene could have had the opposite effect.[487] The court could have decided the murderer was incorrigible, thus a suitable candidate for life in prison.)

Psychiatrist Daniel Amen, author of *Change Your Brain/ Change Your Life*, confirms that some brain pathologies lead to violence: he has examined fifty violent criminals and found that the "cingulate gyrus, curving through the center of the brain, is hyperactive in murderers."[488] Other factors contributing to criminal proclivity include a low heart rate, atypical brain wave patterns in childhood, and "neurological, biochemical, and metabolic abnormalities . . . [which] turn up disproportionately in offenders who are especially brutal or violent."[489]

Violent males often have low levels of the chemical serotonin in the brain, a condition that has a high rate of heritability but that may, in part, stem from malnutrition, physical abuse, and high levels of lead. Low serotonin "has been found in violent populations, such as children who torture animals, children who are unusually hostile toward their mothers, and people who score high for aggression on standardized tests."[490] As touched on earlier, the National Institute of Health conducted a study on the serotonin levels of prison inmates. It determined with an 84 percent accuracy who would return to crime upon release.

Individuals with XYY syndrome have a predisposition toward violence. This condition does not stem from economic or racial barriers. In other words, there is no environmental explanation for the "supermales" with this extra Y chromosome. XYY is connected to a reduced IQ and an elevated risk of eventual criminal incarceration by a factor of ten.[491]

There were many attempts—from the late 1800s until the mid-1900s[492]—to relate violence to biology, but these efforts failed to illustrate anything other than prejudice and error. Today, "science has a new understanding of the roots of violence . . . (in that) you need a particular environment imposed on a particular biology to turn a child into a killer."[493] There is great sensitivity over the issue of equating intelligence or other heritable, neurodevelopmental "imperfections" with "deviant" or criminal behavior. This sensitivity pertains to racism.

Racism and other hierarchical biases surfaced within the theories of Cesare Lombroso and other influential nineteenth-century criminologists who falsely concluded that certain people were more immoral than others because of arrested development. Lombroso argued that criminals were atavistic beings—those with a birth defect, of sorts, whose development had stagnated at a rudimentary level, leaving them to crave evil for its own sake and violence as a personal pleasure. According to Lombroso, a person would pass through the "lower" races, such as African American and Asian, before reaching the epitome of physical, mental, and moral perfection: the White European. Lombroso's theory is condemned for instigating the eugenics movement of the early twentieth century and providing a rationalization for European imperialism. During the Holocaust, Nazis used his principle to conclude that the physical characteristics of the Jews constituted "proof" of their subhuman status.

The dubiousness behind the theories of Lombroso and others who connect biological tendencies with "deviant" behavior rests on how the empirical data is obtained, applied, and categorized. *Without moral overtones, racist assumptions, and the erroneous grouping of individuals into arbitrary categories, investigations of this sort would not be problematic.* In fact, empirical information about an extra-long chromosome or a low IQ could be quite useful. Recognition that a brain lesion is, for example, the precursor to violent outbursts not only provides a possible therapy for modifying the erratic behavior but also dissolves the "moral" condemnation that is ordinarily associated with such acts. The person is no longer viewed as an "evil" perpetrator of an atrocity but instead as a victim of "bad" genes.

For more details on how biological and environmental factors affect a person's behavior, criminal tendencies, beliefs, values, habits, likes, and dislikes, see Chapter 3 of this book.

Author Biography

Charlotte Laws is an award-winning and bestselling writer. She has authored seven books, contributed to four academic anthologies, and written 135 articles that have appeared in various publications, including the *Washington Post*, the *Los Angeles Times*, *Newsweek*, *Huffington Post*, *Salon*, and the *New York Daily News*.

Laws has a Ph.D. in Social Ethics from the University of Southern California, two master's degrees, and two BA degrees. She completed postdoctoral study at Oxford University, England.

Laws was a Greater Valley Glen Councilmember for eight years and currently stars in the Netflix series *The Most Hated Man on the Internet*. She was voted one of the "30 fiercest women in the world" by Buzzfeed and worked as a pundit on NBC and BBC television. She has appeared on CNN, *The Late Show*, Fox News, *Oprah*, *Larry King Live*, MSNBC, and *Nightline*, and has been featured in the *New York Times*, the *San Francisco Chronicle*, the *Atlanta Journal-Constitution*, and the *Guardian*.

Laws was a lecturer at the FBI Academy in Quantico, teaching animal rights philosophy to police chiefs and law enforcement managers from around the world. She is the recipient of the Los Angeles Animal Humanitarian Award and lives in Los Angeles with her husband, her two rescue dogs, and her five rescue hens.

"Charlotte Laws is unquestionably a maverick . . . [Her writing] is a page-turner . . ."

Atlanta Jewish Times

"Dr. Laws is a champion of the underdog."

New York Post

"Charlotte Laws is a tenacious bulldog when she latches onto something."

Atlanta Journal-Constitution

"Laws is a woman of many talents . . . [and] a hero."

Newsweek

Notes

Introduction

1 Jacques Derrida interview on YouTube. “Jacques Derrida and The Question of the Animal.” *https://www.youtube.com/watch?v=Ry49Jr0TFjk#:~:text=Here%2C%20Derrida%20explains%20his%20long,these%20beings%2C%20culminating%20in%20today's* (Internet search on Feb. 29, 2024).

2 David Ernst, “Donald Trump Is The First President To Turn Postmodernism Against Itself,” *The Federalist* (January 23, 2017) at *https://thefederalist.com/2017/01/23/donald-trump-first-president-turn-postmodernism/* (Internet search on Feb. 29, 2024).

3 See Isaac Bashevis Singer quotes on Goodreads. https://www.goodreads.com/quotes/188451-what-do-they-know-all-these-scholars-all-these-philosophers-all (Internet search on Jan. 5, 2024).

4 John Yang, Winston Wilde and Kaisha Young, “Alarming spate of racehorse deaths draws scrutiny of industry safety practices,” *PBS* (May 20, 2023). See https://www.pbs.org/newshour/show/alarming-spate-of-racehorse-deaths-draws-scrutiny-of-industry-safety-practices (Internet search on Jan. 5, 2024).

5 Oliver Milman, “Meat accounts for nearly 60% of all greenhouse gases from food production, study finds,” *The Guardian* (Sept. 13, 2021). See https://www.theguardian.com/environment/2021/sep/13/meat-greenhouses-gases-food-production-study (Internet search on Jan. 5, 2024).

6 Brian Kateman, “Why Some Environmentalists Still Fail To Promote Meat Reduction Answer To The Climate Crisis,” *Forbes* (Sept. 18, 2019). See https://www.forbes.com/sites/briankateman/2019/09/18/why-some-environmentalists-still-fail-to-promote-meat-reduction-as-an-answer-to-the-climate-crisis/?sh=1c5b68a86453 (Internet search on Jan. 5 2024).

7 Gary L. Francione, "Green Party, Extinction Rebellion, and Others: Stop Ignoring the Vegan Solution," *Medium* (Feb. 28, 2019). See https://gary-francione.medium.com/green-party-extinction-rebellion-and-others-stop-ignoring-the-vegan-solution-b174a98e6527 (Internet search on Jan. 5, 2024).

8 Mark Pratt, "6 Dr. Seuss books will stop being published because of racist imagery," *PBS* (March 2, 2021). See https://www.pbs.org/newshour/arts/6-dr-seuss-books-will-stop-being-published-because-of-racist-imagery (Internet search on Jan. 5, 2024).

Chapter One

9 Marjorie Spiegel, *The Dreaded Comparison* (Philadelphia: New Society Publishers, 1988), p. 97.

10 Michele Feder and Michael Alan Park, "Animal Rights: An Evolutionary Perspective," *The Humanist* 50, p. 44.

11 Robert Jay Lifton, *The Nazi Doctors* (USA: Basic Books, 1986), p. 351.

12 Ibid., 361.

13 Ibid., 271.

14 Marjorie Spiegel, *The Dreaded Comparison* (Philadelphia: New Society Publishers, 1988), pp. 61–64.

15 Hans Ruesch, *The Naked Empress: The Great Medical Fraud* (Italy: CIVIS, 1982), pp. 84–96.

16 G. Cowley, "What Do Monkeys Know?" *Newsweek*, 117:57, May 13, 1991. See *https://www.newsweek.com/what-do-monkeys-know-201666* (Internet search on April 4, 2024). See also Sanjana Gajbhiye, "How Bees Interpret Their 'Waggle Dance' Language in the Dark," Earth.com (March 26, 2024) See *https://www.earth.com/news/bees-perform-waggle-dance-to-share-the-location-of-food/* (Internet search on April 4, 2024).

17 Leo Sands, "Did Animals in Turkey, Syria Sense the Quake Early? Here's the Science," *The Washington Post*, February 7, 2023. See *https://www.washingtonpost.com/science/2023/02/07/animals-turkey-syria-sense-earthquake/* (Internet search on April 6, 2024).

18 Allison Futterman, "The 5 Senses Animals Have that Humans Don't," *Discover* (October 12, 2023). See *https://www.discovermagazine.com/planet-earth/the-5-senses-animals-have-that-humans-dont* (Internet search on April 8, 2024).

19 Judith Burns, "Butterfly 'GPS' Found in Antennae," *BBC News* (Sep-

tember 25, 2009). See http://news.bbc.co.uk/2/hi/8273069.stm (Search on April 8, 2024). Also see Hadley Leggett, "Butterflies Use Antenna GPS to Guide Migration," *Wired* (September 24, 2000). See *https://www.wired.com/2009/09/monarch-migration/* (Internet search on April 8, 2024).

20 Frans de Waal, "The Animal Noble Prizes of the Decade," *Huffington Post* (December 6, 2017). See *https://www.huffpost.com/entry/the-animal-noble-prizes-o_b_400977* (Internet search on April 8, 2024).

21 Nicola Davis, "Orangutan Seen Treating Wound with Medicinal Herb in First for Wild Animals," *The Guardian* (May 2, 2024). See *https://www.theguardian.com/science/article/2024/may/02/orangutan-seen-treating-wound-with-medicinal-herb-in-first-for-wild-animals-max-planck-institute-sumatra* (Internet search on May 7, 2024).

22 Editor, "What the Nose Knows," *New York Times*, Opinion section (January 21, 2006). See *https://www.nytimes.com/2006/01/24/opinion/what-the-nose-knows.html* (Internet search on April 8, 2024).

23 Editor, "Research Suggests Dogs Can Be Trained to Sniff out Cancer in Other Dogs," University of Wisconsin-Madison (December 20, 2023). See *https://www.vetmed.wisc.edu/research-suggests-dogs-can-be-trained-to-sniff-out-cancer-in-other-dogs/* (Internet search on April 8, 2024).

24 Editor, "Sounds Trouble Like," *The Age* (March 4, 2007). See http://www.theage.com.au/news/in-depth/sounds-trouble-like/2007/03/03/1172868805142.html (Internet search on April 8, 2024).

25 Norman Miller, "The Animals that Detect Disasters," *BBC* (February 14, 2022). See *https://www.bbc.com/future/article/20220211-the-animals-that-predict-disasters* (Internet search on April 8, 2024).

26 Stephen Jay Gould, *The Mismeasure of Man* (New York: W.W. Norton and Company, 1981), p. 31. Also see Stephen Jay Gould, *Hen's Teeth and Horse's Toes* (New York: W. W. Norton & Company, 1983), pp. 291—309.

27 Richard A. Watson, "Self-Consciousness and the Rights of Nonhuman Animals and Nature," *The Animal Rights/Environmental Ethics Debate*, ed. Eugene C. Hargrove (New York: State University of New York Press, 1992), p. 32.

28 S.F. Sapontzis, *Morals, Reason, and Animals* (Philadelphia: Temple University Press, 1987), p. 217.

29 Natalie Angier, "Smart, Curious, Ticklish. Rats?" *The New York Times*. Science section, July 24, 2007. See http://www.nytimes.com/2007/07/24/science/24angi.html (Internet search on April 6, 2024).

30 Paul Taylor, "The Ethics of Respect for Nature," *The Animal Rights/Environmental Ethics Debate,* ed. Eugene C. Hargrove (New York: State University of New York Press, 1992), pp. 112–113.

31 Editor, "Clever Kanzi, Pygmi Chimp," *Discover*, 12:20, March 1991.

32 Eugene Linden, "Can Animals Think?" *Time*, 141:57, August 29, 1999. See *https://content.time.com/time/magazine/article/0,9171,30198,00.html* (Internet search on April 8, 2024).

33 Sue Savage-Rumbaugh, *Kanzi: The Ape at the Brink of the Human Mind* (Mount Vernon, NY: Trade Paper Press, October 1, 1994).

34 Editor, "Kanzi the Chimpanzee Can Start Fires and Cook, Making Him one of the World's Smartest Monkeys," *New York Daily News* (December 30, 2011). See *https://www.nydailynews.com/2011/12/30/kanzi-the-chimpanzee-can-start-fires-and-cook-making-him-one-of-the-worlds-smartest-monkeys/* (Internet search on April 8, 2024).

35 Editor, "Monkeys Play by the Numbers," *Science News*, 139:383, June 15, 1991. Also see Weiming Sun, Baoming Li, and Chaolin Ma, "Rhesus Monkeys Have a Counting Ability and Can Count from One to Six," *Brain Science* 11, no. 8 (July 30, 2021): 1011, https://doi.org/10.3390/brainsci11081011.

36 Editor, "Pigs Are Gentle Creatures with Surprising Intelligence," Humane Society of the United States. See *https://www.humanesociety.org/animals/pigs* (Internet search on April 8, 2024).

37 Morten Brekkevold, "Suckers for Learning: Why Octopuses Are So Intelligent," *The Conversation* (July 6, 2021). See *https://theconversation.com/suckers-for-learning-why-octopuses-are-so-intelligent-162122* (Internet search on April 8, 2024).

38 Peter Godfrey-Smith, "The Mind of an Octopus," *Scientific American* (January 1, 2017) See *https://www.scientificamerican.com/article/the-mind-of-an-octopus/* (Internet search on April 8, 2024).

39 Shaina Mateev, "Octopuses: More Like Us Than They Appear," *The Commentator* (May 2, 2021). See *https://yucommentator.org/2021/05/octopuses-more-like-us-than-they-appear/* (Internet search on April 8, 2024).

40 Mike Lovett, "Parrot Whose Skills Dazzled Scientists Dies at 31," *Arizona Daily Star* (September 12, 2007). See *https://tucson.com/news/local/education/college/parrot-whose-skills-dazzled-scientists-dies-at-31/article_83cd1ec0-ad27-5549-b975-e89780267bad.html* (Internet search on April 8, 2024).

41 Mark Wexler, "Thinking About Dolphins," National Wildlife Federation (April 1, 1994). See *https://www.nwf.org/Magazines/National-Wildlife/1994/Thinking-About-Dolphins* (Internet search on April 8, 2024).

42 S. Dingfelder, "Sea Lion Smarts," American Psychological Association (March 2007). See *https://www.apa.org/gradpsych/2007/03/sealion* (Internet search on April 8, 2024).

43 P.M. Seyfarth and D.L. Cheney, "Meaning and Mind in Monkeys," *Scientific American*, 267, (Dec. 1992), 122–128. See *https://www.scientificamerican.com/article/meaning-and-mind-in-monkeys/* (Internet search on April 8, 2024).

44 D.R. Griffin, "Essay: Animal Thinking," *Scientific American*, 265, 144, (Nov. 1, 1991). See *https://www.scientificamerican.com/article/essay-animal-thinking/* (Internet search on April 8, 2024).

45 "Dog Understands 1022 Words: Super Smart Animals," *BBC Earth* (May 31, 2017). See *https://www.youtube.com/watch?v=Ip_uVTWfXyI* (Internet search on April 8, 2024).

46 Frans de Waal, "The Animal Noble Prizes of the Decade," *Huffington Post* (December 6, 2017). See *https://www.huffpost.com/entry/the-animal-noble-prizes-o_b_400977* (Internet search on April 8, 2024).

47 D.R. Griffin, "Essay: Animal Thinking," *Scientific American*, 265, 144, (Nov. 1, 1991). See *https://www.scientificamerican.com/article/essay-animal-thinking/* (Internet search on April 8, 2024).

48 John A. Fisher, "Taking Sympathy Seriously: A Defense of Our Moral Psychology Toward Animals," *The Animal Rights/Environmental Ethics Debate*, ed. Eugene C. Hargrove (New York: State University of New York Press, 1992), p. 239.

49 Ibid., 239.

50 S.F. Sapontzis, *Morals, Reason, and Animals* (Philadelphia: Temple University Press, 1987), p. 212.

51 Robert Baird and Stuart Rosenbaum, *Animal Experimentation* (New York: Prometheus Books, 1991), p. 145.

52 Mary Midgley, "The Significance of Species," *The Animal Rights/Environmental Ethics Debate*, ed. Eugene C. Hargrove (New York: State University of New York Press, 1992), p. 122.

53 Ibid., 128.

54 Editor, "Tortoise, Hippo Friendship Deepens Post Tsunami," Reuters (August 9, 2007). See *https://www.reuters.com/article/idUSN28296637/* (Internet search on April 12, 2024).

55 Liam Miller, "Abandoned Piglet Is Lost and Hound: Giant Farm Dog Saves Baby Pig's Bacon by Adopting It as One of Its Own." *Daily Mail* (September 4, 2009). See *http://www.dailymail.co.uk/news/article-1210909/Abandoned-piglet-lost-hound-Giant-farm-dog-saves-baby-pigs-bacon-adopting-own.html* (Internet search on April 12, 2024).

56 Mary Midgley, "The Significance of Species," *The Animal Rights/Environmental Ethics Debate,* ed. Eugene C. Hargrove (New York: State University of New York Press, 1992), pp. 134-135.

57 James Rachels, *The End of Life* (Oxford, UK: Oxford University Press, 1986), p. 75.

58 Tom Regan and Peter Singer, *Animal Rights and Human Obligations* (Upper Saddle River, NJ: Prentice-Hall, Inc., 1989), pp. 115–118.

59 Deborah Slicer, "Your Daughter or Your Dog?" *Ecological Feminist Philosophies*, ed. Karen J. Warren (Bloomington: Indiana University Press, 1996) p. 99.

60 Ibid., 99–101.

61 Later, I argue that the AR movement is guilty of a prejudice I call "sentientism" when they ignore the needs and desires of living beings who are not thought to feel pain.

62 This "Afghanistan argument" fails, as will be discussed in a later chapter.

63 Peter Singer, *Animal Liberation* (New York: Random House, 1990), p. 5.

64 Peter Singer, *In Defense of Animals*, (New York: Harper and Row, 1985), p. 5.

65 Henry Spira is sometimes referred to as the founder of the animal rights movement. He was a former student of Peter Singer and encouraged his professor to expand a 1973 essay about nonhumans into *Animal Liberation*, the current "bible" of the AR movement. Spira put Singer's philosophical ideas into action by persuading the American Museum of Natural History to "end 18 years of sex experiments on maimed and disfigured cats" (see *Animal People*, October 1998, p. 21), by convincing several cosmetic companies to abolish animal testing, by pressuring the USDA to overturn face-branding of cattle, and by pushing McDonald's restaurant to purchase meat only from suppliers who comply with basic animal welfare standards. For further infor-

mation on Spira, see Peter Singer, *Ethics into Action* (Lanham, MD: Rowman & Littlefield Publishers, Inc., 1998).

66 Peter Singer, *In Defense of Animals*, (New York: Harper and Row, 1985), p. 14.

67 George P. Cave, "Animals, Heidegger, and the Right to Life," *Environmental Ethics* 4, no. 3 (Fall 1982): 250.

68 Peter Singer, *In Defense of Animals* (New York: Harper and Row, 1985), p. 7.

69 S.F. Sapontzis, *Morals, Reason, and Animals* (Philadelphia: Temple University Press, 1987), p. 220.

70 James Rachels, *The End of Life* (Oxford, UK: Oxford University Press, 1986), p. 75.

71 Tom Regan, *A Case for Animal Rights* (Oakland: University of California Press, 1983), p. 324.

Chapter Two

72 B.F. Skinner, *Walden Two* (New York: Macmillan Publishing Company, 1976), np.

73 Sigmund Freud discusses this in the book *New Introductory Lectures on Psychoanalysis*. Trans. W.J.H. Sprott (New York: W.W. Norton & Company, 1933).

74 It should be noted that I have always lacked this "free will feeling." When I do thought experiments, envisioning myself at an exact time and place in the past with the information available to me at that particular moment (as well as acknowledging the emotions rushing through my head), I realize I made the only decision that I could. It is important to try to put oneself in that exact circumstance with the thoughts that one had at the time. Otherwise, one can fall victim to self-delusion.

75 Baruch Spinoza, *The Ethics and Selected Letters* (Indianapolis, IN: Hackett Publishing Company, 1982), p. 108.

76 Mike Wehner, "Your Brain Makes Decisions Before You Even Realize It." *New York Post* (March 7, 2019). See https://nypost.com/2019/03/07/your-brain-makes-decisions-before-you-even-realize-it/ (Internet search on January 5, 2024).

77 Dennis Overbye, "Free Will: Now You Have It, Now You Don't," *New York Times* (January 2, 2007). See https://www.nytimes.com/2007/01/02/

science/02free.html (Internet search on January 23, 2024).

78 Mike Wehner, "Your Brain Makes Decisions Before You Even Realize It." *New York Post* (March 7, 2019). See *https://nypost.com/2019/03/07/your-brain-makes-decisions-before-you-even-realize-it/* (Internet search on January 5, 2024)

79 Editor, "The Zombie Within." *New Scientist* (September 5, 1998). See *https://www.newscientist.com/article/mg15921505-500-the-zombie-within/* (Internet search on January 23, 2024)

80 Descartes argued that freedom stems from the pineal gland, as this body part is present in humans and absent in other species.

81 Jacques Thiroux, *Ethics: Theory and Practice* (Upper Saddle River, NJ: Prentice Hall, 1995), p. 128.

82 Ibid., 128.

83 Gary Watson, *Free Will* (Oxford, UK: Oxford University Press, 1982), p. 1.

84 Eric Hoffer, *Next Nature* (2006). See https://nextnature.net/story/2006/notnatural-and-notmechanical-human (Internet search on January 23, 2024).

85 Crispin Sartwell, "Humans Are Animals. Let's Get Over It." *New York Times* (February 23, 2021). See *https://www.nytimes.com/2021/02/23/opinion/humans-animals-philosophy.html* (Internet search on August 8, 2024).

86 John D. Caputo, *Against Ethics* (Bloomington: Indiana University Press, 1993), pp. 134–137.

87 Ibid., 135.

88 Ibid., 136.

89 Ibid., 136.

Chapter Three

90 Roger Koenig-Robert and Joel Pearson, "Decoding the Contents and Strength of Imagery Before Volitional Engagement," *Scientific Reports* (2019). See *https://www.nature.com/articles/s41598-019-39813-y* (Internet search on January 31, 2024). Also see Mike Wehner, "Your Brain Makes Decisions Before You Even Realize It," *New York Post* (March 7, 2019). See https://nypost.com/2019/03/07/your-brain-makes-decisions-before-you-even-realize-it/ (Internet search on January 31, 2024).

91 Editor, "The Zombie Within," *New Scientist* (September 5, 1998). See *https://www.newscientist.com/article/mg15921505-500-the-zombie-within/* (Internet search on January 31, 2024).

92 Valerie Ulene, "In Search of Lasting Happiness," *LA Times* (January 31, 2011). See *http://articles.latimes.com/2011/jan/31/health/la-he-the-md-happiness-20110131* (Internet search on January 23, 2024).

93 Ed Edelson, "Popular or Not? Your Genes May Help Decide," *ABC News* (January 26, 2009). See *http://abcnews.go.com/Health/Healthday/story?id=6737071&page=1* (Internet search on January 23, 2024).

94 Julie Steenhuysen, "Gene Switch Altered Sex Orientation of Worms," Reuters (October 26, 2007). See *http://www.reuters.com/article/idUSN2535476120071025* (Internet search on January 23, 2024).

95 Excerpted from *60 Minutes II*, CBS, February 10, 1999. Transcript printed by Burrelles Information Services, p. 10. See also Philip A. Vernon, Vanessa C. Villani, Leanne C. Vickers and Julie Aitken Harris, "A Behavioral Genetic Investigation of the Dark Triad and the Big 5," *Science Direct* 44, no. 2 (January 2008). See *https://www.sciencedirect.com/science/article/abs/pii/S0191886907003054* (Internet search on April 14, 2024).

96 Noam Shpancer, "Is Morality Genetic?" *Psychology Today* (November 2, 2021). See *https://www.psychologytoday.com/us/blog/insight-therapy/202111/is-morality-genetic* (Internet search on July 27, 2024).

97 Benedict Carey, "Some Politics May Be Etched in the Genes," *New York Times* (June 21, 2005). See *http://www.nytimes.com/2005/06/21/science/21gene.html* (Internet Search on January 23, 2024).

98 Cynthia Fazio, "Study Finds Link between Genetics and Coffee Intake," *Medical Xpress* (June 18, 2024). See *https://medicalxpress.com/news/2024-06-link-genetics-coffee-intake.html* (Internet search on June 20, 2024). You can find the original study in *Nature* (June 11, 2024) at *https://www.nature.com/articles/s41386-024-01870-x* (Internet search on June 20, 2024).

99 Maria Cheng, "Food Aversion?" Associated Press (August 27, 2010). Also see Lauren J. Young, "Your Genes May Influence What You Like to Eat," *Scientific American* (August 1, 2023). See *https://www.scientificamerican.com/article/your-genes-may-influence-what-you-like-to-eat/* (Internet search on January 23, 2024). Also see "Taste for Specialty Foods Is in Our Genes, Study Shows," University of Edinburgh (2022). See *https://www.ed.ac.uk/news/2022/taste-for-food-is-in-our-genes-study-shows* (Internet search on January 23, 2024).

100 Steven Pinker, "My Genome, My Self," *New York Times* (January 7, 2009). See *http://www.nytimes.com/2009/01/11/magazine/11Genome-t.html* (Internet search on January 23, 2024).

101 Dr. Mackelroy, *Dateline*, MSNBC, November 27, 1998, 7:30 pm. PST.

102 George Howe Colt, "Were You Born That Way?" *Life* (April 1998), p. 48.

103 Adam Rogers, "Thinking Differently: Brain Scans Give New Hope of Diagnosing ADHA," *Newsweek* (December 7, 1998), p. 60.

104 Paul Bloom, "The Moral Life of Babies," *New York Times* (May 5, 2010). See *http://www.nytimes.com/2010/05/09/magazine/09babies-t.html* (Internet search on January 23, 2024).

105 Editor, "Magnetism 'Can Modify Morality,'" *BBC News* (March 30, 2010). See *http://news.bbc.co.uk/2/mobile/health/8593748.stm* (Internet search on June 24, 2024).

106 Eric Bland, "Study: Magnets Can Alter Morality," *NBC News* (March 29, 2010). See *https://www.nbcnews.com/health/health-news/study-magnets-can-alter-morality-flna1c9449359* (Internet search on June 24, 2024).

107 Excerpted from *60 Minutes II*, CBS (February 10, 1999). Transcript printed by Burrelles Information Services, p. 10.

108 Robert Reinhold, "Study Says Criminal Tendencies May Be Inherited," *New York Times* (January 8, 1982). See *http://www.nytimes.com/1982/01/08/us/study-says-criminal-tendencies-may-be-inherited.html* (Internet search on September 17, 2010).

109 Elizabeth Kandel, Sarnoff A. Mednick, Lis Kirkegaard-Sorenson, Barry Hutchings, Joachim Knop, Raben Rosenberg, and Fini Schulsinger, "IQ as a Protective Factor for Subjects at High Risk for Antisocial Behavior," *Journal of Consulting and Clinical Psychology* 56 (1988): 224–226.

110 R.J. Herrnstein, "Criminogenic Traits," *Crime*, eds. James Q. Wilson and Joan Petersilia (San Francisco: Institute for Contemporary Studies, 1995), p. 56.

111 Kathleen McAuliffe, "Born to Believe: Your Values about God, Home and Country May Be Influenced by Your Genes," *Omni*, October 1992, 25. *https://www.kmcauliffe.com/_files/ugd/f0f6ae_c14e4084d-22a4b1697d8687dc888e59b.pdf*

112 Ibid., 26. Some twin studies have found that genes even "shape whether

an individual will favor or oppose capital punishment." See Sharon Begley, "Decoding the Human Body," *Newsweek,* April 10, 2000, 57.

113 Sharon Begley, "Rewiring Your Gray Matter," *Newsweek*, January 1, 2000, 65.

114 J.M. Darley and C.D. Batson, "From Jerusalen to Jericho: A Study of Situational and Dispositional Variables in Helping Behavior," *Journal of Personality and Social Psychology* 27 (1): 100. Also see Sara Lyons-Padilla, "Take Time to be a Good Samaritan," Stanford University. See *https://sparq.stanford.edu/solutions/take-time-be-good-samaritan* (Internet search on June 25, 2024).

115 Kendra Cherry, "The Asch Conformity Experiments," *Verywell Mind* (November 13, 2023) See *https://www.verywellmind.com/the-asch-conformity-experiments-2794996* (Internet search on June 25, 2024).

116 Saul Mcleod, "Stanley Milgram Shock Experiment," *Simply Psychology* (November 14, 2023). See *https://www.simplypsychology.org/milgram.html* (Internet search on June 25, 2024).

117 Saul Mcleod, "Stanford Prison Experiment: Zimbardo's Famous Study," *Simply Psychology* (November 17, 2023). See *https://www.simplypsychology.org/zimbardo.html* (Internet search on June 25, 2024).

118 Matthew Barakat, "20 Years Later, Abu Ghraib Detainees Get Their Day in US Court," Associated Press (April 11, 2024). See *https://apnews.com/article/abu-ghraib-lawsuit-caci-virginia-contractor-torture-47bca65df10c62b672944692a139e012* (Internet search on June 25, 2024).

119 Stephen Hawking, *The Grand Design* (New York: Bantam Books, 2010), pp. 31–32.

120 David Bohm, "Postmodern Science and a Postmodern World." *Ecology*, ed. Carolyn Merchant. Atlantic Highlands, NJ: Humanities Press, 1994, p. 342.

121 Ibid., 348.

122 Arthur J. Minton, "Theories About Human Freedom," *Philosophy and Science: The Wide Range of Interaction*, ed. Frederick E. Mosedale (Upper Saddle River, NJ: Prentice-Hall, Inc., 1979), p. 120.

123 Andrew Watson, "Quantum Spookiness Wins, Einstein Loses in Photon Test," *Science* 277 (July 25, 1997): 481.

124 Lewis Schipper, *Spinoza's Ethics: The View From Within* (New York:

Peter Lang, 1993), p. 12.

125 Ian Stewart, *Does God Play Dice?* (Cambridge, MA: Basil Blackwell, 1989), pp. 17, 289.

126 Ibid., 293–295.

127 Ibid., 299–300.

128 Philipp Frank, *Philosophy of Science* (Upper Saddle River, NJ: Prentice-Hall, Inc., 1957), p. 245.

129 N. R. Hanson, *Patterns of Discovery* (Cambridge, UK: Cambridge University Press, 1958), p. 173.

130 Dietrich Schroeer, "Recent Physics and Limits of Knowledge," *Philosophy of Science: The Wide Range of Interaction*, ed. Frederick E. Mosedale (Upper Saddle River, NJ: Prentice Hall, 1979), p. 152.

131 David Bohm, "Postmodern Science and a Postmodern World," *Ecology,* ed. Carolyn Merchant. Atlantic Highlands, NJ: Humanities Press, 1994, p. 346.

132 This randomness would not just exist on the subatomic level but would translate into macro-randomness because large objects would be composed of erratic subatomic particles.

133 Rene Descartes, *Meditations on First Philosophy* (Indianapolis, IN: Hackett Publishing Company, 1979), p. 15.

134 Thomas Nagel, "Moral Luck," *Free Will*, ed. Gary Watson (Oxford, UK: Oxford University Press, 1982), p. 181.

135 Jeffrey M. Jones, "Belief in God in U.S. Dips to 81%, a New Low." Gallup (June 17, 2022). See *https://news.gallup.com/poll/393737/belief-god-dips-new-low.aspx* (Internet search on February 2, 2024).

Chapter Four

136 W. T. Stace writes, "It is certain that if there is no free will there can be no morality. Morality is concerned with what men ought and ought not do." See W. T. Stace, "The Problem of Free Will," *Philosophy and Contemporary Issues*, eds. John R. Burr and Milton Goldinger (New York: Macmillan Publishing Co., Inc., 1980), p. 32.

137 John Hospers, "What Means This Freedom?" *Determinism and Freedom in the Age of Modern Science*, ed. Sidney Hook (New York: Collier Publishing, 1958), p. 133.

138 Stuart Hampshire, *Spinoza* (Harmondsworth, UK: Penguin Books, 1951), p. 121.

139 Peter Van Inwagen, "The Incompatibility of Free Will and Determinism," *Free Will*, ed. Gary Watson (Oxford, UK: Oxford University Press, 1982), p. 50.

140 Baruch Spinoza, *The Ethics and Selected Letters* (Indianapolis: Hackett Publishing Company, 1982), p. 191.

141 "Responsible," *Webster's New Collegiate Dictionary* (Springfield, MA: G. & C. Merriam Company, Publishers, 1949), p. 722.

142 David Ludden, "Can We Have Justice Without Free Will?" *Psychology Today* (July 27, 2020). See https://www.psychologytoday.com/us/blog/talking-apes/202007/can-we-have-justice-without-free-will (Internet search on January 26, 2024).

143 Ernest Becker, "The Fragile Fiction," *The Birth and Death of Meaning* (New York: The Free Press/ Simon & Schuster, 1971).

144 Peter Berger, *The Sacred Canopy* (New York: Doubleday and Company, 1967), p. 4.

145 Marvin Harris, *Cows, Pigs, Wars, and Witches: The Riddles of Culture* (New York: Vintage Books, 1974), p. 188.

146 Ibid., 233.

147 Ibid., 233.

148 Friedrich Nietzsche, *Beyond Good and Evil* (New York: Vintage Books, 1989), p. 60.

149 Ibid., 67.

150 Sigmund Freud, *Civilization and Its Discontents* (New York: W.W. Norton & Company, 1961), p. 77.

151 Sigmund Freud, *The Future of An Illusion* (New York: W.W. Norton & Company, 1961), pp. 59–63.

152 Karl Marx, *The Marx-Engels Reader*, ed. Robert C. Tucker (New York: W.W. Norton & Company, 1978), p. 54.

153 John Stuart Mill, "Utility of Religion," *Essential Works of John Stuart Mill*, ed. Max Lerner (New York: Bantam Books, 1961), p. 410.

154 Ludwig Wittgenstein, "A Lecture on Ethics," *Discovering Philosophy*,

ed. Matthew Lipman (New York: Meredith Corporation, 1969), p. 138.

155 Ibid., 139.

156 William K. Frankena, *Ethics*, 2nd Edition (Upper Saddle River, NJ: Prentice-Hall, Inc., 1973), pp. 9–10.

157 *Unsolved Mysteries*, Lifetime Television, Season 1, number 21, April 12, 1989.

158 Ludwig Wittgenstein, "A Lecture on Ethics," *Discovering Philosophy*, ed. Matthew Lipman (New York: Meredith Corporation, 1969), p. 139.

159 Jeffrey Stout, *Ethics After Babel* (Boston: Beacon Press, 1988), p. 35.

160 Immanuel Kant, *Groundwork of the Metaphysic of Morals* (New York: Harper and Row, 1964), p. 34.

161 John Locke, *The Second Treatise of Government* (Indianapolis: The Bobbs-Merrill Company, Inc., 1952), p. 5.

162 Few people say that the Nazis merely disobeyed international law. Most people believe they acted in an immoral or evil way.

163 John Stuart Mill, "Utilitarianism," *Essential Works of John Stuart Mill*, ed. Max Lerner (New York: Bantam Books, 1961), pp. 216–217.

164 John Stuart Mill, *Utilitarianism*, ed. Oskar Piest (New York: Bobbs-Merrill, 1957), p. 10.

165 Anthropologist Laila Williamson says, "Infanticide has been practiced on every continent and by people on every level of cultural complexity . . . . Rather than being an exception, it has been the rule." See Laila Williamson, "Infanticide: An Anthropological Analysis," *Infanticide and the Value of Life*, ed. Marvin Kohl (New York: Prometheus Books, 1978), pp. 61–75.

166 Peter Singer, *Ethics Into Action: Henry Spira and the Animal Rights Movement* (New York: Rowan & Littlefield Publishers, Inc., 1998), p. 187.

167 "Hedonism," *Encyclopedia of Philosophy*, vol. 3 (New York: Macmillan Publishing Company, Inc., 1967), p. 432.

168 James Rachels, "Egoism and Moral Skepticism," *Vice & Virtue in Everyday Life*, ed. Christina Sommers & Fred Sommers (Fort Worth, TX: Harcourt Brace Jovanovich College Publishers, 1993), pp. 458-463.

169 Nonhuman living beings are considered part of society.

170 "Happiness" is defined very broadly to mean that the interests, needs, or

desires of living things are satisfied.

171 "Perspective" is meant to apply to even those living beings who may lack what is commonly called "perspective," such as a comatose person, an insect, or a tree. We can attribute a perspective to these living things by surmising what would be in their best interest; we can become impartial observers or place ourselves behind a non-anthropocentric veil of ignorance and try to make an unbiased decision.

172 James Rachels, *The End of Life* (Oxford, UK: Oxford University Press, 1986), p. 64.

173 I use the words *interests*, *needs*, *desires*, and *wants* interchangeably to signify that a being (or living thing), whether conscious or not, potentially has a stake in a particular outcome or state of affairs. This "stake" may be in favor of life, happiness, relief from pain, propagation of one's species, nourishment, flourishing, or other goals.

174 Anthony Flew, *A Dictionary of Philosophy* (New York: St. Martin's Press, 1979), p. 251.

175 Ibid., 266.

176 All living things necessarily seek the expected utility (for themselves); this may or may not coincide with actual utility.

177 I use this word loosely. Some living things, such as plants, might not be able to "perceive" but could be said to thrive, flourish, perish, or otherwise undergo a better or worse state of affairs.

178 This term is meant loosely, so as to also apply to trees or any possibly unconscious living things. Later in this book, I will allude to scientific data that supports the fact that trees and insects are most likely conscious and sentient.

Chapter Five

179 Huston Smith, "Postmodernism and World's Religions," Inaugural Symposium of the International Institute of Islamic Thought and Civilization, Malaysia, August 1994. Also see Vaclav Havel, "The Search for Meaning in a Global Civilization," Philadelphia Liberty Medal acceptance speech, Philadelphia, July 4, 1994, or Vaclav Havel, "The Search for Meaning in a Global Civilization," *The Truth about the Truth*, ed. Walter Truett Anderson (New York: G.P. Putnam's Sons, 1995), pp. 232–238.

180 Robert Frodeman, "Radical Environmentalism and the Political Roots of Postmodernism: Differences That Make a Difference," *Postmodern Envi-*

ronmental Ethics, ed. Max Oelschlaeger (Albany: State University of New York Press, 1995), p. 122.

181 Max Oelschlaeger, Introd., *Postmodern Environmental Ethics* (Albany: State University of New York Press, 1995), p. 6.

182 Steven Best and Douglas Kellner, *The Postmodern Turn* (New York: Guilford Press, 1997), p. 6.

183 Friedrich Nietzsche, *Beyond Good and Evil* (New York: Random House, Inc., 1996), pp. 60, 83, 85, 101, and 102.

184 Ibid., 115.

185 Walter Truett Anderson, "Four Different Ways to be Absolutely Right," *The Truth about the Truth,* ed. Walter Truett Anderson (New York: G.P. Putnam's Sons, 1995), p. 113.

186 Wade Clark Roof, *A Generation of Seekers* (San Francisco: HarperCollins Publishers, 1993).

187 Jeet Heer, "America's First Postmodern President," *New Republic* (July 8, 2017). See *https://newrepublic.com/article/143730/americas-first-postmodern-president* (Internet search on March 1, 2024).

188 Peter Franklin, "Donald Trump Was America's First Post-modern President," *UnHerd* (January 13, 2021). See *https://unherd.com/newsroom/donald-trump-was-americas-first-post-modern-president/* (Internet search on March 1, 2024).

189 Charles Lane, "Take Trump Seriously and Literally," *The Washington Post* (November 16, 2016). See *https://www.washingtonpost.com/opinions/take-trump-seriously-and-literally/2016/11/16/cbdcf2c8-ac25-11e6-8b45-f8e493f06fcd_story.html* (Internet search on March 1, 2024).

190 David Ernst, "Donald Trump Is the First President to Turn Postmodernism Against Itself," *The Federalist* (January 23, 2017). See *https://thefederalist.com/2017/01/23/donald-trump-first-president-turn-postmodernism/* (Internet search on March 1, 2024).

191 "Create," *Merriam-Webster Dictionary* (New York: G. & C. Merriam Company, 1974), p. 176.

192 This term is used loosely. It applies to humans as well as nonhuman animals and other living things who may not be able to "regard" in the way that humans do.

193 Gary Steiner, *Animals and the Limits of Postmodernism* (New York:

Columbia University Press, 2013), pp. 3–4.

194 Gary L. Francione, "Woke Animal Rights Means No Animal Rights, Part 1," *Medium* (May 16, 2021). See *https://gary-francione.medium.com/woke-animal-rights-means-no-animal-rights-bf1e420e0404* (Internet search on March 14, 2024).

195 Ibid.

196 Matthew Scully, "The Animal-Protection Movement Is Everything That 'Woke' Activism Isn't," *National Review* (October 4, 2020). See *https://www.nationalreview.com/2020/10/the-animal-protection-movement-is-everything-that-woke-activism-isnt/* (Internet search on March 15, 2024).

197 Russell Goldman, "Here's a List of 58 Gender Options for Facebook Users," *ABC News* (February 13, 2014). See *https://abcnews.go.com/blogs/headlines/2014/02/heres-a-list-of-58-gender-options-for-facebook-users* (Internet search on March 12, 2024).

198 Editor, "Civil Service Tells Staff There Are 'More than 100 Genders,'" *Christian* (June 10, 2022). See *https://www.christian.org.uk/news/civil-service-tells-staff-there-are-more-than-100-genders/* (Internet search on March 12, 2024).

199 "List of Genders." See *https://gender.fandom.com/wiki/List_of_Genders* (Internet search on March 12, 2024).

200 Alex Hershaft, "What Tears us Apart," The Vegan Blog (May 25, 2021). See *https://theveganblog.org/48-how-we-tear-ourselves-apart* (Internet search on March 14, 2024).

201 When I talk about my "animal rights theory," I am referring to legal rights, not "moral" rights.

202 Matthew Scully, "The Animal-Protection Movement Is Everything That 'Woke' Activism Isn't," *National Review* (October 4, 2020). See *https://www.nationalreview.com/2020/10/the-animal-protection-movement-is-everything-that-woke-activism-isnt/* (Internet search on March 15, 2024).

203 Rebecca Olds, "Today's Turkey Traditions, Explained: How Many Turkeys Are Killed for Thanksgiving?" *The Deseret News* (November 18, 2023). See *https://www.deseret.com/2023/11/18/23950898/how-many-turkeys-are-killed-each-year-for-thanksgiving/* (Internet search on March 15, 2024).

204 Chas Newkey-Burden, "If You Go to Firework Displays, You Don't Love Animals," *The Independent* (November 5, 2022). See *https://www.independent.co.uk/voices/firework-displays-bonfire-night-animal-cruelty-*

b2218348.html (Internet search on March 15, 2024).

205 Paige Austin, "Fireworks Cause Hazardous Air Quality in Woodland Hills," *The Patch* (July 5, 2024). See *https://patch.com/california/woodland-hills/fireworks-cause-hazardous-air-quality-woodland-hills* (Internet search on July 8, 2024).

206 New Root Institute. Numbers taken from USDA Livestock and Meat Domestic Data (April 28, 2020). See *https://www.newrootsinstitute.org/facts/number-of-animals-killed* (Internet search on March 15, 2024).

207 Marina Bolotnikova and Kenny Torrella, "9 Charts that Show US Factory Farming Is Even Bigger than You Realize," *Vox* (February 24, 2024). See *https://www.vox.com/future-perfect/24079424/factory-farming-facts-meat-usda-agriculture-census* (Internet search on March 16, 2024).

208 Marina Bolotnikova, "Humanity Is Failing One of Its Greatest Moral Tests," *Vox* (August 7, 2024). See *https://www.vox.com/future-perfect/363550/factory-farming-human-progress-sustainable-food-movement* (Internet search on August 8, 2024).

209 Lewis Bollard, "We Love Animals. Why Do We Torture Them?" Farm Animal Welfare Research Newsletter (July 18, 2024). See *https://farmanimalwelfare.substack.com/p/we-love-animals-why-do-we-torture* (Internet search on August 9, 2024).

Chapter Six

210 Julia Shapero, "Belief in God, the Devil Falls to a New Low: Gallup," *The Hill* (July 20, 2023). See *https://thehill.com/changing-america/respect/diversity-inclusion/4107968-belief-in-god-the-devil-falls-to-new-low-gallup/* (Internet search on April 13, 2024).

211 Jennifer Robison, "The Devil and the Demographic Details," *Gallup* (February 25, 2003). See *https://news.gallup.com/poll/7858/devil-demographic-details.aspx* (Internet search on April 13, 2024).

212 Jacob Ausubel, "Christians, Religiously Unaffiliated Differ on Whether Most Things in Society Can Be Divided into Good, Evil," *Pew Research Center* (December 21, 2021). See *https://www.pewresearch.org/short-reads/2021/12/21/christians-religiously-unaffiliated-differ-on-whether-most-things-in-society-can-be-divided-into-good-evil/* (Internet search on April 13, 2024).

213 Kim Hart, "Democrats See Republicans as Racist, Sexist," *Axios* (November 2, 2018). See *https://www.axios.com/2018/11/12/poll-democrats-and-republicans-hate-each-other-racist-ignorant-evil* (Internet search on

April 13, 2024).

214 David Brooks, "The Source of Trump's Appeal," *New York Times* (July 11, 2024). See *https://www.nytimes.com/2024/07/11/opinion/trump-biden-authoritarianism.html* (Internet search on July 12, 2024).

215 David Wisniewski, "Free Will Beliefs Are Better Predicted by Dualism than Determinism Beliefs across Different Cultures," *PLOS ONE* (September 11, 2019). See *https://journals.plos.org/plosone/article?id=10.1371/journal.pone.0221617* (Internet search on April 13, 2024).

216 Ralph Lewis, "What Actually Is Evil? And What Makes People Carry Out Evil Acts?" *Psychology Today* (June 10, 2021). See *https://www.psychologytoday.com/us/blog/finding-purpose/202106/what-actually-is-evil-and-what-makes-people-carry-out-evil-acts* (Internet search on April 14, 2024). Also see Shafiqullah Ahadi, "The Normalization of Evil and Social Indifferences in a Government of the Masses," *8 AM Media* (May 8, 2023). See *https://8am.media/eng/the-normalization-of-evil-and-social-indifferences-in-a-government-of-the-masses/* (Internet search on April 14, 2024).

217 Francesco Bernardini, Laura Scarponi, Luigi Attademo, Philippe Hubain, Gwenole Loas and Orin Devinsky, "Musical Anhedonia: A Review," *Journal of Psychopathology* (June 8, 2020). See *https://old.jpsychopathol.it/wp-content/uploads/2020/12/08_Bernardini-1.pdf* (Internet search on April 13, 2024).

218 Editor, "People Can Recover and Thrive after Mental Illness and Substance Use Disorders," *Association for Psychological Science* (April 29, 2022). See *https://www.psychologicalscience.org/observer/thrive-after-mental-illness* (Internet search on April 13, 2024).

219 Kristina Kopic, "Mental Illness as a Moral Failing," *Ruderman Foundation* (December 15, 2016). See *https://rudermanfoundation.org/mental-illness-as-a-moral-failing/* (Internet search on April 13, 2024).

220 Advertisement of a Charles Manson documentary on MSNBC, April 11, 2000, 3:15 PM, PST.

221 Harold Schechter & David Everitt, *A-Z Encyclopedia of Serial Killers* (New York: Pocket Books, 1996), pp. 14–15.

222 Michael Newton, *Encyclopedia of Serial Killers* (New York: CheckMark Books, 2000), p. 126.

223 Ibid., 107.

224 David Robson, "Psychology: The Man who Studies Everyday Evil,"

BBC (January 30, 2015) See *https://www.bbc.com/future/article/20150130-the-man-who-studies-evil* (Internet search on April 13, 2024).

225 Arne Naess, *Ecology, community and lifestyle* (Cambridge, UK: Cambridge University Press, 1989), pp. 89–91.

226 In later chapters, I will discuss the human-populated area called Bioland and what it means to be a "protectable living being."

227 Dero A. Saunders, Introduction, *The Decline and Fall of the Roman Empire* by Edward Gibbon (New York: Penguin Classics, 1985), p. 4.

228 Howard Bloom, *The Lucifer Principle* (New York: The Atlantic Monthly Press, 1955), p. 88.

229 Friedrich Nietzsche, *Beyond Good and Evil* (New York: Vintage Books, 1989), p. 81.

230 Baruch Spinoza, *The Ethics and Selected Letters* (Indianapolis, IN: Hackett Publishing Company, 1982), p. 185.

231 John Stuart Mill, "Utility of Religion," in *Essential Works of John Stuart Mill* (New York: Bantam Books, 1961), p. 418.

232 Alan Ryan, *J.S. Mill* (London: Routledge & Kegan Paul, 1974), p. 134.

233 John Stuart Mill argues that " . . .human individuality is a necessary element to man's well-being." See John Stuart Mill, "Essay on Liberty," *Masterpieces of World Philosophy*, ed. Frank N. Magill (New York: HarperCollins Publishers, 1990), p. 396.

234 Alan Ryan, *J.S. Mill* (New York: Routledge & Kegan Paul, 1974), p. 135.

Chapter Seven

235 Harriet Ritvo, "The Animal Connection," *The Boundaries of Humanity: Humans, Animals, Machines*, eds. James J. Sheehan and Morton Sosna (Berkeley: University of California Press, 1991), p. 69.

236 James J. Sheehan and Morton Sosna, *The Boundaries of Humanity: Humans, Animals, Machines* (Berkeley: University of California Press, 1991), p. 32.

237 Davydd J. Greenwood, *The Taming of Evolution: The Persistence of Nonevolutionary Views in the Study of Humans* (Ithaca, NY: Cornell University Press, 1984), pp. 146–147.

238 Carl N. Degler, *In Search of Human Nature* (Oxford, UK: Oxford University Press, 1991), p. 281.

239 Karl Barth, *Church Dogmatics III*, 2 (Edinburgh, UK: T. and T. Clark, 1960), p. 609.

240 James M. Gustafson, *Ethics from a Theocentric Perspective*, vol. I (Chicago: University of Chicago Press, 1981), pp. 90–91.

241 Ken Wilber, "The Great Chain of Being," *Journal of Humanistic Psychology* 33, no. 3 (Summer 1993): 53. Also see Harriet Ritvo, "The Animal Connection," *The Boundaries of Humanity: Humans, Animals, Machines* (Berkeley: University of California Press, 1991), pp. 69–70. Ritvo says, "Recent research suggests that most ordinary Americans explicitly endorse . . . [speciesism]."

242 "Free Will," *The World Book Encyclopedia*, vol. 7 (Chicago: Field Enterprises Educational Corporation, 1969), p. 427.

243 John Bartlett, *Familiar Quotations* (Boston: Little, Brown and Company, 1980), p. 902

244 George Burden, "One in Eleven Odds: The Deadly Risk of Being U.S. President," *Life As A Human* (June 9, 2020). See http://lifeasahuman.com/2010/arts-culture/history/one-in-eleven-odds-the-deadly-risk-of-being-us-president/ (Internet search on April 20, 2024).

245 "Amoral," *Webster's New Collegiate Dictionary* (Springfield, MA: G. & C. Merriam Co., Publishers, 1949), p. 30.

246 "Amoral," *Webster's Encyclopedic Unabridged Dictionary of the English Language* (New York: Gramercy Books, 1989), p. 49.

247 Sterling A. Brown, "Negro Character as Seen by White Authors," *Dark Symphony: Negro Literature in America* (New York: New York Free Press, 1968), pp. 155–156. Also see Stephen Jay Gould, *Hen's Teeth and Horse's Toes* (New York: W. W. Norton & Company, 1983), p. 305.

248 "Indian Wars," *World Book Encyclopedia*, vol. 10 (Chicago: Field Enterprises Educational Corporation, 1969), pp. 144–149.

249 R.R. Cobb, *An Inquiry Into the Law of Negro Slavery in the United States of America* (1858).

250 Some thesauri list *evil*, *depraved*, *sinful*, *wicked*, and *corrupt* as synonyms for both *immoral* and *amoral*.

251 R. S. Peters, *Authority, Responsibility and Education* (London: George

Allen & Unwin LTD, 1959), p. 13.

252 Tom Regan, *The Case for Animal Rights* (Berkeley: University of California Press, 1983), p. 233.

253 Ibid., 151.

254 Ibid., 152.

255 Ibid., 285.

256 Daisie and Michael Radner, *Animal Consciousness* (New York: Prometheus Books, 1996), p. 217.

257 "Baby," *The World Book Encyclopedia*, vol. 2 (Chicago: Field Enterprises Educational Corporation, 1969), pp. 5–6.

258 "Potential," *Webster's Encyclopedic Unabridged Dictionary of the English Language* (New York: Gramercy Books, 1989), p. 1125.

259 Ibid., 1125.

260 David Suzuki, Forword, *Natures Outcasts: A New Look at Living Things We Love to Hate* by Des Kennedy (Pownal, VT: Storey Communications, Inc., 1993), p. viii.

261 Baruch Spinoza, *The Ethics and Selected Letters* (Indianapolis, IN: Hackett Publishing Company, 1982), p. 201.

262 Andrea Wulf, "The Forgotten Father of Environmentalism," *The Atlantic* (December 23, 2015). See *https://www.theatlantic.com/science/archive/2015/12/the-forgotten-father-of-environmentalism/421434/* (Internet search on April 23, 2024).

263 Vance Lehmkuhl, "You Care More About Animals Than You Do About People," *North American Vegetarian Society*. See *https://navs-online.org/articles/care-animals-people/* (Internet search on April 23, 2024).

264 Julia Janicki, Katy Daigle, and Sudev Kiyada, "On the Brink," Reuters (December 23, 2022). See *https://www.reuters.com/graphics/GLOBAL-ENVIRONMENT/EXTINCT/lbvgggdgevq/* (Internet search on April 23, 2024).

265 John A. Vucetich, "Are Humans and Nature Fundamentally One and the Same?" *Center for Humans and Nature.* See *https://humansandnature.org/are-humans-and-nature-fundamentally-one-and-the-same/* (Internet search on April 23, 2024).

266 Ibid.

267 Melissa S. Tulin, *Aardvarks to Zebras* (New York: Citadel Press, 1995), p. 70.

268 Thomas H. Maugh, II, "Tiny Water Flea has the Longest Genome," *LA Times* (February 6, 2011). See http://articles.latimes.com/2011/feb/06/science/la-sci-water-flea-20110206 (Internet search on April 24, 2024).

269 Bob Holmes, "Chimps 'More Evolved' than Humans," *New Scientist* (April 16, 2007). See http://www.newscientist.com/article/dn11611-chimps-more-evolved-than-humans.html (Internet search on April 24, 2024).

270 Chantal van Ham, "In the Spirit of Nature, Everything Is Connected," *International Union for Conservation of Nature* (January 25, 2018). See *https://www.iucn.org/news/europe/201801/spirit-nature-everything-connected* (Internet search on April 24, 2024).

271 Des Kennedy, *Nature's Outcasts* (Pownal, VT: Storey Communications, Inc., 1993), p. 5.

272 M.L. Kreithen and D.B. Quine, "Infrasound Detection by the Homing Pigeon," *Journal of Comparative Physiology* 129 (1979): 1–4.

273 Theodore Xenophon Barber, *The Human Nature of Birds* (New York: St. Martin's Press, 1993), p. 69.

274 Ibid., 143.

275 David George Gordon, *The Compleat Cockroach* (Berkeley, CA: Ten Speed Press, 1996), p. 33.

276 Charles W. Petit and Laura Tangley, "The Invisible Emperors," *U.S. News and World Report*, November 8, 1999, p. 73.

277 Bernard E. Rollin, *Animal Rights and Human Morality* (New York: Prometheus Books, 1981), pp. 62–63.

278 "Pet Statistics," *The American Society for the Prevention of Cruelty to Animals*. See *https://www.aspca.org/helping-people-pets/shelter-intake-and-surrender/pet-statistics* (Internet search on April 24, 2024).

Chapter Eight

279 "Interests" are not merely about consciousness or awareness. They correspond to the potential needs or desires of a living thing (whether this be a human, nonhuman animal, plant, insect, etc.). Interests are associated with, yet not limited to, the personal advantages brought about by life, happiness, relief from pain, propagation of one's species, nourishment, and/or flourishing.

280 "Alienate" and "Alienation," *Webster's New Collegiate Dictionary* (Springfield, MA: G. & C. Merriam Co., Publishers, 1949), p. 22.

281 Erich Fromm, *Marx's Concept of Man* (New York: Frederick Ungar, 1961), p. 46.

282 Erich Fromm, *The Sane Society* (New York: Fawcett Premier Books, 1955), p. 30.

283 Erich Fromm, *Escape from Freedom* (New York: Avon Books, 1941), p. 50.

284 Rebecca Hall, *Voiceless Victims* (London: Wildwood House, 1984), p. xii.

285 Arnold S. Kaufman, "On Alienation," *Inquiry* 8, no. 2 (Summer 1965): 143.

286 Lewis Feuer, "What Is Alienation? The Career of a Concept," *New Politics* 1, no. 3 (Spring 1962): 132.

287 Kenneth Keniston, *The Uncommitted: Alienated Youth in American Society* (New York: Harcourt, Brace & World, 1965), p. 452.

288 Arne Naess, "The Shallow and the Deep, Long-Range Ecology Movement: A Summary," *Inquiry* 16 (1973): 95–100.

289 Ariel Salleh, "Class, Race, and Gender Discourse in the Ecofeminism/ Deep Ecology Debate," *Environmental Ethics* 15, no. 3 (Fall 1993): 225.

290 Mary Daly, *Pure Lust* (San Francisco: HarperSanFrancisco, 1984), p. 351.

291 Winthrop D. Jordan, *The White Man's Burden* (London: Oxford University Press, 1974), p. 61.

292 Robert J. Lifton with Eric Markusen, "Genocidal Ideology: Trauma and Cure," *On Prejudice: A Global Perspective*, ed. Daniela Gioseffi (New York: Doubleday, 1993), p. 285.

293 Ibid., 288.

294 J. Baird Callicott, "Animal Liberation: A Triangular Affair," *The Animal Rights/Environmental Ethics Debate*, ed. Eugene C. Hargrove (New York: State University of New York Press, 1992), p. 57.

295 Peter Singer, *Animal Liberation* (New York: Random House, Inc., 1990), pp. 7–8.

296 W.K. Frankena, "Ethics and the Environment," *Ethics and Problems of the 21st Century*, ed. K.E. Goodpastor and K.M. Sayre. (Notre Dame, IN: University of Notre Dame Press, 1979), pp. 11–15.

297 Joel Feinberg, "The Rights of Animals and Unborn Generations," *Philosophy and Environmental Crisis*, ed. William T. Blackstone (Athens: University of Georgia Press, 1974), pp. 49, 52.

298 Bernard Rollin, *Animal Rights and Human Morality* (New York: Prometheus Books, 1981), p. 42.

299 Spence Carlton, "Human Needs Are Not More Important than Animal Rights," *Animal Rights: Opposing Viewpoints*, ed. Janelle Rohr (San Diego, CA: Greenhaven Press, 1989), p. 44.

300 Tom Regan, "The Case for Animal Rights," *Animal Rights and Human Obligations*, ed. Tom Regan and Peter Singer (Upper Saddle River, NJ: Prentice Hall, 1989), p. 112.

301 Tom Regan, *A Case for Animal Rights* (Berkeley: University of California Press, 1983), p. 319. Regan also includes rocks and glaciers on his list of natural objects that may someday be determined conscious.

302 Michael W. Fox, *Inhumane Society* (New York: St. Martin's Press, 1990), p. 228.

303 Ibid., 120.

304 Ibid., 121.

305 S.F. Sapontzis, *Morals, Reason, and Animals* (Philadelphia: Temple University Press, 1987), p. 76. Also see page 84.

306 Edward Maitland, *Anna Kingsford: Her Life, Letters, Diary and Work*, Vol. 2 (London: Redway, 1896), pp. 223–224.

307 Martin Luther King, Jr., "Letter from the Birmingham City Jail," in *Applied Ethics: A Multicultural Approach*, eds. Larry May & Shari Collins Sharratt (Upper Saddle River, NJ: Prentice Hall, 1994), p. 234.

308 Karen J. Warren, "Feminism and Ecology: Making Connections," *Environmental Ethics* 9 (1987): 18.

309 Karen J. Warren, "The Power and Promise of Ecological Feminism," in *Applied Ethics: A Multicultural Approach*, eds. Larry May & Shari Collins Sharratt (Upper Saddle River, NJ: Prentice-Hall, Inc., 1994), p. 115.

310 Victoria Lee Erickson, *Where Silence Speaks* (Minneapolis, MN: For-

tress Press, 1993), p. 166. See also page 198.

311 Rosemary Radford Ruether, *Sexism and God-Talk: Toward a Feminist Theology* (Boston: Beacon Press, 1983), p. 32.

312 Greta Gaard, *Ecofeminism: Women, Animals, Nature* (Philadelphia: Temple University Press, 1993), p. 61.

313 Carol J. Adams, *The Sexual Politics of Meat* (New York: The Continuum Publishing Company, 1992), p. 16.

314 Ibid., 70.

315 Ibid., 153.

316 Robert D. Bullard, *Dumping in Dixie* (Boulder, CO: Westview Press, 1994), pp. 58, 66, 94, 124.

317 H.J. McCloskey, "Rights," *Philosophical Quarterly* 15 (1965): 253.

318 The "other minds problem" argues that we can never really know what is in the minds of other people.

319 Peter Tompkins and Christopher Bird, *The Secret Life of Plants* (New York: Harper & Row, 1973), p. xi.

320 Evan Bush, "Scientists Push New Paradigm of Animal Consciousness, Saying Even Insects May Be Sentient," *NBC News* (April 2024). See *https://www.nbcnews.com/science/science-news/animal-consciousness-scientists-push-new-paradigm-rcna148213* (Internet search on April 26, 2024).

321 The Canadian Press, "Conscious, Sentient Thought Likely for Many or Most Animals: Scientists," *Victoria News* (April 23, 2024). See *https://www.vicnews.com/trending-now/conscious-sentient-thought-likely-for-many-or-most-animals-scientists-7348678* (Internet search on April 26, 2024).

322 Marc Bekoff, "Insect Sentience: Science, Pain, Ethics, and Welfare," *Psychology Today* (March 30, 2023). See *https://www.psychologytoday.com/us/blog/animal-emotions/202303/insect-sentience-science-pain-ethics-and-welfare* (Internet search on April 26, 2024).

323 Alexander Lee, "The Intelligence of Earthworms," *History Today* (June 6, 2020). See *https://www.historytoday.com/archive/natural-histories/intelligence-earthworms* (Internet search on April 26, 2024).

324 Tam Hunt, "Where Does Consciousness Come From? It Could All Be Vibrations," *PsyPost* (April 26, 2024). See *https://www.psypost.org/where-does-consciousness-come-from-it-could-all-be-vibrations/* (Internet search on

April 26, 2024).

325 Mark Bekoff, "The Future of Animal Sentience: Colorado Can Lead the Way," *The Marc Bekoff Blog* (November 20, 2022). See *https://marcbekoff.com/marcs-essays/f/the-future-of-animal-sentience-colorado-can-lead-the-way* (Internet search on April 26, 2024).

326 Ibid.

327 Marc Bekoff, "Insect Sentience: Science, Pain, Ethics, and Welfare," *Psychology Today* (March 30, 2023). See *https://www.psychologytoday.com/us/blog/animal-emotions/202303/insect-sentience-science-pain-ethics-and-welfare* (Internet search on April 26, 2024).

328 The Canadian Press, "Conscious, Sentient Thought Likely for Many or Most Animals: Scientists," *Victoria News* (April 23, 2024). See *https://www.vicnews.com/trending-now/conscious-sentient-thought-likely-for-many-or-most-animals-scientists-7348678* (Internet search on April 26, 2024).

329 Evan Bush, "Scientists Push New Paradigm of Animal Consciousness, Saying Even Insects May Be Sentient," *NBC News* (April 2024). See *https://www.nbcnews.com/science/science-news/animal-consciousness-scientists-push-new-paradigm-rcna148213* (Internet search on April 26, 2024).

330 The Canadian Press, "Conscious, Sentient Thought Likely for Many or Most Animals: Scientists," *Victoria News* (April 23, 2024). See *https://www.vicnews.com/trending-now/conscious-sentient-thought-likely-for-many-or-most-animals-scientists-7348678* (Internet search on April 26, 2024).

331 Michelle Starr, "Plants Really Do 'Scream.' We've Simply Never Heard It Until Now," *Science Alert* (April 2, 2024). See *https://www.sciencealert.com/plants-really-do-scream-weve-simply-never-heard-it-until-now* (Internet search on May 1, 2024).

332 Editor, "Plant Consciousness: The Fascinating Evidence Showing Plants Have Human Level Intelligence, Feelings, Pain and More." See *http://www.esalq.usp.br/lepse/imgs/conteudo_thumb/Plant-Consciousness---The-Fascinating-Evidence-Showing-Plants-Have-Human-Level-Intelligence--Feelings--Pain-and-More.pdf* (Internet search on May 1, 2024).

333 Justin Faerman, "The Man Who Talked to Plants: The Visionary Research of Cleve Backster," *Conscious Lifestyle Magazine* (Fall 2014). See *https://www.consciouslifestylemag.com/cleve-backster-research-plants/* (Internet search on May 1, 2024).

334 K. Yokawa, T. Kagenishi, A. Pavlovic, S. Gall, M. Weiland, S. Mancuso and F. Baluska, "Anesthetics Stop Diverse Plant Organ Movements, Af-

fect Endocytic Vesicle Recycling and ROS Homeostasis, and Block Action Potentials in Venus Flytraps," *Botany* (December 11, 2017). See *https://academic.oup.com/aob/article/122/5/747/4722571?login=false* (Internet search on May 1, 2024).

335 Zoe Schlanger, "The Mysteries of Plant 'Intelligence,'" *The Atlantic* (June 2024). See *https://www.theatlantic.com/magazine/archive/2024/06/plant-consciousness-intelligence-light-eaters/678207/* (Internet search on May 1, 2024).

336 Natalie Lawrence, "The Radical New Experiments that Hint at Plant Consciousness," *New Scientist* (August 24, 2024). See *https://www.newscientist.com/article/mg25534012-800-the-radical-new-experiments-that-hint-at-plant-consciousness/* (Internet search on May 1, 2024).

337 Ibid.

338 Christopher D. Stone, "Should Trees Have Standing? Toward Legal Rights for Natural Objects," *The Environmental Ethics and Policy Book*, eds. Donald VanDeVeer & Christine Pierce (Belmont, CA: Wadsworth Publishing Company, 1994), p. 117.

339 Steven Sapontzis, *Morals, Reason, and Animals* (Philadelphia: Temple University Press, 1987), p. 74.

340 Jessica Damiano, "Unearthing Your Potato Harvest: How Do You Know When to Dig?" Associated Press (August 9, 2022). See *https://apnews.com/article/gardening-d99ae88544f9531f7cb4384dfc3e2a07* (Internet search on May 3, 2024).

341 Jemina Weber, "'Vegans Don't Realize Billions of Animals Are Killed Growing Crops' Says Farmer," *Plant Based News* (July 4, 2019). See *https://plantbasednews.org/culture/billions-animals-killed-growing-crops/* (Internet search on May 3, 2024).

342 Ibid.

Chapter Nine

343 Michael Tobias, "Jainism and Ecology: Views of Nature, Nonviolence, and Vegetarianism," in *Worldviews and Ecology: Religion, Philosophy and the Environment*, eds. Mary Evelyn Tucker and John A. Grim (New York: Orbis Books, 1994), p. 138. There are about 30,000 adherents of Jainism in America.

344 "Jainism in the United States." Wikipedia. See https://en.wikipedia.org/wiki/Jainism_in_the_United_States (Internet search on May 14, 2024).

345 George Woodcock, *Mohandas Gandhi* (New York: The Viking Press, 1971), p. 60.

346 Hermann Jacobi, "The Gaina Sutras," in *Sacred Books of the East* ed. F. Max Muller (Oxford, UK: Clarendon Press, 1884), pp. 79–90.

347 Shri Kunda Kunda Acharya, *Samayasara* (New York: AMS Press, 1974), p. 6.

348 Christopher Key Chapple, *Nonviolence to Animals, Earth, and Self in Asian Traditions* (New York: State University of New York Press, 1993), p. 10. Also see Sagarmal Jain, *Saman Suttam* (India: Sarva Seva Sangh Prakashan, 1993), p. 57. Jainism offers, "Killing a living being is killing oneself; showing compassion to a living being is showing compassion to oneself. He who does his own good, should avoid causing harm to a living being."

349 Christopher Key Chapple, *Nonviolence to Animals, Earth, and Self in Asian Traditions* (New York: State University of New York Press, 1993), pp. 86–87, 93. See also p. 44.

350 H. R. Kapadia, *Introduction to Haribhadra Suri's Anekantajayapataka with His Own Commentary and Municandra Suri's Supercommentary* (Baroda: Oriental Institute, 1947), p. cxiv.

351 Christopher Key Chapple, *Nonviolence to Animals, Earth, and Self in Asian Traditions* (New York: State University of New York, 1993), p. 111.

352 Pravin K. Shah, *Essence of World Religions* (Cary, NC: Jain Study Center, 1994), p. 5.

353 Nathmal Tatia, *Studies in Jaina Philosophy* (India: P.V. Research Institute, 1951), p. 18. "Evil" is meant in a non-absolute sense.

354 Michael Tobias, "Jainism and Ecology: Views of Nature, Nonviolence, and Vegetarianism," in *Worldviews and Ecology: Religion, Philosophy, and the Environment*, eds. Mary Evelyn Tucker and John A. Grim (New York: Orbis Books, 1994), p. 139.

355 Nathmal Tatia, *Studies in Jaina Philosophy* (India: P.V. Research Institute, 1951), pp. 21–22. A Jain monk "must use . . . [nonviolent] language when describing nature [i.e., when speaking about vegetables, trees, or wild fruits]." See Hermann Jacobi, *Jaina Sutras*, 1 (New Delhi, India: Motilal Banarsidass, 1980), pp. 152–156. Also see Sagarmal Jain, *Saman Suttam* (India: Sarva Seva Sangh Prakasham, 1993), p. 149.

356 Knut A. Jacobsen, "The Institutionalization of the Ethics of 'Non-Injury'

toward All 'Beings' in Ancient India." *Environmental Ethics* 16, no. 3 (Fall 1994): 294.

357 Sagarmal Jain, *Saman Suttam* (India: Sarva Seva Sangh Prakasham, 1993), p. 145.

358 Ibid., 145–147.

359 Nathmal Tatia, *Studies in Jaina Philosophy* (India: P.V. Research Institute, 1951), p. 19.

360 Michael Tobias, "Jainism and Ecology: Views of Nature, Nonviolence, and Vegetarianism," in *Worldviews and Ecology: Religion, Philosophy, and the Environment*, eds. Mary Evelyn Tucker and John A. Grim (New York: Orbis Books, 1994), p. 141.

361 Sagarmal Jain, *Saman Suttam* (India: Sarva Seva Sangh Prakashan, 1993), p. 117.

362 Balwant Nevaskar, *Capitalists without Capitalism* (Westport CT: Greenwood Publishing Corporation, 1971), p. 158.

363 Michael Tobias, "Jainism and Ecology: Views of Nature, Nonviolence, and Vegetarianism," in *Worldviews and Ecology: Religion, Philosophy, and the Environment*, eds. Mary Evelyn Tucker and John A. Grim (New York: Orbis Books, 1994), p. 142.

364 Christopher Key Chapple, *Nonviolence to Animals, Earth, and Self in Asian Traditions* (New York: State University of New York Press, 1993), p. 10.

365 Michael Tobias, "Jainism and Ecology: Views of Nature, Nonviolence, and Vegetarianism," in *Worldviews and Ecology: Religion, Philosophy, and the Environment*, eds. Mary Evelyn Tucker and John A. Grim (New York: Orbis Books, 1994), p. 143.

366 An orthodox Jain is told that it is best to eat food that has been partially eaten by other animals or fruit that has already fallen from a tree.

367 Sagarmal Jain, *Saman Suttam* (India: Sarva Seva Sangh Prakashan, 1993), p. 57. As an aside, there are a few AR philosophers who recommend rescuing wild animals from predators, a practice that, if universally adopted, would insert humans into the role of kingmaker or savior, designating who lives and who dies, choosing between the hungry and their prey. This would increase the *difficulty quotient* exponentially, making it harder to be an AR activist. If the movement progresses toward a concern for all living entities, as this text recommends, the idea of picking winners and losers in the wilder-

ness would be a nonstarter, an onerous and absurd task. In *The Case for Animal Rights*, Tom Regan comes close to suggesting the removal of predators from natural systems. (Berkeley: University of California Press, 1983), pp. 361–362. Also, I dined with philosopher Peter Singer in June 2007, and he intimated that people might someday need to go into the wilderness to rescue animals. See *Philosophy Now* (Issue 67) at *https://philosophynow.org/issues/67/Guess_Whos_Coming_To_Dinner_The_controversial_Peter_Singer* (Internet search on May 16, 2024).

368 They believe that if humans are not going to live in the desert, they should live in cities so as to negatively impact as few nonhumans as possible.

369 Knut A. Jacobsen, "The Institutionalization of the Ethics of 'Non-Injury' towards All 'Beings' in Ancient India," *Environmental Ethics* 16, no. 3 (Fall 1994): 296.

370 John Robbins, *Diet for a New America* (Walpole, NH: Stillpoint Publishing, 1987).

371 Crystal Heath, "19th-Century Animal Rights Activists Had a Lot of Moxie. Here's How to Get It Back," *Vox* (August 9, 2024). See *https://www.vox.com/future-perfect/363275/meat-industry-lobbying-usda-animal-rights-progressive-movement-vegetarianism* (Internet search on August 9, 2024).

Chapter Ten

372 Nikolas Kompridis, "Technology's Challenge to Democracy," *Parrhesia 8* (2009). See *http://www.parrhesiajournal.org/parrhesia08/parrhesia08_kompridis.pdf* (Searched on August 30, 2011).

373 Robert Maynard Hutchins, "Democracy and Human Nature." Excerpt from John Bartlett's *Familiar Quotations* (Boston: Little Brown and Company, 1980), p. 845.

374 Keph Senett, "Following Examples Set by Ecuador and Bolivia, Turkey Is Considering Ecological Constitution," (May 23, 2011). See *http://www.pvpulse.com/en/news/world-news/following-examples-set-by-ecuador-and-bolivia-turkey-is-considering-ecological-constitution* (Searched August 30, 2011). Also see Xinhua Editor, "Feature: Turkey Passes New Law to Protect Animals," *Xinhua* (July 3, 2021). See *http://www.xinhuanet.com/english/europe/2021-07/03/c_1310041502.htm* (Internet search on May 24, 2024).

375 Erin, Evans, "Constitutional Inclusion of Animal Rights in Germany and Switzerland: How Did Animal Protection Become an Issue of National Importance?" *Society and Animals* (2010): 231–250. See *http://www.animalsandsociety.org/assets/443_evansnutshell.pdf* (Internet search on May 24,

2024).

376 Times of India World Desk, "World's First City Where Non-Veg Is Illegal," *Times of India* (July 26, 2024). See *https://timesofindia.indiatimes.com/world/worlds-first-city-where-non-veg-is-illegal/articleshow/111689287.cms* (Internet search on January 28, 2025).

377 Editor, "Italy Praised by American Animal Rights Group," *Italy Magazine* (January 13, 2006). See *https://www.italymagazine.com/featured-story/italy-praised-american-animal-rights-group* (Internet search on May 24, 2024).

378 Bruce Johnston, "Italian Animal Rights Law Puts Lobster Off the Menu," *The Telegraph*, (March 7, 2004). See *http://www.telegraph.co.uk/news/worldnews/europe/italy/1456270/Italian-animal-rights-law-puts-lobster-off-the-menu.html* (Internet search on May 24, 2024).

379 "Meat Consumption Per Capita," *The Guardian* (September 2, 2009). See *http://www.guardian.co.uk/environment/datablog/2009/sep/02/meat-consumption-per-capita-climate-change* (Internet search on May 24, 2024).

380 Animal Welfare Institute, "The Welfare of Birds at Slaughter in the United States," (November 2020), See *https://awionline.org/sites/default/files/publication/digital_download/20TheWelfareBirdsSlaughter.pdf* (Internet search on June 5, 2024).

381 Carol Gilligan, *In a Different Voice: Psychological Theory and Women's Development* (Cambridge, MA: Harvard University Press, 1982), pp. 18–19.

382 Lawrence Kohlberg, *Moral Development and Behavior* (New York: Holt, Rinehart and Winston. 1976), np.

383 Seyla Benhabib, "The Generalized and Concrete Other: The Kohlberg-Gilligan Controversy and Moral Theory," *Women and Moral Theory* (1991), ed. Eva Feder Kittay and Diana T. Meyers (Lanham, MD: Rowman & Littlefield), p. 154.

384 Ibid., 169.

385 Ibid., 168.

386 Susan Moller Okin, "Reason and Feeling in Thinking about Justice," *Feminism and Political Theory*, ed. Cass R. Sunstein (Chicago: University of Chicago, 1989), p. 19.

387 John Rawls, *A Theory of Justice* (Cambridge, MA:Belknap Press of Harvard University Press, 1971), p. 60.

388 Ibid., 17.

389 Ibid., 512.

390 Ibid., 505.

391 Ibid., 137.

392 Lilly-Marlene Russow, "Animals in the Original Position," *Between the Species*, 8, no. 4 (Fall 1992): 224.

393 The "maximin" suggests that society should be arranged so as to benefit the least-advantaged persons. (When I use this term, I am referring to nonhumans as "persons.")

394 Donald VanDeVeer, "Interspecific Justice," *Inquiry* (1979): 371–372.

395 Lilly-Marlene Russow, "Animals in the Original Position," *Between the Species*, 8, no. 4 (Fall 1992): 227.

396 Ibid., 227.

397 John Rawls, *A Theory of Justice* (Cambridge, MA: The Belknap Press of Harvard University Press, 1971), p. 510.

398 Lilly-Marlene Russow, "Animals in the Original Position," *Between the Species*, 8, no. 4 (Fall 1992): 228.

399 James A. Donahue, "The Use of Virtue and Character in Applied Ethics," *Horizons,* 17, no. 2 (Fall 1990): 240.

400 Michael Davis, "Seven Step Method for Ethical Decision-Making." See *https://onlineethics.org/cases/seven-step-method-ethical-decision-making* (Internet search on June 6, 2024).

401 "The Seven Steps Method: A Method for Analyzing Cases in Research Ethics and Research Integrity," The Embassy of Good Science (April 29, 2019). See *https://embassy.science/wiki/Instruction:6b129846-c455-4849-9eaf-0d25f3c5600e*. Also see *https://zenodo.org/records/4905906* (Internet searches on June 6, 2024).

402 Michael Davis, *Ethics and the University* (London: Routledge, 1999), pp. 166–167.

403 Within this book, "society" does not merely define a group of human beings but refers to a community inclusive of all living things.

404 Benedict de Spinoza, *A Theologico-Political Treatise, A Political Treatise* (New York: Dover Publications, Inc., 1951), p. 261.

Chapter Eleven

405 John B. Cobb, Jr., *Matters of Life and Death* (Louisville, KY: John Knox Press, 1991), pp. 25, 29.

406 George Sessions, Preface, *Deep Ecology for the 21st Century*, ed. George Sessions (Boston: Shambhala, 1995) p. xiii. Also see Louis P. Pojman, *Environmental Ethics* (Boston: Jones and Bartlett Publishers, 1994), pp. 84–102.

407 Bill Devall, "The Deep Ecology Movement," *Ecology*, ed. Carolyn Merchant (Atlantic Highlands, NJ: Humanities Press, 1994), pp. 133–135.

408 Aldo Leopold, "The Land Ethic," *Environmental Ethics and Policy Book*, eds. D. VanDeVeer and C. Pierce (Boston: Wadsworth, 1994), p. 139.

409 Aldo Leopold, *A Sand County Almanac: And Sketches Here and There* (Oxford, UK: Oxford University Press, 1989), p. 146.

410 Tom Regan, *The Case for Animal Rights* (Berkeley: University of California, 1983), p. 361.

411 J. Baird Callicott, "Animal Liberation: A Triangular Affair," *The Animal Rights/Environmental Ethics Debate*, ed. Eugene C. Hargrove (New York: State University of New York Press, 1992), p. 43.

412 J.R. Absher, "We Support Hunting But . . ." (March 25, 2010). See *https://www.outdoorlife.com/blogs/newshound/2010/03/sierra-club-we-support-hunting/* (Internet search on June 11, 2024).

413 Janet Albrechtsen, "Climate Change Cure Is Warm and Fuzzy," *The Republic* (January 2, 2008). See *https://freerepublic.com/focus/f-news/1950796/posts* (Internet search on June 11, 2024).

414 Shoba Rao, "Kangaroos to be Killed in Canberra under Culling Program," *The Telegraph* (May 19, 2008). See *http://www.dailytelegraph.com.au/news/national/kangaroos-to-be-killed-in-canberra-under-culling-program/story-e6freuzr-1111116381352* (Internet search on August 26, 2011).

415 Claire Fenwicke, "Review Comments 'Extremely Impressive' Kangaroo Cull Program to Protect Threatened Species," *Riotact* (May 15, 2024). See *https://the-riotact.com/review-commends-extremely-impressive-kangaroo-cull-program-to-protect-threatened-species/770079* (Internet search on June 11, 2024).

416 Karen Collier, "Greenpeace Urges Kangaroo Consumption to Fight Global Warming," *Herald Sun* (October 10, 2007). See http://www.

heraldsun.com.au/news/national/eat-a-roo-save-the-world/story-e6fr-f7l6-1111114612144 (Internet search on July 29, 2011). Also see Jennifer Marohasy, "Eat Kangaroos to Help Save the Planet – Greenpeace" (October 11, 2007). See *https://jennifermarohasy.com/2007/10/eat-kangaroos-to-help-save-the-planet-greenpeace/* (Internet search on June 11, 2024).

417 George Sessions, "Ecocentrism and the Anthropocentric Detour," *Deep Ecology for the 21st Century*, ed. George Sessions (Boston: Shambhala, 1995), p. 157.

418 George Sessions, "Arne Naess on Deep Ecology and Ecosophy," *Deep Ecology for the 21st Century* (Boston: Shambhala, 1995), p. 188.

419 Eugene C. Hargrove, Preface, *The Animal Rights/Environmental Ethics Debate*, ed. Eugene C. Hargrove (New York: State University of New York Press, 1992), p. xi.

420 David Henry Thoreau, *Natural History of Massachusetts*, 3 Dial 19 (1842). See *https://archive.vcu.edu/english/engweb/transcendentalism/authors/thoreau/nathist.html pp. 20-21* (Internet search on June 13, 2024).

421 William O. Douglas, *Points of Rebellion* (New York: Random House, January 1, 1970), pp. 50–51.

422 Surveillance tools would need to be made in such a way as to not negatively impact the environment.

423 On occasion, law enforcement may need to enter Ecoland to arrest intruders. Plus, there could be some emergency situations in which firefighters will need to put out flames that threaten Bioland.

424 Balthasar Gracian, *The Pocket Oracle and Art of Prudence* (New York: Penguin Classics, March 29, 2011).

425 John Robbins, *Diet for a New America* (Walpole, NH: Stillpoint Publishing, 1987), pp. 360, 362.

426 World Wildlife Fund, "The Effects of Deforestation." See *https://www.wwf.org.uk/learn/effects-of/deforestation* (Internet search on June 12, 2024).

427 United States Census Bureau, "National Wilderness Month: September 2023" (September 2023). See *https://www.census.gov/newsroom/stories/wilderness-month.html* (Internet search on June 13, 2024).

428 Alecks Phillips, "Area Twice the Size of California to be Allowed to Return to Nature," *Newsweek* (January 30, 2024). See *https://www.newsweek.com/area-twice-size-california-return-nature-rewilding-climate-*

change-1865221# (Internet search on June 26, 2024).

429 Team of the Delegation to Turkiye, "Stop Fires! 90 Percent of Forest Fires Are Caused by Humans," (October 10, 2023). See *https://www.eeas.europa.eu/delegations/t%C3%BCrkiye/stop-fires-90-cent-forest-fires-are-caused-humans_en?s=230* (Internet search on June 13, 2024).

430 California Wildlife Conservation Board, "Natural Heritage Preservation Tax Credit Program," See *https://wcb.ca.gov/Programs/Natural-Heritage-Preservation-Tax-Credit* (Internet search on June 12, 2024).

431 Land Trust Alliance, "State Tax Credits for Donation of a Conservation Easement." See *https://www.landcan.org/article/state-tax-credits-for-donation-of-a-conservation-easement/1616#* (Internet search on June 13, 2024).

432 Zayna Syed, "Why It Matters that Humans and Nature Are Growing Apart," *Popular Science* (January 4, 2023). See *https://www.popsci.com/environment/humans-nature-relationship-decline/* (Internet search on June 20, 2024).

433 Sue Reid, "Europe's Plummeting Birth Rate Timebomb: To Keep a Stable Population, Countries Need a Birthrate of 2.1 Babies per Woman. The Continent Races a 'Staggering Social Change,' writes Sue Reid," *The Daily Mail* (June 19, 2024). See *https://www.dailymail.co.uk/news/article-13547253/Europes-plummeting-birth-rate-timebomb-stable-population-countries-need-birth-rate-2-1-babies-woman-continent-faces-staggering-social-change-writes-SUE-REID.html* (Internet search on June 20, 2024).

434 "Biocentric," *Webster's Encyclopedic Unabridged Dictionary of the English Language* (New York: Gramercy Books, 1989), p. 149.

435 Paul Taylor, "Biocentric Egalitarianism," *Environmental Ethics*, ed. Louis P. Pojman (Boston: Jones and Bartlett Publishers, 1994), p. 76.

436 Jim Cameron, "Why Traffic Signals Are Red, Yellow, Green—and Expensive," (December 31, 2023) *CT Mirror*. See *https://ctmirror.org/2023/12/31/why-traffic-signals-are-red-green-and-expensive/* (Internet search on June 15, 2024).

437 PETA, "Facts and Statistics About Animal Testing," (2022). See *https://www.peta.org/issues/animals-used-for-experimentation/animals-used-experimentation-factsheets/animal-experiments-overview/* (Internet search on June 15, 2024). Also see K. Taylor, N. Gordon, G. Langley, and W. Higgins, "Estimates for Worldwide Laboratory Animal Use in 2005," *Alternatives to Laboratory Animals* 36 (2008): 327–342.

438 Daniel G. Hackam and Donald A. Redelmeier, "Translation of Research

Evidence from Animals to Human," *The Journal of the American Medical Association* 296 (2006): 1731–1732.

439 Michael B. Bracken, "Why Animal Studies Are Often Poor Predictors of Human Reactions to Exposure," *Journal of the Royal Society of Medicine* (March 1, 2009). See *https://www.ncbi.nlm.nih.gov/pmc/articles/PMC2746847/* (Internet search on June 15, 2024).

440 Ana Goni-Lessan, Dan Rorabaugh, and Mike Snider, "Florida Bans Lab-Grown Meat as Other States Weigh It: What's Their Beef with Cultured Meat?" *USA Today* (May 5, 2024). See *https://www.usatoday.com/story/money/food/2024/05/05/florida-lab-grown-meat-ban/73569976007/* (Internet search on June 16, 2024). It should be noted that Governor Ron DeSantis appears to be relatively good on policy related to protecting animals, so it is unclear why he took such a strong stance against cultured meat. Also see Cecilia Nowell, "'Political Efforts': The Republican States Trying to Ban Lab-Grown Meat," *The Guardian* (April 9, 2024). See *https://www.theguardian.com/environment/2024/apr/09/us-states-republicans-banning-lab-grown-meat* (Internet search on June 16, 2024).

441 Tweet, November 2, 2022.

442 "Industry Profile: Agricultural Services/Products," Open Secrets (2024). See *https://www.opensecrets.org/federal-lobbying/industries/summary?id=A07* (Internet search on June 17, 2024).

443 Joshua Hawkins, "Four High School Students Invented a Device that Prevents Roadkill," BGR (October 7, 2024). See *https://bgr.com/tech/four-high-school-students-invented-a-device-that-prevents-roadkill/* (Internet search on December 19, 2024).

444 Alexandra Romero, "See Renderings of the Wildlife Crossing over the 101 Freeway in Agoura Hills," *NBC Los Angeles* (April 17, 2024). See *https://www.nbclosangeles.com/local/see-renderings-of-the-wildlife-crossing-over-the-101-freeway-in-agoura-hills/3390691/* (Internet search on June 20, 2024).

445 Catrin Einhorn, "Bridges and Tunnels in Colorado Are Helping Animals Commute," *New York Times* (March 25, 2025). See *https://www.nytimes.com/2025/03/25/climate/wildlife-crossings-colorado.html* (Internet search on April 30, 2025).

446 Sean Riley, "Edible Beer Packaging from Eco-Friendly Ingredients," Packaging World (October 19, 2023). See *https://www.packworld.com/sustainable-packaging/article/22876685/beer-packaging-from-ecofriendly-beer-ingredients* (Internet search on July 10, 2024).

447 Rachel Kurzius and Jaclyn Peiser, "Your Fridge Isn't Built to Last. Here's Why," *Washington Post* (July 2, 2024). See *https://www.washingtonpost.com/home/2024/07/02/why-refrigerator-oven-dishwasher-break/* (Internet search on August 8, 2024).

448 Rachel Wolfe, "The Lifespan of Large Appliances Is Shrinking," *Wall Street Journal* (February 20, 2024). See *https://www.wsj.com/personal-finance/the-lifespan-of-large-appliances-is-shrinking-e5fb205b* (Internet search on August 6. 2024).

449 Sabrina Moreno and Karri Peifer, "The Current: Our Nearly Full Landfills," *Axios* (June 25, 2024). See *https://www.axios.com/local/richmond/2024/06/25/the-current-our-nearly-full-landfills* (Internet search on August 6, 2024). Also see Ryan Brainard, "Linn County Landfill Will Be Full 8 Years Earlier than Expected," *98.1 KHAK* (July 12, 2024). See *https://khak.com/linn-county-landfill-closing/* (Internet search on August 6, 2024).

450 Hiroko Tabuchi, "'Garbage Lasagna': Dumps Are a Big Driver of Warming, Study Says," *New York Times* (March 28, 2024). See *https://www.nytimes.com/2024/03/28/climate/landfills-methane-emissions.html* (Internet search on August 6, 2024).

Chapter Twelve

451 Vivek Ramaswamy ran for president in the 2024 Republican presidential primary and was assisting the 2025 Trump administration via the Department of Government Efficiency (DOGE) until January 27, 2025, when he resigned so he could run for governor of Ohio. Dr. Ben Carson ran for president in 2016 and then served as the Secretary of Housing and Urban Development from 2017 to 2021. Tulsi Gabbard was a member of the House of Representatives from January 2013 to January 2021. She was chosen by President Donald Trump to be the Director of National Intelligence and was confirmed for this post in January 2025.

452 Adams was a Democrat until April 2025, when he became an independent candidate.

453 Dennis Kucinich was an Ohio congressman for 16 years. He was also the mayor of Cleveland, a member of the Ohio senate, and sought the Democratic nomination for president of the United States in 2004 and 2008.

454 Josh James, "Sen. Paul Presses FDA for Action on Law Ending Mandatory Animal Testing on Drugs," *WUKY* (November 21, 2024). See *https://www.wuky.org/local-regional-news/2023-11-21/sen-paul-presses-fda-for-action-on-law-ending-mandatory-animal-testing-on-drugs* (Internet search on June 18, 2024).

455 Kimbery K. Smith, *Governing Animals* (Oxford, UK: Oxford University Press, 2012), p. 110.

456 Hannah Sentenac, "Time to Change Your Voter Registration: There's a Vegan Political Party," Harm.less (July 1, 2015). See *https://www.bharmless.com/time-to-change-your-voter-registration-theres-a-vegan-political-party/* (Internet search on June 19, 2024).

457 Editor, "American Dietary Preferences Are Split across Party Lines," *The Economist* (November 22, 2008). See *https://www.economist.com/graphic-detail/2018/11/22/american-dietary-preferences-are-split-across-party-lines* (Internet search on June 19, 2024).

458 Editor, "Political Parties." See *https://www.mountvernon.org/george-washington/the-first-president/political-parties/* (Internet search on June 20, 2024).

459 Sparsha Saha, "Why Don't Politicians Talk about Meat? The Political Psychology of Human-Animal Relations in Elections," *Frontiers in Psychology* (June 23, 2023). See *https://www.ncbi.nlm.nih.gov/pmc/articles/PMC10327565/* (Internet search on June 21, 2024).

460 Alex Smith, "The Coming 'Meat Vortex,'" *The Breakthrough Institute* (November 30, 2021). See *https://thebreakthrough.org/journal/no-15-winter-2022/meat-vortex-alternative-protein* (Internet search on June 21, 2024).

461 Ibid.

462 Ibid.

463 Jeffrey M. Jones, "In U.S., 4% Identify as Vegetarian, 1% as Vegan," *Gallup* (August 24, 2023). See *https://news.gallup.com/poll/510038/identify-vegetarian-vegan.aspx#* (Internet search on June 21, 2024).

464 Lewis Bollard, "We Love Animals. Why Do We Torture Them?" Farm Animal Welfare Research Newsletter (July 18, 2023). See *https://farmanimalwelfare.substack.com/p/we-love-animals-why-do-we-torture* (Internet search on August 9, 2024).

465 Will Kymlicka and Sue Donaldson, "Animal Rights, Multiculturalism, and the Left," *Journal of Social Philosophy* 45, no. 1 (Spring 2014): 118.

466 Congress, "Recognizing the Duty of the Federal Government to Create a Green New Deal," 117th Congress (2021-2022). See *https://www.congress.gov/bill/117th-congress/house-resolution/332* (Internet search on June 21, 2024).

467 My memoir, *Rebel in High Heels*, details my fight against revenge porn. Also, a docuseries on Netflix called *The Most Hated Man on the Internet* outlines my struggles and success.

468 Editor, "Innovations Take Time to Catch On," *Economic Times* (February 9, 2004). See *https://economictimes.indiatimes.com/innovations-take-time-to-catch-on/articleshow/483059.cms* (Internet search on June 22, 2024).

469 Justin McCarthy, "U.S. Same-Sex Marriage Support Holds at 71% High," *Gallup* (June 5, 2023). See *https://news.gallup.com/poll/506636/sex-marriage-support-holds-high.aspx* (Internet search on June 22, 2024).

470 This was before Tucker Carlson left Fox News.

471 Megan Brenan and Jeffrey M. Jones, "Ethics Ratings of Nearly All Professions Down in U.S.," *Gallup* (January 22, 2024). See *https://news.gallup.com/poll/608903/ethics-ratings-nearly-professions-down.aspx* (Internet search on June 18, 2024).

Appendix

472 Richard J. Herrnstein and Charles Murray, *The Bell Curve: Intelligence and Class Structure in American Life* (New York: Free Press, 1994). See also David C. Rowe, *The Limits of Family Influence: Genes, Experience, and Behavior* (New York: Guilford Press, 1994). See also Robert Plomin, Michael F. Scheier, C.S. Bergman, N.L. Pederen, J.R. Nesselroade, and Gerald E. McClearn, "Optimism, Pessimism and Mental Health," *Personality and Individual Differences* 13 (1992): 922.

473 Paul D. Lipsitt, Stephen L., Buka and Lewis P. Lipsitt. "Early Intelligence Scores and Subsequent Delinquency: A Prospective Study," *American Journal of Family Therapy* 18 (1990): 197–208.

474 Alfred Blumenstein, David P. Farrington, and Soumyo Moitra, "Delinquency Careers: Innocents, Desisters, and Persisters," *Crime and Justice: A Review of Research*, eds. Michael H. Tonry and Norval Morris (Chicago: University of Chicago Press, 1985), pp. 187–219.

475 James Q. Wilson and Richard J. Herrnstein, *Crime and Human Nature* (New York: Simon & Schuster, 1985).

476 Howard Reichel and David Magnusson, *The Relationship of Intelligence to Registered Criminality* (University of Stockholm Reports from the Department of Psychology 676, 1988).

477 Emmy E. Werner, "High Risk Children in Young Adulthood: A Longitudinal Study from Birth to 32 Years," *American Journal of Orthopsy* 59

(1989): 72–81.

478 R.J. Herrnstein, "Criminogenic Traits," *Crime*, eds. James Q Wilson and Joan Petersilia (San Francisco: Institute for Contemporary Studies, 1995), p. 43.

479 Ibid., 47.

480 Avshalom Caspi, "Personality in the Life Course," *Journal of Personality and Social Psychology* 53 (1987): 1203–1213.

481 Marvin E. Wolfgang, Leonard Savitz, and Norman Johnson, *The Sociology of Crime and Delinquency* (New York: John Wiley and Sons, Inc., 1962), pp. 176–177.

482 M.M. Mesulam, "Frontal Cortex and Behaviors," *Annals of Neurology* 19 (1986): 319–323.

483 Patricia A Brennan, Sarnoff A. Mednick, and Jan Volavka, "Biomedical Factors in Crime," *Crime* (San Francisco: Institute for Contemporary Studies, 1995), p. 79.

484 David M. Ferguson, Joseph M. Boden, L. John Horwood, Allison Miller, and Martin A. Kennedy, "Moderating Role of the MAOA Genotype in Antisocial Behavior," *British Journal of Psychiatry* (January 2, 2018). See *http://bjp.rcpsych.org/content/200/2/116.abstract* (Internet search on January 26, 2024).

485 Steve Connor, "Do Your Genes Make You a Criminal?" *The Independent* (February 12, 1995). See *http://www.independent.co.uk/news/uk/do-your-genes-make-you-a-criminal-1572714.html* (Internet search on January 26, 2024).

486 Ewen Callaway, "Murderer with 'Aggression Genes' Gets Sentence Cut," *New Scientist* (November 3, 2009). See *http://www.newscientist.com/article/dn18098-murderer-with-aggression-genes-gets-sentence-cut.html* (Internet search on January 26, 2024).

487 Gareth Huw Davies, "Is Crime in the Blood – The Case of the Mean Genes," *Radio Times* (May 1996). See *http://media.gn.apc.org/members/3/index10.html* (Internet search on September 17, 2010.

488 Sharon Begley, "Why the Young Kill" *Newsweek* (May 3, 1999), p. 34.

489 R.J. Herrnstein, "Criminogenic Traits," *Crime*, eds. James Q. Wilson and Joan Petersilia (San Francisco: Institute for Contemporary Studies, 1995), p. 57.

490 R. Wright, "The Biology of Violence," *New Yorker* (March 5, 1995), p. 69. Also see L.A. Gottschalk, T. Rebello, M.S. Buchsbaum, H.G. Tucker, and E.L. Hodges, "Abnormalities in Hair Trace Elements as Indicators of Aberrant Behavior," *Comprehensive Psychiatry* 28 (1991): 212–223.

491 R.J. Herrnstein, "Criminogenic Traits," *Crime*, eds. James Q. Wilson and Joan Petersilia (San Francisco: Institute for Contemporary Studies, 1995). p. 57.

492 Due to the eugenics movement, 60,000 people were sterilized for so-called defects (e.g., feeble-mindedness), and in the early 1900s, fifteen states had laws that allowed the sterilization of criminals. Also see Stephen Jay Gould, *The Mismeasure of Man* (New York: W.W. Norton and Company, 1981), pp. 94–95, for Bischoff's study on the brains of assassins, murderers, and thieves.

493 Sharon Begley, "Why The Young Kill," *Newsweek* (3 May 1999), p. 32.

Bibliography

Absher, J.R. March 25, 2020. "We Support Hunting But . . ." *Outdoor Life*. Website *https://www.outdoorlife.com/blogs/newshound/2010/03/sierra-club-we-support-hunting/* (accessed on June 11, 2024).

Acharya, Shri Kunda Kunda. 1974. *Samayasara*. New York: AMS Press.

Adams, Carol. 1992. *The Sexual Politics of Meat*. New York: The Continuum Publishing Company.

Ahadi, Shafiqullah. May 8, 2023. "The Normalization of Evil and Social Indifferences in a Government of the Masses." *8 AM Media*. Website *https://8am.media/eng/the-normalization-of-evil-and-social-indifferences-in-a-government-of-the-masses/* (accessed on April 14, 2024).

Albrechtsen, Janet. January 2, 2008. "Climate Change Cure Is Warm and Fuzzy." *The Republic*. Website https://freerepublic.com/focus/f-news/1950796/posts (accessed on June 11, 2024).

The American Society for the Prevention of Cruelty to Animals. "Pet Statistics." Website *https://www.aspca.org/helping-people-pets/shelter-intake-and-surrender/pet-statistics* (accessed on April 24, 2024).

Anderson, Walter Truett. 1995. *The Truth About The Truth*. New York: G.P. Putnam's Sons.

Angier, Natalie. July 24, 2007. "Smart, Curious, Ticklish. Rats?" *The New York Times*. Science Section. Website http://www.nytimes.com/2007/07/24/science/24angi.html (accessed on April 6, 2024).

Animal Welfare Institute. November 2020. "The Welfare of Birds at Slaughter in the United States." Website https://awionline.org/

sites/default/files/publication/digital_download/20TheWelfareBirdsSlaughter.pdf (accessed on June 5, 2024).

Austin, Paige. July 5, 2024. "Fireworks Cause Hazardous Air Quality In Woodland Hills." *The Patch*. Website https://patch.com/california/woodlandhills/fireworks-cause-hazardous-air-quality-woodland-hills (accessed on July 8, 2024).

Ausubel, Jacob. December 21, 2021. "Christians, Religiously Unaffiliated Differ on Whether Most Things in Society Can Be Divided into Good, Evil." *Pew Research Center*. Website https://www.pewresearch.org/short-reads/2021/12/21/christians-religiously-unaffiliated-differ-on-whether-most-things-in-society-can-be-divided-into-good-evil/ (accessed on April 13, 2024).

Baird, Robert and Stuart Rosenbaum. 1991. *Animal Experimentation*. New York: Prometheus Books.

Barakat, Matthew. April 11, 2024. "20 years later, Abu Ghraib detainees get their day in US court." *Associated Press*. Website https://apnews.com/article/abu-ghraib-lawsuit-caci-virginia-contractor-torture-47bca65df10c62b672944692a139e012 (accessed on June 25, 2024).

Barber, Theodore Xenophon. 1993. *The Human Nature of Birds*. New York: St. Martin's Press.

Barth, Karl. 1960. *Church Dogmatics*. Edinburgh: T. & T. Clark.

Bartlett, John. 1980. *Familiar Quotations*. Boston: Little, Brown and Company.

BBC Editor. May 31, 2017. "Dog Understands 1022 Words: Super Smart Animals." *BBC Earth*. Website *https://www.youtube.com/watch?v=Ip_uVTWfXyI* (accessed on April 8, 2024).

BBC News Editor. March 30, 2020. "Magnetism 'Can Modify Morality.'" *BBC News*. Website http://news.bbc.co.uk/2/mobile/health/8593748.stm (accessed on June 24, 2024).

Becker, Ernest. 1971. "The Fragile Fiction." *In The Birth and Death of Meaning*. New York: The Free Press/Simon & Schuster.

Begley, Sharon. April 10, 2000. "Decoding the Human Body." *Newsweek*.

----------. January 1, 2000. "Rewiring Your Gray Matter." *Newsweek*.

----------. May 3, 1999. "Why The Young Kill." *Newsweek*.

Bekoff, Marc. March 30, 2023. "Insect Sentience: Science, Pain, Ethics, and Welfare." *Psychology Today*. Website *https://www.psychologytoday.com/us/blog/animal-emotions/202303/insect-sentience-science-pain-ethics-and-welfare* (accessed on April 26, 2024).

----------. November 20, 2022. "The Future of Animal Sentience: Colorado Can Lead the Way." *The Marc Bekoff Blog*. Website *https://marcbekoff.com/marcs-essays/f/the-future-of-animal-sentience-colorado-can-lead-the-way* (accessed on April 26, 2024).

Benhabib, Seyla. 1991. "The Generalized and Concrete Other: The Kohlberg-Gilligan Controversy and Moral Theory." *Women and Moral Theory*. Eds. Eva Feder Kittay & Diana T. Meyers. Lanham, MD: Rowman & Littlefield.

Berger, Peter L. 1967. *The Sacred Canopy*. New York: Anchor Books.

Bernardini, Francesco, Laura Scarponi, Luigi Attademo, Philippe Hubain, Gwenole Loas and Orin Devinsky. June 8, 2020. "Musical Anhedonia: A Review." *Journal of Psychopathology*. Website https://old.jpsychopathol.it/wp-content/uploads/2020/12/08_Bernardini-1.pdf (accessed on April 13, 2024).

Best, Steven and Douglas Kellner. 1997. *The Postmodern Turn*. New York: The Guilford Press.

Bland, Eric. March 29, 2010. "Study: Magnets Can Alter Morality." *NBC News*. Website https://www.nbcnews.com/health/health-news/study-magnets-can-alter-morality-flna1c9449359 (accessed on June 24, 2024).

Bloom, Howard. 1955. *The Lucifer Principle*. New York: The Atlantic Monthly Press.

Bloom, Paul. May 5, 2020. "The Moral Life of Babies." *New York Times*. Website *http://www.nytimes.com/2010/05/09/magazine/09babies-t.html* (accessed on January 23, 2024.

Blumenstein, David P. Farrington and Soumyo Moitra. 1985. "Delinquency Careers: Innocents, Desisters, and Persisters." *Crime and Justice: A Review of Research*. Eds. Michael H. Tonry and Norval Morris. Chicago: University of Chicago Press.

Bohm, David. 1994. "Postmodern Science and a Postmodern

World." *Ecology*. Ed. Carolyn Merchant. Atlantic Highlands, NJ: Humanities Press.

Bollard, Lewis. July 18, 2023. "We Love Animals. Why Do We Torture Them?" Farm Animal Welfare Research Newsletter. Website *https://farmanimalwelfare.substack.com/p/we-love-animals-why-do-we-torture* (accessed on August 9, 2024).

Bolotnikova, Marina. August 7, 2024. "Humanity Is Failing One of Its Greatest Moral Tests." *Vox*. Website *https://www.vox.com/future-perfect/363550/factory-farming-human-progress-sustainable-food-movement* (accessed on August 8, 2024).

Bolotnikova, Marina, and Kenny Torrella. February 24, 2024. "9 Charts that Show us Factory Farming Is Even Bigger than You Realize." *Vox*. Website *https://www.vox.com/future-perfect/24079424/factory-farming-facts-meat-usda-agriculture-census* (accessed on March 16, 2024).

Bracken, Michael B. March 1, 2009. "Why Animal Studies Are Often Poor Predictors of Human Reactions to Exposure." *Journal of the Royal Society of Medicine*. Website *https://www.ncbi.nlm.nih.gov/pmc/articles/PMC2746847/* (accessed on June 15, 2024).

Brainard, Ryan. July 12, 2024. "Linn County Landfill Will Be Full 8 Years Earlier than Expected." 98.1 KHAK. Website *https://khak.com/linn-county-landfill-closing/* (accessed on August 6, 2024).

Brekkevold, Morten. July 6, 2021. "Suckers for Learning: Why Octopuses Are So Intelligent." *The Conversation*. Website https://theconversation.com/suckers-for-learning-why-octopuses-are-so-intelligent-162122 (accessed on April 8, 2024).

Brenan, Megan, and Jeffrey M. Jones. January 22, 2024. "Ethics Ratings of Nearly All Professions Down in U.S." *Gallup*. Website https://news.gallup.com/poll/608903/ethics-ratings-nearly-professions-down.aspx (accessed on June 18, 2024).

Brennan, Patricia A., Sarnoff A. Mednick and Jan Volavka. 1995. "Biomedical Factors in Crime." *Crime*. San Francisco: Institute for Contemporary Studies.

Brooks, David. July 11, 2024. "The Source of Trump's Appeal." *New York Times*. Website https://www.nytimes.com/2024/07/11/opinion/trump-biden-authoritarianism.html (accessed on July 12, 2024).

Brown, Sterling A. 1968. "Negro Character as Seen by White Authors." *Dark Symphony: Negro Literature in America*. New York: New York Free Press.

Bullard, Robert D. 1994. *Dumping in Dixie*. Boulder, CO: Westview Press.

Burden, George. June 9, 2020. "One in Eleven Odds: The Deadly Risk of Being U.S. President." *Life As A Human*. Website http://lifeasahuman.com/2010/arts-culture/history/one-in-eleven-odds-the-deadly-risk-of-being-us-president/ (accessed on April 20, 2024).

Burns, Judith. September 25, 2009. "Butterfly 'GPS' Found in Antennae." *BBC News*. Website http://news.bbc.co.uk/2/hi/8273069.stm (access on April 8, 2024).

Burrell, David B. 1977. "From System to Story: An Alternative Pattern for Rationality in Ethics." *Truthfulness and Tragedy*. Ed. Stanley Hauerwas. Notre Dame, IN: University of Notre Dame Press.

Bush, Evan. April 2024. "Scientists Push New Paradigm of Animal Consciousness, Saying Even Insects May Be Sentient." *NBC News*. Website *https://www.nbcnews.com/science/science-news/animal-consciousness-scientists-push-new-paradigm-rcna148213* (accessed on April 26, 2024).

California Wildlife Conservation Board. "Natural Heritage Preservation Tax Credit Program." Website https://wcb.ca.gov/Programs/Natural-Heritage-Preservation-Tax-Credit (accessed on June 12, 2024).

Callaway, Ewen. November 3, 2009. "Murderer with 'Aggression Genes' Gets Sentence Cut." *New Scientist*. Website http://www.newscientist.com/article/dn18098-murderer-with-aggression-genes-gets-sentence-cut.html (accessed on January 26, 2024).

Callicott, J. Baird. 1992. "Animal Liberation: A Triangular Affair." *The Animal Rights/Environmental Ethics Debate*. Ed. Eugene C. Hargrove. New York: State University of New York Press.

Cameron, Jim. December 31, 2023. "Why Traffic Signals Are Red, Yellow, Green—and Expensive." *CT Mirror*. Website https://ctmirror.org/2023/12/31/why-traffic-signals-are-red-green-and-expensive/ (accessed on June 15, 2024).

The Canadian Press. April 23, 2024. "Conscious, Sentient Thought Likely for Many or Most Animals: Scientists." *Victoria News*. Website https://www.vicnews.com/trending-now/conscious-sentient-thought-likely-for-many-or-most-animals-scientists-7348678 (accessed on April 26, 2024).

Caputo, John D. 1993. *Against Ethics*. Bloomington: Indiana University Press.

Carey, Benedict. June 21, 2005. "Some Politics May Be Etched in the Genes." *New York Times*. Website http://www.nytimes.com/2005/06/21/science/21gene.html (accessed on January 23, 2024).

Carlton, Spence. 1989. "Human Needs Are Not More Important Than Animal Rights." *Animal Rights: Opposing Viewpoints*. Ed. Janelle Rohr. San Diego: Greenhaven Press.

Caspi, Avshalom. 1987. "Personality in the Life Course." *Journal of Personality and Social Psychology* 53 (6): 1203–1213.

Cave, George P. 1982. "Animals, Heidegger, and the Right to Life." *Environmental Ethics* 4, no. 3 (Fall): .249–254.

Chapple, Christopher Key. 1993. *Nonviolence to Animals, Earth, and Self in Asian Traditions*. New York: State University of New York Press.

Cheng, Maria. August 27, 2010. "Food Aversion?" Associated Press.

Cherry, Kendra. November 13, 2023. "The Asch Conformity Experiments." *Verywell Mind*. Website https://www.verywellmind.com/the-asch-conformity-experiments-2794996 (accessed on June 25, 2024).

Cobb, R.R. 1858. *An Inquiry into the Law of Negro Slavery in the United States of America*.

Cobb, John B., Jr. 1991. *Matters of Life and Death*. Louisville, KY: Westminster/John Knox Press.

Collier, Karen. October 10, 2007. "Greenpeace Urges Kangaroo Consumption to Fight Global Warming," *Herald Sun*. Website http://www.heraldsun.com.au/news/national/eat-a-roo-save-the-world/story-e6frf7l6-1111114612144 (accessed on July 29, 2011).

Colt, George Howe. April 1998. "Were You Born That Way?" *Life*.

Congress. 2021–2022. "Recognizing the Duty of the Federal Government to Create a Green New Deal." *117th Congress.* Website https://www.congress.gov/bill/117th-congress/house-resolution/332 (accessed on June 21, 2024).

Connor, Steve. February 12, 1995. "Do Your Genes Make You a Criminal?" *The Independent.* Website http://www.independent.co.uk/news/uk/do-your-genes-make-you-a-criminal-1572714.html (accessed on January 26, 2024).

Cowley, G. May 13, 1991. "What Do Monkeys Know?" *Newsweek.*

Daly, Mary. 1984. *Pure Lust.* San Francisco: HarperSanFrancisco.

Damiano, Jessica. August 9. 2022. "Unearthing Your Potato Harvest: How Do You Know When to Dig?" Associated Press. Website https://apnews.com/article/gardening-d99ae88544f9531f-7cb4384dfc3e2a07 (accessed on May 3, 2024).

Darley, J.M. and C.D. Batson. "From Jerusalen to Jericho: A Study of Situational and Dispositional Variables in Helping Behavior." *Journal of Personality and Social Psychology* 27 (1).

Dateline. November 27, 1998. MSNBC.

Davies, Gareth Huw. May 1996. "Is Crime in the Blood – The Case of the Mean Genes." *Radio Times.* Website http://media.gn.apc.org/members/3/index10.html (accessed on September 17, 2010.

Davis, Michael. 1999. *Ethics and the University.* London: Routledge.

----------. "Seven Step Method for Ethical Decision-Making." Website https://onlineethics.org/cases/seven-step-method-ethical-decision-making (accessed on June 6, 2024).

Davis, Nicola. May 2, 2024. "Orangutan Seen Treating Wound with Medicinal Herb in First for Wild Animals." *The Guardian.* Website https://www.theguardian.com/science/article/2024/may/02/orangutan-seen-treating-wound-with-medicinal-herb-in-first-for-wild-animals-max-planck-institute-sumatra (accessed on May 7, 2024).

Degler, Carl N. 1991. *In Search of Human Nature.* Oxford, UK: Oxford University Press.

Derrida, Jacques. Interview on YouTube. "Jacques Derrida and the Question of the Animal." *https://www.youtube.com/watch?v=Ry49JrOTFjk#:~:text=Here%2C%20Derrida%20explains%20his%20 long,these%20beings%2C%20culminating%20in%20today's* (access on February 29, 2024).

Descartes, Rene. 1979. *Meditations on First Philosophy*. Indianapolis: Hackett Publishing Company, Inc.

Devall, Bill. 1994. "The Deep Ecology Movement." *Ecology*. Ed. Carolyn Merchant. Atlantic Highlands, NJ: Humanities Press.

Dingfelder, S. March 2007. "Sea Lion Smarts." *American Psychological Association*. Website *https://www.apa.org/gradpsych/2007/03/sealion* (accessed on April 8, 2024).

Discover Editor. March 1991. "Clever Kanzi, Pygmy Chimp." *Discover*. 12:20.

Donahue, James A. 1990. "The Use of Virtue and Character in Applied Ethics." *Horizons* 17, no. 2 (Fall).

Douglas, William O. 1970. *Points of Rebellion*. New York: Random House.

Economist editor. November 22, 2008. "American dietary preferences are split across party lines." *The Economist*. Website *https://www.economist.com/graphic-detail/2018/11/22/american-dietary-preferences-are-split-across-party-lines* (accessed on June 19, 2024).

Edelson, Ed. January 26, 2009. "Popular or Not? Your Genes May Help Decide." *ABC News* Website *http://abcnews.go.com/Health/Healthday/story?id=6737071&page=1* (accessed on January 23, 2024).

Editor. March 4, 2007. "Sounds Trouble Like." *The Age*. Website http://www.theage.com.au/news/in-depth/sounds-trouble-like/2007/03/03/1172868805142.html (accessed on April 8, 2024).

Editor. April 29, 2022. "People Can Recover and Thrive After Mental Illness and Substance Use Disorders." *Association for Psychological Science*. Website https://www.psychologicalscience.org/observer/thrive-after-mental-illness (accessed on April 13, 2024).

Editor. June 10, 2022. "Civil Service Tells Staff There Are 'More than 100 Genders.'" *Christian*. Website *https://www.christian.org.uk/news/civil-service-tells-staff-there-are-more-than-100-genders/* (accessed on March 12, 2024).

Editor. February 9, 2004. "Innovations Take Time to Catch On." *Economic Times*. Website https://economictimes.indiatimes.com/innovations-take-time-to-catch-on/articleshow/483059.cms (accessed on June 22, 2024).

Editor. "Plant Consciousness: The Fascinating Evidence Showing Plants Have Human Level Intelligence, Feelings, Pain and More." Website http://www.esalq.usp.br/lepse/imgs/conteudo_thumb/Plant-Consciousness---The-Fascinating-Evidence-Showing-Plants-Have-Human-Level-Intelligence--Feelings--Pain-and-More.pdf (accessed on May 1, 2024).

Editor. "Pigs Are Gentle Creatures With Surprising Intelligence." *Humane Society of the United States*. Website https://www.humanesociety.org/animals/pigs (accessed on April 8, 2024).

Editor. January 13, 2006. "Italy Praised by American Animal Rights Group." *Italy Magazine*. Website https://www.italymagazine.com/featured-story/italy-praised-american-animal-rights-group (accessed on May 24, 2024).

Editor. "Political Parties." Website *https://www.mountvernon.org/george-washington/the-first-president/political-parties/* (accessed on June 20, 2024).

Editor. December 20, 2023. "Research Suggests Dogs Can Be Trained to Sniff Out Cancer in Other Dogs." University of Wisconsin-Madison. Website *https://www.vetmed.wisc.edu/research-suggests-dogs-can-be-trained-to-sniff-out-cancer-in-other-dogs/* (accessed on April 8, 2024).

Einhorn, Catrin. March 25, 2025. "Bridges and Tunnels in Colorado Are Helping Animals Commute." *New York Times*. Website *https://www.nytimes.com/2025/03/25/climate/wildlife-crossings-colorado.html* (accessed on April 30, 2025).

Embassy of Good Science. April 29, 2019. "The Seven Steps Method: A Method for Analyzing Cases in Research Ethics and Research Integrity." The Embassy of Good Science. Website *https://embassy.science/wiki/Instruction:6b129846-c455-4849-9eaf-0d25f3c5600e* Also see *https://zenodo.org/records/4905906* (accessed on June 6, 2024).

The Encyclopedia of Philosophy. 1967. Vols. I, II, and III. New York: Macmillan Publishing Company, Inc.

Erickson, Victoria Lee. 1993. *Where Silence Speaks*. Minneapolis: Fortress Press.

Ernst, David. January 23, 2017. "Donald Trump Is The First President to Turn Postmodernism Against Itself." *The Federalist*. Website https://thefederalist.com/2017/01/23/donald-trump-first-president-turn-postmodernism/ (accessed on February 29, 2024).

Evans, Erin. 2010. "Constitutional Inclusion of Animal Rights in Germany and Switzerland: How Did Animal Protection Become an Issue of National Importance?" *Society and Animals*. Website *http://www.animalsandsociety.org/assets/443_evansnutshell.pdf* (accessed on May 24, 2024)

Faerman, Justin. Fall 2014. "The Man Who Talked to Plants: The Visionary Research of Cleve Backster." *Conscious Lifestyle Magazine*. Website *https://www.consciouslifestylemag.com/cleve-backster-research-plants/* (accessed on May 1, 2024).

Fazio, Cynthia. June 18, 2024. "Study Finds Link Between Genetics and Coffee Intake." *Medical Xpress*. Website *https://medicalxpress.com/news/2024-06-link-genetics-coffee-intake.html* (accessed on June 20, 2024).

Feder, Michele and Michael Alan Park. "Animal Rights: An Evolutionary Perspective." *The Humanist* 50.

Feinberg, Joel. 1974. "The Rights of Animals and Unborn Generations." *Philosophy and Environmental Crisis*. ed. William T. Blackstone. Athens: University of Georgia Press.

Fenwicke, Claire. May 15, 2024. "Review Comments 'Extremely Impressive' Kangaroo Cull Program to Protect Threatened Species." *Riotact*. Website *https://the-riotact.com/review-commends-extremely-impressive-kangaroo-cull-program-to-protect-threatened-species/770079* (accessed on June 11, 2024).

Ferguson, David M., Joseph M. Boden, L. John Horwood, Allison Miller, and Martin A. Kennedy. January 2, 2018. "Moderating Role of the MAOA Genotype in Antisocial Behavior." Cambridge University Press. *British Journal of Psychiatry*. Website http://bjp.rcpsych.org/content/200/2/116.abstract (access on January 26, 2024).

Feuer, Lewis Samuel. Spring 1962. "What Is Alienation? The Career of a Concept." *New Politics* 1, no. 3.

Fisher, John A. 1992. "Taking Sympathy Seriously: A Defense of Our Moral Psychology Towards Animals." *The Animal Rights/ Environmental Ethics Debate*. New York: State University of New York Press.

Flew, Anthony. 1979. *A Dictionary of Philosophy*. New York: St. Martin's Press.

Fox, Michael W. 1990. *Inhumane Society*. New York: St. Martin's Press.

Francione, Gary L. February 28, 2019. "Green Party, Extinction Rebellion, and Others: Stop Ignoring the Vegan Solution," *Medium*. Website https://gary-francione.medium.com/green-party-extinction-rebellion-and-others-stop-ignoring-the-vegan-solution-b174a98e6527 (accessed on January 5, 2024).

----------. May 16, 2024. "Woke Animal Rights Means No Animal Rights, Part 1." *Medium*. Website https://gary-francione.medium.com/woke-animal-rights-means-no-animal-rights-bf1e420e0404 (accessed on March 14, 2024).

Frank, Philipp. 1957. *Philosophy of Science: The Link Between Science and Philosophy*. New Jersey: Prentice-Hall, Inc.

Frankena, William K. 1973. *Ethics*. 2nd ed. Upper Saddle River, NJ: Prentice-Hall, Inc.

----------. 1979. "Ethics and the Environment." *Ethics and Problems of the 21st Century*. ed. K.E. Goodpastor and K.M. Sayre. Notre Dame, IN: University of Notre Dame Press.

Franklin, Peter. January 13, 2021. "Donald Trump Was America's First Post-Modern President," *UnHerd*. Website https://unherd.com/newsroom/donald-trump-was-americas-first-post-modern-president/ (accessed on March 1, 2024).

Freud, Sigmund. 1961. *Civilization and Its Discontents*. New York: W.W. Norton & Company.

----------. 1961. *The Future of an Illusion*. New York: W.W. Norton & Company.

----------. 1933. *New Introductory Psychoanalysis*. Trans. W.H.J. Sprott. New York: W.W. Norton & Company.

Frodeman, Robert. 1995. "Radical Environmentalism and the Political Roots of Postmodernism: Differences That Make a Difference." *Postmodern Environmental Ethics*. ed. Max Oelschlaeger Albany: State University of New York Press.

Fromm, Eric. 1941. *Escape from Freedom*. New York: Avon Books.

----------. 1961. *Marx's Concept of Man*. New York: Frederick Ungar.

----------. 1955. *The Sane Society*. New York: Fawcett Premier Books.

Futterman, Allison. October 12, 2023. "The 5 Senses Animals Have That Humans Don't." *Discover Magazine*. Website https://www.discovermagazine.com/planet-earth/the-5-senses-animals-have-that-humans-dont (accessed on April 8, 2024).

Gaard, Greta. 1993. *Ecofeminism: Women, Animals, Nature*. Philadelphia: Temple University Press.

Gibbon, Edward. 1985. *The Decline and Fall of the Roman Empire*. New York: Penguin Classics.

Gilligan, Carol. 1982. *In a Different Voice: Psychological Theory and Women's Development*. Cambridge, MA: Harvard University Press.

Godfrey-Smith, Peter. January 1, 2017. "The Mind of an Octopus." *Scientific American*. Website *https://www.scientificamerican.com/article/the-mind-of-an-octopus/* (accessed on April 8, 2024).

Goldman, Russell. February 13, 2014. "Here's a List of 58 Gender Options for Facebook Users." *ABC News*. Website https://abcnews.go.com/blogs/headlines/2014/02/heres-a-list-of-58-gender-options-for-facebook-users (accessed on March 12, 2024).

Goni-Lessan, Ana, Dan Rorabaugh and Mike Snider. May 5, 2024. "Florida Bans Lab-Grown Meat as Other States Weigh It: What's Their Beef with Cultured Meat?" *USA Today*. Website *https://www.usatoday.com/story/money/food/2024/05/05/florida-lab-grown-meat-ban/73569976007/* (accessed on June 16, 2024).

Gordon, David George. 1996. *The Compleat Cockroach*. Berkeley, CA: Ten Speed Press.

Gottschalk, L.A., T. Rebello, M.S. Buchsbaum, H.G. Tucker and E.L. Hodges. 1991. "Abnormalities in Hair Trace Elements as

Indicators of Aberrant Behavior." *Comprehensive Psychiatry* no. 28.

Gould, Stephen Jay. 1983. *Hen's Teeth and Horse's Toes*. New York: W.W. Norton & Company.

----------. 1981. *The Mismeasure of Man*. New York: W.W. Norton & Company.

Gracian, Balthasar. March 29, 2011. *The Pocket Oracle and Art of Prudence*. New York: Penguin Classics.

Greenwood, Davydd J. 1984. *The Taming of Evolution: The Persistence of Nonevolutionary Views in the Study of Humans*. Ithaca, NY: Cornell University Press.

Griffin, D.R. November 1991. "Essay: Animal Thinking." *Scientific American*. Website https://www.scientificamerican.com/article/essay-animal-thinking/ (accessed on April 8, 2024).

Guardian Editor. September 2, 2009. "Meat Consumption Per Capita." *The Guardian*. Website http://www.guardian.co.uk/environment/datablog/2009/sep/02/meat-consumption-per-capita-climate-change (accessed on May 24, 2024).

Gustafson, James M. 1981. *Ethics from a Theocentric Perspective*. Chicago: University of Chicago Press.

Hackam, Daniel G. 2006. "Translation of Research Evidence from Animals to Human." *The Journal of the American Medical Association* 296.

Hall, Rebecca. 1984. *Voiceless Victims*. London: Wildwood House.

Ham, Chantal van. January 25, 2018. "In the Spirit of Nature, Everything Is Connected." *International Union for Conservation of Nature*. Website https://www.iucn.org/news/europe/201801/spirit-nature-everything-connected (accessed on April 24, 2024).

Hampshire, Stuart. 1987. *Spinoza: An Introduction to His Philosophical Thought*. London: Penguin Books.

Hanson, N.R. 1958. *Patterns of Discovery*. Cambridge, UK: Cambridge University Press.

Hargrove, Eugene C., ed. 1992. *The Animal Rights/Environmental Ethics Debate*. New York: State University of New York Press.

Harris, Marvin. 1989. *Cows, Pigs, Wars, and Witches: The Riddles of Culture*. New York: Vintage Books.

Hart, Kim. November 2, 2018. "Democrats See Republicans as Racist, Sexist." *Axios*. Website https://www.axios.com/2018/11/12/poll-democrats-and-republicans-hate-each-other-racist-ignorant-evil (accessed on April 13, 2024).

Havel, Vaclav. July 4, 1994. "The Search for Meaning in a Global Civilization." This speech was made after acceptance of the Philadelphia Liberty Medal, Philadelphia.

----------. 1995. "The Search for Meaning in a Global Civilization." *Truth about the Truth*. Ed. Walter Anderson. New York: G.P. Putnam's Sons.

Hawking, Stephen. 2010. *The Grand Design*. New York: Bantam Books.

Hawkins, Joshua. October 7, 2024. "Four High School Students Invented a Device that Prevents Roadkill." *BGR*. Website *https://bgr.com/tech/four-high-school-students-invented-a-device-that-prevents-roadkill/* (accessed on December 19, 2024).

Heath, Crystal. April 9, 2024. "19th-Century Animal Rights Activists Had a Lot of Moxie. Here's How to Get It Back." *Vox*. Website *https://www.vox.com/future-perfect/363275/meat-industry-lobbying-usda-animal-rights-progressive-movement-vegetarianism* (accessed on August 9, 2024).

Heer, Jeet. July 8, 2017. "America's First Postmodern President." *New Republic*. Website *https://newrepublic.com/article/143730/americas-first-postmodern-president* (accessed on March 1, 2024).

Herrnstein, R.J. 1995. "Criminogenic Traits." *Crime*. Eds. James Q. Wilson and Joan Petersilia. San Francisco: Institute for Contemporary Studies.

Herrnstein, Richard J. and Charles Murray. 1994. *The Bell Curve: Intelligence and Class Structure in American Life*. New York: Free Press.

Hershaft, Alex. May 25, 2021. "What Tears Us Apart." *The Vegan Blog*. Website https://theveganblog.org/48-how-we-tear-ourselves-apart (accessed on March 14, 2024).

Hoffer, Eric. 2006. *Next Nature*. Website https://nextnature.net/

story / 2006 / notnatural-and-notmechanical-human (accessed on January 23, 2024).

Holmes, Bob. April 16, 2007. "Chimps 'More Evolved' than Humans." *New Scientist.* Website http: / / www.newscientist. com / article / dn11611-chimps-more-evolved-than-humans.html (accessed on April 24, 2024).

Hospers, John. 1958. "What Means This Freedom?" *Determinism and Freedom in the Age of Modern Science,* ed. Sidney Hook. New York: Collier Publishing.

Hunt, Tam. April 26, 2024. "Where Does Consciousness Come From? It Could All Be Vibrations." *PsyPost.* Website https: / / www. psypost.org / where-does-consciousness-come-from-it-could-all-be-vibrations / (accessed on April 26, 2024).

Hutchins, Robert Maynard. 1980. "Democracy and Human Nature." *Familiar Quotations.* John Bartlett. Boston: Little Brown and Company.

Inwagen, Peter Van. 1982. "The Incompatibility of Free Will and Determinism," *Free Will,* ed. Gary Watson. Oxford, UK: Oxford University Press.

Isaac Bashevis Singer. Quotes on Goodreads. Website *https://www. goodreads.com/quotes/188451-what-do-they-know-all-these-scholars-all-these-philosophers-all* (access on January 5, 2024).

Jacobi, Hermann. 1980. *Jaina Sutras.* New Delhi: Motilal Banarsidass.

Jacobsen, Knut A. Fall 1994. "The Institutionalization of the Ethics of 'Non-Injury' toward All 'Beings' in Ancient India." *Environmental Ethics* 16, no. 3.

Jain, Sagarmal. 1993. *Saman Suttam.* India: Sarva Seva Sangh Prakashan.

"Jainism." Wikipedia. Website https: / / en.wikipedia.org / wiki / Jainism_in_the_United_States (accessed on May 14, 2024).

James, Josh. November 21, 2024. "Sen. Paul Presses FDA for Action on Law Ending Mandatory Animal Testing on Drugs." *WUKY.* Website *https://www.wuky.org/local-regional-news/2023-11-21/ sen-paul-presses-fda-for-action-on-law-ending-mandatory-animal-testing-on-drugs* (accessed on June 18, 2024).

Janicki, Julia, Katy Daigle, and Sudev Kiyada. December 23, 2022.

"On the Brink." Reuters. Website https://www.reuters.com/graphics/GLOBAL-ENVIRONMENT/EXTINCT/lbvgggdgevq/ (accessed on April 23, 2024)

Johnston, Bruce. March 7, 2004. "Italian Animal Rights Law Puts Lobster Off the Menu." *The Telegraph.* Website http://www.telegraph.co.uk/news/worldnews/europe/italy/1456270/Italian-animal-rights-law-puts-lobster-off-the-menu.html (accessed on May 24, 2024).

Jones, Jeffrey M. June 17, 2022. "Belief in God in U.S. Dips to 81%, a New Low." *Gallup.* Website *https://news.gallup.com/poll/393737/belief-god-dips-new-low.aspx* (accessed on February 2, 2024).

----------. August 24, 2023. "In U.S., 4% Identify as Vegetarian, 1% as Vegan." *Gallup.* Website *https://news.gallup.com/poll/510038/identify-vegetarian-vegan.aspx#* (accessed on June 21, 2024).

Jordan, Winthrop D. 1974. *The White Man's Burden.* London: Oxford University Press.

Kandel, Elizabeth, Sarnoff A. Mednick, Lis Kirkegaard-Sorenson, Barry Hutchings, Joachim Knop, Raben Rosenberg, and Fini Schulsinger. 1988. "IQ as a Protective Factor for Subjects at High Risk for Antisocial Behavior." *Journal of Consulting and Clinical Psychology* 56.

Kant, Immanuel. 1964. *Groundwork of the Metaphysic of Morals.* New York: Harper & Row.

Kapadia, H.R. 1947. "Introduction." *Anekantajayapataka.* Author Haribhadra Sur. With his own Commentary and Municandra Suri's Supercommentary. Baroda: Oriental Institute.

Kateman, Brian. September 18, 2019. "Why Some Environmentalists Still Fail to Promote Meat Reduction Answer to the Climate Crisis," *Forbes.* Website https://www.forbes.com/sites/briankateman/2019/09/18/why-some-environmentalists-still-fail-to-promote-meat-reduction-as-an-answer-to-the-climate-crisis/?sh=1c5b68a86453 (access on January 5, 2024).

Kaufman, Arnold S. 1965. "On Alienation." *Inquiry* 8, no. 2 (Summer).

Keniston, Kenneth. 1965. *The Uncommitted: Alienated Youth in American Society.* New York: Harcourt, Brace & World.

Kennedy, Des. 1993. *Nature's Outcasts: A New Look at Living Things We Love to Hate*. Pownal, VT: Storey Communications, Inc.

King, Martin Luther. 1994. "Letter from the Birmingham City Jail." *Applied Ethics: A Multicultural Approach*. Ed. Larry May and Shari Collins Sharratt. Upper Saddle River, NJ: Prentice-Hall.

Koenig-Robert, Roger and Joel Pearson. 2019. "Decoding the Contents and Strength of Imagery Before Volitional Engagement." *Scientific Reports*. Website *https://www.nature.com/articles/s41598-019-39813-y* (accessed on January 31, 2024).

Kohlberg, Lawrence. 1976. *Moral Development and Behavior*. New York: Holt, Rinehart and Winston.

Kompridis, Nikolas. 2009. "Technology's Challenge to Democracy." *Parrhesia 8*. Website *http://www.parrhesiajournal.org/parrhesia08/parrhesia08_kompridis.pdf* (accessed on August 30, 2011).

Kopic, Kristina. December 15, 2016. "Mental Illness as a Moral Failing." Ruderman Foundation. Website *https://rudermanfoundation.org/mental-illness-as-a-moral-failing/* (accessed on April 13, 2024).

Kreithen, M.L. and D.B. Quine. 1979. "Infrasound Detection by the Homing Pigeon." *Journal of Comparative Physiology* 129.

Kurzius, Rachel and Jaclyn Peiser. July 2, 2024. "Your Fridge Isn't Built to Last. Here's Why." *Washington Post*. Website *https://www.washingtonpost.com/home/2024/07/02/why-refrigerator-oven-dishwasher-break/* (accessed on August 8, 2024).

Kymlicka, Will, and Sue Donaldson. March 18, 2014. "Animal Rights, Multiculturalism, and the Left." *Journal of Social Philosophy* 45 (1): 116–135.

Land Trust Alliance. "State Tax Credits for Donation of a Conservation Easement." Website *https://www.landcan.org/article/state-tax-credits-for-donation-of-a-conservation-easement/1616#* (accessed on June 13, 2024).

Lane, Charles. November 16, 2016. "Take Trump Seriously and Literally." *The Washington Post*. Website *https://www.washingtonpost.com/opinions/take-trump-seriously-and-literally/2016/11/16/cbdcf2c8-ac25-11e6-8b45-f8e493f06fcd_story.html* (accessed on March 1, 2024).

Lawrence, Natalie. August 24, 2024. "The Radical New Experiments that Hint at Plant Consciousness." *New Scientist*. Website https: / / www.newscientist.com / article / mg25534012-800-the-radical-new-experiments-that-hint-at-plant-consciousness / (accessed on May 1, 2024).

Laws, Charlotte. 2008. "Guess Who's Coming to Dinner? The Controversial Peter Singer!" *Philosophy Now*. Website *https://philosophynow.org/issues/67/Guess_Whos_Coming_To_Dinner_The_controversial_Peter_Singer* (accessed on July 13, 2024).

----------. 2015. *Rebel in High Heels*. Anaheim, CA: Stroud House Publishing.

Lee, Alexander. June 6, 2020. "The Intelligence of Earthworms." *History Today*. Website https: / / www.historytoday.com / archive / natural-histories / intelligence-earthworms (accessed on April 26, 2024).

Leggett, Hadley. September 24, 2000. "Butterflies Use Antenna GPS to Guide Migration." *Wired*. Website *https://www.wired.com/2009/09/monarch-migration/* (accessed on April 8, 2024).

Lehmkuhl, Vance. "You Care More About Animals than You Do About People." *North American Vegetarian Society*. Website https: / / navs-online.org / articles / care-animals-people / (accessed on April 23, 2024).

Leopold, Aldo. 1949. *A Sand County Almanac*. New York: Oxford University Press.

----------. 1994. "The Land Ethic." *Environmental Ethics and Policy Book*. Eds. D. VanDeVeer and C. Pierce. Boston: Wadsworth.

Lewis, M.D., Ralph. June 10, 2021. "What Actually Is Evil? And What Makes People Carry Out Evil Acts?" *Psychology Today*. Website *https://www.psychologytoday.com/us/blog/finding-purpose/202106/what-actually-is-evil-and-what-makes-people-carry-out-evil-acts* (accessed on April 14, 2024).

Lifton, Robert Jay. 1986. *The Nazi Doctors*. New York: Basic Books.

Lifton, Robert J. with Eric Markusen. 1993. "Genocidal Ideology: Trauma and Cure." *On Prejudice: A Global Perspective*. Ed. Daniela Gioseffi. New York: Doubleday.

Linden, Eugene. August 29, 1999. "Can Animals Think?" *Time*.

141:57. Website https://content.time.com/time/magazine/article/0,9171,30198,00.html (accessed on April 8, 2024).

Lipsitt, Paul D., Stephen L. Buka and Lewis P. Lipsitt. 1990. "Early Intelligence Scores and Subsequent Delinquency: A Prospective Study." *The American Journal of Family Therapy*. No. 18.

"List of Genders." Website *https://gender.fandom.com/wiki/List_of_Genders* (accessed on March 12, 2024).

Locke, John. 1952. *The Second Treatise of Government*. Indianapolis: The Bobbs-Merrill Company, Inc.

Lovett, Mike. September 12, 2007. "Parrot Whose Skills Dazzled Scientists Dies at 31." *Arizona Daily Star*. Website https://tucson.com/news/local/education/college/parrot-whose-skills-dazzled-scientists-dies-at-31/article_83cd1ec0-ad27-5549-b975-e89780267bad.html (accessed on April 8, 2024).

Ludden, David. July 27, 2020. "Can We Have Justice Without Free Will?" *Psychology Today*. Website https://www.psychologytoday.com/us/blog/talking-apes/202007/can-we-have-justice-without-free-will (accessed on January 26, 2024).

Lyons-Padilla, Sara. "Take Time to Be a Good Samaritan." Stanford University. Website https://sparq.stanford.edu/solutions/take-time-be-good-samaritan (accessed on June 25, 2024).

Maitland, Edward. 1896. *Anna Kingsford: Her Life, Letters, Diary and Work*. Vol. 2. London: Redway.

Marohasy, Jennifer. October 11, 2007. "Eat Kangaroos to Help Save the Planet – Greenpeace." Website https://jennifermarohasy.com/2007/10/eat-kangaroos-to-help-save-the-planet-greenpeace/ (accessed on June 11, 2024).

Marx, Karl. 1978. *The Marx-Engels Reader*. Ed. Robert C. Tucker. New York: W.W. Norton & Company.

Mateev, Shaina. May 2, 2021. "Octopuses: More Like Us than They Appear." *The Commentator*. Website https://yucommentator.org/2021/05/octopuses-more-like-us-than-they-appear/ (accessed on April 8, 2024).

Maugh, Thomas H. II. February 6, 2011. "Tiny Water Flea Has the Longest Genome." *LA Times*. Website http://articles.latimes.

com/2011/feb/06/science/la-sci-water-flea-20110206 (accessed on April 24, 2024).

McAuliffe, K. October 1992. "Born to Believe: Your Values about God, Home, and Country May Be Influenced by Your Genes." *Omni* 25.

McCarthy, Justin. June 5, 2023. "U.S. Same-Sex Marriage Support Holds at 71% High." *Gallup*. Website *https://news.gallup.com/poll/506636/sex-marriage-support-holds-high.aspx* (accessed on June 22, 2024).

McCloskey, H.J. 1965. "Rights." *Philosophical Quarterly* 15.

Mcleod, Saul. November 17, 2023. "Stanford Prison Experiment: Zimbardo's Famous Study." *Simply Psychology*. Website https://www.simplypsychology.org/zimbardo.html (accessed on June 25, 2024).

----------. November 14, 2023. "Stanley Milgram Shock Experiment." *Simply Psychology*. Website https://www.simplypsychology.org/milgram.html (accessed on June 25, 2024).

Merriam-Webster Dictionary. 1974. Ed. Henry Bosley Woolf. New York: Pocket Books.

Mesulam, M.M. 1986. "Frontal Cortex and Behaviors." *Annals of Neurology* no. 19.

Midgley, Mary. 1983. *Animals and Why They Matter*. Athens: University of Georgia Press.

----------. 1992. "The Significance of Species." *The Animal Rights/Environmental Ethics Debate*. Ed. Eugene C. Hargrove. New York: State University of New York Press.

Mill, John Stuart. *Essential Works of John Stuart Mill*. Ed. Max Lerner. New York: Bantam Books, 1961.

----------. 1990. "Essay on Liberty." *Masterpieces of World Philosophy*. ed. Frank N. Magill. New York: HarperCollins Publishers.

----------. 1957. *Utilitarianism*. Ed. Oskar Piest. New York: Bobbs-Merrill.

Miller, Liam. September 4, 2009. "Abandoned Piglet is lost and hound: Giant farm dog saves baby pig's bacon by adopting it as one of its own." *Daily Mail*. Website http://www.dailymail.co.uk/news/article-1210909/

Abandoned-piglet-lost-hound-Giant-farm-dog-saves-baby-pigs-bacon-adopting-own.html (accessed on April 12, 2024).

Miller, Norman. February 14, 2022. "The Animals That Detect Disasters." *BBC*. Website *https://www.bbc.com/future/article/20220211-the-animals-that-predict-disasters* (accessed on April 8, 2024).

Milman, Oliver. September 13, 2021. "Meat Accounts for Nearly 60% of all Greenhouse Gases from Food Production, Study Finds." *The Guardian*. Website https://www.theguardian.com/environment/2021/sep/13/meat-greenhouses-gases-food-production-study (accessed on January 5, 2024).

Minton, Arthur J. 1979. "Theories about Human Freedom." *Philosophy and Science: The Wide Range of Interaction*. Ed. Frederick E. Mosedale. Upper Saddle River, NJ: Prentice-Hall, Inc.

Moreno, Sabrina and Karri Peifer. June 25, 2024. "The Current: Our Nearly Full Landfills." *Axios*. Website *https://www.axios.com/local/richmond/2024/06/25/the-current-our-nearly-full-landfills* (accessed on August 6, 2024).

MSNBC Documentary. April 11, 2000. "Charles Manson." Advertisement.

Naess, Arne. 1989. *Ecology, community and lifestyle*. Cambridge, UK: Cambridge University Press.

----------. 1973. "The Shallow and the Deep, Long-Range Ecology Movement: A Summary." *Inquiry* 16.

Nagel, Thomas. 1982. "Moral Luck." *Free Will*. Ed. Gary Watson. Oxford, UK: Oxford University Press.

Nature Editor. June 11, 2024. *Nature*. Website *https://www.nature.com/articles/s41386-024-01870-x* (accessed on June 20, 2024).

Nevaskar, Balwant. 1971. *Capitalists without Capitalism*. Westport, CT: Greenwood Publishing Corporation.

Newkey-Burden, Chas. November 5, 2022. "If You Go to Firework Displays, You Don't Love Animals." *The Independent*. Website *https://www.Independent.co.uk/voices/firework-displays-bonfire-night-animal-cruelty-b2218348.html* (accessed on March 15, 2024).

New Root Institute. April 28, 2020. Numbers Taken from USDA

Livestock and Meat Domestic Data. Website *https://www.newrootsinstitute.org/facts/number-of-animals-killed* (accessed on March 15, 2024).

New Scientist Editor. September 5, 1998. "The Zombie Within." *New Scientist*. Website https://www.newscientist.com/article/mg15921505-500-the-zombie-within/ (accessed on January 23, 2024)

Newton, Michael. 2000. *Encyclopedia of Serial Killers*. New York: CheckMark Books.

New York Daily News Editor. December 30, 2011. "Kanzi the Chimpanzee Can Start Fires and Cook, Making Him One of the World's Smartest Monkeys." *New York Daily News*. Website https://www.nydailynews.com/2011/12/30/kanzi-the-chimpanzee-can-start-fires-and-cook-making-him-one-of-the-worlds-smartest-monkeys/ (accessed on April 8, 2024).

New York Times Editor. January 21, 2006. "What the Nose Knows." *New York Times*. Opinion Section Website *https://www.nytimes.com/2006/01/24/opinion/what-the-nose-knows.html* (accessed on April 8, 2024).

Nietzsche, Friedrich. 1989. *Beyond Good and Evil*. Trans. Walter Kaufmann. New York: Vintage Books.

Nowell, Cecilia. April 9, 2024. "'Political Efforts': The Republican States Trying to Ban Lab-Grown Meat." *The Guardian*. Website https://www.theguardian.com/environment/2024/apr/09/us-states-republicans-banning-lab-grown-meat (accessed on June 16, 2024).

Oelschlaeger, Max. 1995. *Postmodern Environmental Ethics*. Albany: State University of New York Press.

Olds, Rebecca. November 18, 2023. "Today's Turkey Traditions, Explained: How Many Turkeys Are Killed for Thanksgiving?" *The Deseret News*. Website https://www.deseret.com/2023/11/18/23950898/how-many-turkeys-are-killed-each-year-for-thanksgiving/ (accessed on March 15, 2024).

Open Secrets. 2024. "Industry Profile: Agricultural Services / Products." *Open Secrets*. Website *https://www.opensecrets.org/*

federal-lobbying/industries/summary?id=A07 (accessed on June 17, 2024).

Overbye, Dennis. January 2, 2007. "Free Will: Now You Have It, Now You Don't." *New York Times*. Website https://www.nytimes.com/2007/01/02/science/02free.html (accessed on January 23, 2024).

PETA. 2022. "Facts and Statistics About Animal Testing." Website *https://www.peta.org/issues/animals-used-for-experimentation/animals-used-experimentation-factsheets/animal-experiments-overview/* (accessed on June 15,

Peters, R. 1959. *Authority, Responsibility and Education*. London: Peters.

Petit, Charles W., and Laura Tangley. November 8, 1999. "The Invisible Emperors." *U.S. News & World Report*.

Phillips, Alecks. January 30, 2024. "Area Twice the Size of California to be Allowed to Return to Nature." *Newsweek*. Website *https://www.newsweek.com/area-twice-size-california-return-nature-rewilding-climate-change-1865221#* (accessed on June 26, 2024).

Pinker, Steven. January 7, 2009. "My Genome, My Self." *New York Times*. Website *http://www.nytimes.com/2009/01/11/magazine/11Genome-t.html* (accessed on January 23, 2024).

Plomin, Robert, Michael F. Scheier, C.S. Bergman, N.L. Pederman, J.R. Nesselroade and Gerald E. McClearn. 1992. "Optimism, Pessimism, and Mental Health." *Personality and Individual Differences*. No. 13.

Pojman, Louis P. 1994. *Environmental Ethics*. Boston: Jones and Bartlett Publishers.

Pratt, Mark. March 2, 2021. "6 Dr. Seuss Books Will Stop Being Published because of Racist Imagery." *PBS*. Website https://www.pbs.org/newshour/arts/6-dr-seuss-books-will-stop-being-published-because-of-racist-imagery (accessed on January 5, 2024).

Rachels, James. 1986. *The End of Life*. Oxford, UK: Oxford University Press.

----------. 1993. "Egoism and Moral Skepticism." *Vice & Virtue in*

Everyday Life. ed. Christina Sommers & Fred Sommers. New York: Harcourt Brace Jovanovich College Publishers.

Radner, Daisie and Michael Radner. 1996. *Animal Consciousness*. New York: Prometheus Books.

Rao, Shoba. May 19, 2008. "Kangaroos to Be Killed in Canberra under Culling Program." *The Telegraph*. Website http://www.dailytelegraph.com.au/news/national/kangaroos-to-be-killed-in-canberra-under-culling-program/story-e6freuzr-1111116381352 (accessed on August 26, 2011).

Rawls, John. 1971. *A Theory of Justice*. Cambridge, MA: Harvard University Press.

Regan, Tom. 1983. *The Case for Animal Rights*. Berkeley: University of California Press.

Regan, Tom and Peter Singer. 1989. *Animal Rights and Human Obligations*. 2nd Ed. Upper Saddle River, NJ: Prentice-Hall, Inc.

Reichel, Howard and David Magnusson. 1988. *The Relationship of Intelligence to Registered Criminality*. University of Stockholm Reports from the Department of Psychology 676, Stockhold, Sweden.

Reid, Sue. June 19, 2024. "Europe's Plummeting Birth Rate Timebomb: To Keep a Stable Population, Countries Need a Birthrate of 2.1 Babies per Woman. The Continent Races a 'Staggering Social Change,' writes Sue Reid." *The Daily Mail*. Website https://www.dailymail.co.uk/news/article-13547253/Europes-plummeting-birth-rate-timebomb-stable-population-countries-need-birth-rate-2-1-babies-woman-continent-faces-staggering-social-change-writes-SUE-REID.html (accessed on June 20, 2024).

Reinhold, Robert. January 8, 1982. "Study Says Criminal Tendencies May Be Inherited." *New York Times*. Website http://www.nytimes.com/1982/01/08/us/study-says-criminal-tendencies-may-be-inherited.html (accessed on September 17, 2010.

Reuters Editor. August 9, 2007. "Tortoise, Hippo Friendship Deepens Post Tsunami." Reuters. Website https://www.reuters.com/article/idUSN28296637/ (accessed on April 12, 2024).

Riley, Sean. October 19, 2023. "Edible Beer Packaging from Eco-Friendly Ingredients." *Packaging World*. Website https://www.

packworld.com/sustainable-packaging/article/22876685/beer-packaging-from-ecofriendly-beer-ingredients (accessed on July 10, 2024).

Ritvo, Harriet. 1991. "The Animal Connection." *The Boundaries of Humanity: Humans, Animals, Machines*. Eds. James J. Sheehan and Morton Sosna. Berkeley: University of California Press.

Robbins, John. 1987. *Diet for a New America*. Walpole, NH: Stillpoint Publishing.

Robison, Jennifer. February 25, 2003. "The Devil and the Demographic Details." *Gallup*. Website *https://news.gallup.com/poll/7858/devil-demographic-details.aspx* (accessed on April 13, 2024).

Robson, David. January 30, 2015. "Psychology: The Man Who Studies Everyday Evil." *BBC*. Website https://www.bbc.com/future/article/20150130-the-man-who-studies-evil (accessed on April 13, 2024).

Rogers, Adam. December 7, 1998. "Thinking Differently." *Newsweek*.

Rollin, Bernard. 1981. *Animal Rights and Human Morality*. New York: Prometheus Books.

Romero, Alexandra. April 17, 2024. "See Renderings of the Wildlife Crossing over the 101 Freeway in Agoura Hills." *NBC Los Angeles*. Website https://www.nbclosangeles.com/local/see-renderings-of-the-wildlife-crossing-over-the-101-freeway-in-agoura-hills/3390691/ (accessed on June 20, 2024).

Roof, Wade Clark. 1993. *A Generation of Seekers*. San Francisco: HarperCollins Publishers.

Rowe, David C. 1994. *The Limits of Family Influence: Genes, Experience, and Behavior*. New York: Guilford Press.

Ruesch, Hans. 1982. *The Naked Empress: The Great Medical Fraud*. Italy: CIVIS.

Ruether, Rosemary Radford. 1983. *Sexism and God-Talk: Toward a Feminist Theology*. Boston: Beacon Press.

Russow, Lilly-Marlene. Fall 1992. "Animals in the Original Position." *Between the Species* 8, no. 4.

Ryan, Alan. 1974. *J.S. Mill*. London: Routledge & Kegan Paul.

Saha, Sparsha. June 23, 2023. "Why Don't Politicians Talk about Meat? The Political Psychology of Human-Animal Relations in Elections." *Frontiers in Psychology*. Website https://www.ncbi.nlm.nih.gov/pmc/articles/PMC10327565/ (accessed on June 21, 2024).

Salleh, Ariel. Fall 1993. "Class, Race, and Gender Discourse in the Ecofeminism/Deep Ecology Debate." *Environmental Ethics* 15, no. 3.

Sands, Leo. February 7, 2023. "Did Animals in Turkey, Syria Sense the Quake Early? Here's the Science." *The Washington Post*. Website *https://www.washingtonpost.com/science/2023/02/07/animals-turkey-syria-sense-earthquake/* (accessed on April 6, 2024).

Sapontzis, S.F. 1987. *Morals, Reason, and Animals*. Philadelphia: Temple University Press.

Sartwell, Crispin. February 23, 2021. "Humans Are Animals. Let's Get Over It." *New York Times*. Website *https://www.nytimes.com/2021/02/23/opinion/humans-animals-philosophy.html* (accessed on August 8, 2024).

Saunders, Dero A. 1985. *The Decline and Fall of the Roman Empire*. Introduction. Edward Gibbon. New York: Penguin Classics.

Savage-Rumbaugh, Sue. October 1, 1994. *Kanzi: The Ape at the Brink of the Human Mind*. Trade Paper Press.

Schechter, Harold and David Everitt. 1996. *A-Z Encyclopedia of Serial Killers*. New York: Pocket Books.

Schipper, Lewis. 1993. *Spinoza's Ethics: The View from Within*. New York: Peter Lang.

Schlanger, Zoe. June 2024. "The Mysteries of Plant 'Intelligence'." *The Atlantic*. Website *https://www.theatlantic.com/magazine/archive/2024/06/plant-consciousness-intelligence-light-eaters/678207/* (accessed on May 1, 2024).

Schroeer, Dietrich. 1979. "Recent Physics and Limits of Knowledge." *Philosophy of Science: The Wide Range of Interaction*. Ed. Frederick E. Mosedale. Upper Saddle River, NJ: Prentice-Hall.

Science News Editor. June 15, 1991. "Monkeys Play by the Numbers," *Science News* 139: 383.

Scully, Matthew. October 4, 2020. "The Animal-Protection Movement

Is Everything that 'Woke' Activism Isn't." *National Review*. Website https://www.nationalreview.com/2020/10/the-animal-protection-movement-is-everything-that-woke-activism-isnt/ (accessed on March 15, 2024).

Senett, Keph. May 23, 2011. "Following Examples Set by Ecuador and Bolivia, Turkey Is Considering Ecological Constitution." Website *http://www.pvpulse.com/en/news/world-news/following-examples-set-by-ecuador-and-bolivia-turkey-is-considering-ecological-constitution* (accessed August 30, 2011).

Sentenac, Hannah. July 1, 2015. "Time to Change Your Voter Registration: There's a Vegan Political Party." *Harm.less*. Website https://www.bharmless.com/time-to-change-your-voter-registration-theres-a-vegan-political-party/ (accessed on June 19, 2024).

Sessions, George, ed. 1995. *Deep Ecology for the 21st Century*. Boston: Shambhala.

Seyfarth, P.M. and D.L. Cheney. December 1992. "Meaning and Mind in Monkeys." *Scientific American*. Website https://www.scientificamerican.com/article/meaning-and-mind-in-monkeys/ (accessed on April 8, 2024).

Shah, Pravin K. 1994. *Essence of World Religions*. Cary, NC: Jain Study Center.

Shapero, Julia. July 20, 2023. "Belief in God, the Devil Falls to a New Low: Gallup." *The Hill*. Website *https://thehill.com/changing-america/respect/diversity-inclusion/4107968-belief-in-god-the-devil-falls-to-new-low-gallup/* (accessed on April 13, 2024).

Sheehan, James J. and Morton Sosna, eds. 1991. *The Boundaries of Humanity: Humans, Animals, Machines*. Berkeley: University of California Press.

Shpancer, Noam. November 2, 2021. "Is Morality Genetic?" *Psychology Today*. Website *https://www.psychologytoday.com/us/blog/insight-therapy/202111/is-morality-genetic* (accessed on July 27, 2024).

Singer, Peter. 1990. *Animal Liberation*. New York: Random House.

----------. 1998. *Ethics Into Action: Henry Spira and the Animal Rights Movement*. Lanham, MD: Rowman & Littlefield Publishers, Inc.

----------. 1985. *In Defense of Animals*. New York: Harper & Row.

60 Minutes II. February 10, 1999. CBS television.

Skinner, B.F. 1976. *Walden II*. New York: MacMillan Publishing Company.

Slicer, Deborah. 1996. "Your Daughter or Your Dog?" *Ecological Feminist Philosophies*. Ed. Karen J. Warren. Bloomington: Indiana University Press.

Smith, Alex. November 30, 2012. "The Coming 'Meat Vortex.'" *The Breakthrough Institute*. Website https://thebreakthrough.org/journal/no-15-winter-2022/meat-vortex-alternative-protein (accessed on June 21, 2024).

Smith, Huston. August 1994. "Postmodernism and the World Religions." Essay delivered at the Inaugural Symposium of the International Institute of Islamic Thought and Civilization, Malaysia.

Smith, Kimberly K. 2012. *Governing Animals*. Oxford, UK: Oxford University Press.

Spiegel, Marjorie. 1988. *The Dreaded Comparison*. Philadelphia: New Society Publishers.

Spinoza, Baruch. 1982. *The Ethics and Selected Letters*. Trans. Samuel Shirley. Ed. Seymour Feldman. Indianapolis: Hackett Publishing Company.

----------. 1951. *A Theologico-Political Treatise, A Political Treatise*. Trans. R.H.M. Elwes. New York: Dover Publications.

Stace, W.T. 1980. "The Problem of Free Will." *Philosophy and Contemporary Issues*, ed. John R. Burr and Milton Goldinger. New York: Macmillan Publishing Co., Inc.

Starr, Michelle. April 2, 2024. "Plants Really Do 'Scream.' We've Simply Never Heard It Until Now." *Science Alert*. Website https://www.sciencealert.com/plants-really-do-scream-weve-simply-never-heard-it-until-now (accessed on May 1, 2024).

Steiner, Gary. 2013. *Animals and the Limits of Postmodernism*. New York: Columbia University Press.

Stewart, Ian. 1989. *Does God Play Dice?* Cambridge, MA: Basil Blackwell.

Stone, Christopher D. Fall 1987. "Legal Rights and Moral Pluralism." *Environmental Ethics* 9, no. 3.

Stout, Jeffrey. 1988. *Ethics After Babel*. Boston: Beacon Press.

Steenhuysen, Julie. October 26, 2007. "Gene Switch Altered Sex Orientation of Worms." Reuters. Website http://www.reuters.com/article/idUSN2535476120071025 (accessed on January 23, 2024).

Sun, Weiming, Baoming Li & Chaolin Ma. July 30, 2021. "Rhesus Monkeys Have a Counting Ability and Can Count from One to Six." National Institute of Health.

Sunstein, Cass R. 1989. *Feminism and Political Theory*. Chicago: University of Chicago.

Suzuki, David. 1993. *Natures Outcasts: A New Look at Living Things We Love to Hate*. Forward. Des Kennedy. Pownal, VT: Storey Communications, Inc.

Syed, Zayna. January 4, 2023. "Why It Matters that Humans and Nature Are Growing Apart." *Popular Science*. Website https://www.popsci.com/environment/humans-nature-relationship-decline/ (accessed on June 20, 2024).

Tabuchi, Hiroko. March 28, 2024. "'Garbage Lasagna': Dumps Are a Big Driver of Warming, Study Says." *New York Times*. Website *https://www.nytimes.com/2024/03/28/climate/landfills-methane-emissions.html* (accessed on August 6, 2024).

Tatia, Nathmal. 1951. *Studies in Jaina Philosophy*. India: P.V. Research Institute.

Taylor, Paul. 1994. "Biocentric Egalitarianism." *Environmental Ethics*. Ed. Louis P. Pojman. Boston: Jones and Bartlett Publishers.

----------. 1992. "The Ethics of Respect for Nature." *The Animal Rights/Environmental Ethics Debate*. Ed. Eugene C. Hargrove. New York: State University of New York Press.

Taylor, Katy, Nicky Gordon, Gill Langley, and Wendy Higgins. 2008. "Estimates for Worldwide Laboratory Animal Use in 2005." *Alternatives to Laboratory Animals*. 36.

Team of the Delegation to Turkiye. October 10, 2023. "Stop Fires! 90 percent of forest fires are caused by humans." Website https://www.eeas.europa.eu/delegations/t%C3%BCrkiye/

stop-fires-90-cent-forest-fires-are-caused-humans_en?s=230 (accessed on June 13, 2024).

Thiroux, Jacques. 1995. *Ethics: Theory and Practice.* Upper Saddle River, NJ: Prentice-Hall.

Thoreau, Henry David. 1993. "A Plea for Captain John Brown." *Civil Disobedience and Other Essays.* New York: Dover Publications.

----------. 1842. *Natural History of Massachusetts.* 3 Dial 19. Website https://archive.vcu.edu/english/engweb/transcendentalism/authors/thoreau/nathist.html pp. 20-21. (accessed on June 13, 2024).

Times of India. July 26, 2024. "World's First City Where Non-Veg Is Illegal." Website *https://timesofindia.indiatimes.com/world/worlds-first-city-where-non-veg-is-illegal/articleshow/111689287.cms* (accessed on January 28, 2025).

Tobias, Michael. 1994. "Jainism and Ecology: Views of Nature, Nonviolence, and Vegetarianism." *Worldviews and Ecology: Religion, Philosophy and the Environment.* Eds. Mary Evelyn Tucker & John A. Grim. New York: Orbis Books.

Tompkins, Peter and Christopher Bird. 1973. *The Secret Life of Plants.* New York: Harper & Row.

Tulin, Melissa S. 1995. *Aardvarks to Zebras.* New York: Citadel Press.

Ulene, Valerie. January 31, 2011. "In Search of Lasting Happiness." *LA Times.* Website http://articles.latimes.com/2011/jan/31/health/la-he-the-md-happiness-20110131 (accessed on January 23, 2024)

United States Census Bureau. September 2023. "National Wilderness Month: September 2023." Website https://www.census.gov/newsroom/stories/wilderness-month.html (accessed on June 13, 2024).

University of Edinburgh. 2022. "Taste for Specialty Foods Is in our Genes, Study Shows." *University of Edinburgh.* Website *https://www.ed.ac.uk/news/2022/taste-for-food-is-in-our-genes-study-shows* (accessed on January 23, 2024).

Unsolved Mysteries. June 27, 2000. Lifetime television.

VanDeVeer, Donald. 1979. "Interspecific Justice." *Inquiry.*

Vernon, Philip A., Vanessa C. Villani, Leanne C. Vickers and

Julie Aitken Harris. January 2008. "A Behavioral Genetic Investigation of the Dark Triad and the Big 5." *Science Direct* 44, no. 2. Website https://www.sciencedirect.com/science/article/abs/pii/S0191886907003054 (accessed on April 14, 2024).

Vucetich, John A. "Are Humans and Nature Fundamentally One and the Same?" Center for Humans and Nature. Website https://humansandnature.org/are-humans-and-nature-fundamentally-one-and-the-same/ (accessed on April 23, 2024).

Waal, Frans de. December 6, 2017. "The Animal Noble Prizes of the Decade." *Huffington Post*. Website https://www.huffpost.com/entry/the-animal-noble-prizes-o_b_400977 (access on April 8, 2024).

Warren, Karen J. 1987. "Feminism and Ecology: Making Connections." *Environmental Ethics* no. 9.

----------. 1994. "The Power and Promise of Ecological Feminism." *Applied Ethics: A Multicultural Approach*. Eds. Larry May & Shari Collins Sharratt. Upper Saddle River, NJ: Prentice-Hall, Inc.

Watson, Andrew. July 25, 1997. "Quantum Spookiness Wins, Einstein Loses in Photon Test." *Science* 27.

Watson, Gary. 1982. *Free Will*. Oxford, UK: Oxford University Press.

Watson, Richard A. 1992. "Self-Consciousness and the Rights of Nonhuman Animals and Nature." *The Animal Rights/Environmental Ethics Debate*. Ed. Eugene C. Hargrove. New York: State University of New York Press.

Weber, Jemina. July 4, 2019. "'Vegans Don't Realize Billions of Animals Are Killed Growing Crops' Says Farmer." *Plant Based News*. Website *https://plantbasednews.org/culture/billions-animals-killed-growing-crops/* (accessed on May 3, 2024).

Webster's Encyclopedic Unabridged Dictionary of the English Language. 1989. New York: Gramercy Books.

Webster's New Collegiate Dictionary Editor. 1949. *Webster's New Collegiate Dictionary*. Springfield, Mass.: G.& C. Merriam Co., Publishers.

Wehner, Mike. March 7, 2019. "Your Brain Makes Decisions Before You Even Realize It." *New York Post*. Website https://nypost.com/2019/03/07/

your-brain-makes-decisions-before-you-even-realize-it/ (accessed on Jan. 5, 2024).

Werner, Emmy E. 1989. "High Risk Children in Young Adulthood: A Longitudinal Study from Birth to 32 Years." *American Journal of Orthopsy*. No. 59.

Wexler, Mark. April 1, 1994. "Thinking about Dolphins." *National Wildlife Federation*. Website https://www.nwf.org/Magazines/National-Wildlife/1994/Thinking-About-Dolphins (accessed on April 8, 2024).

White, Lynn Jr. 1994. "The Historical Roots of Our Ecological Crisis." *Environmental Ethics*. Ed. Louis P. Poman. Boston: Jones and Bartlett Publishers.

Wilber, Ken. Summer 1993. "The Great Chain of Being." *Journal of Humanistic Psychology*. 33, No. 3.

Williamson, Laila. 1978. "Infanticide: An Anthropological Analysis." *Infanticide and the Value of Life*, ed. Marvin Kohl. New York: Prometheus Books.

Wilson, James Q. and Richard J. Herrnstein. 1985. *Crime and Human Nature*. New York: Simon & Schuster.

Wisniewski, David. September 11, 2019. "Free Will Beliefs Are Better Predicted by Dualism than Determinism Beliefs across Different Cultures." *PLOS ONE*. Website https://journals.plos.org/plosone/article?id=10.1371/journal.pone.0221617 (accessed on April 13, 2024).

Wittgenstein, Ludwig. 1969. "A Lecture on Ethics." *Discovering Philosophy*. Ed. Matthew Lipman. New York: Meredith Corporation.

Wolfe, Rachel. February 20, 2024. "The Lifespan of Large Appliances Is Shrinking." *Wall Street Journal*. Website *https://www.wsj.com/personal-finance/the-lifespan-of-large-appliances-is-shrinking-e5fb205b* (accessed on August 6, 2024).

Wolfgang, Marvin E., Leonard Savitz and Norman Johnson. 1962. *The Sociology of Crime and Delinquency*. New York: John Wiley & Sons, Inc.

Woodcock, George. 1971. *Mohandas Gandhi*. New York: The Viking Press.

The World Book Encyclopedia. 1969. Vol. 3. Chicago: Field Enterprises Educational Corporation.

World Wildlife Fund. "The Effects of Deforestation." Website https://www.wwf.org.uk/learn/effects-of/deforestation (accessed on June 12, 2024).

Wright, R. March 5, 1995. "The Biology of Violence." The New Yorker.

Wulf, Andrea. December 23, 2015. "The Forgotten Father of Environmentalism." *The Atlantic*. Website https://www.theatlantic.com/science/archive/2015/12/the-forgotten-father-of-environmentalism/421434/ (accessed on April 23, 2024).

Xinhua Editor. July 3, 2021. "Feature: Turkey Passes New Law to Protect Animals." *Xinhua*. Website http://www.xinhuanet.com/english/europe/2021-07/03/c_1310041502.htm (accessed on May 24, 2024).

Yang, John, Winston Wilde and Kaisha Young. May 20, 2023), "Alarming Spate of Racehorse Deaths Draws Scrutiny of Industry Safety Practices." *PBS*. Website https://www.pbs.org/newshour/show/alarming-spate-of-racehorse-deaths-draws-scrutiny-of-industry-safety-practices (access on January 5, 2024).

Yokawa, K., T. Kagenishi, A. Pavlovic, S. Gall, M. Weiland, S. Mancuso and F. Baluska. December 11, 2017. "Anesthetics Stop Diverse Plant Organ Movements, Affect Endocytic Vesicle Recycling and ROS Homeostasis, and Block Action Potentials in Venus Flytraps." *Botany*. Website https://academic.oup.com/aob/article/122/5/747/4722571?login=false (accessed on May 1, 2024).

Young, Lauren J. August 1, 2023. "Your Genes May Influence What You Like to Eat." *Scientific American*. Website *https://www.scientificamerican.com/article/your-genes-may-influence-what-you-like-to-eat/* (accessed on January 23, 2024).

Index

www.ingramcontent.com/pod-product-compliance
Lightning Source LLC
Chambersburg PA
CBHW051711020426
42333CB00014B/944